PUBLIC ORDER LAW

Including the Public Order Act 1986

PUBLIC ORDER LAW

Including the Public Order Act 1986

Peter Thornton

Barrister and past chairman of the
National Council for Civil Liberties

First published in Great Britain 1987 by Financial Training Publications Limited,
Holland House, 140-144 Freston Road, London W10 6TR

© Peter Thornton, 1987

ISBN: 1 85185 040 6

Typeset by Rapidset and Design Ltd, London
Printed by Redwood Burn Ltd, Trowbridge

Contents

Preface   ix

Table of Statutes   xi

Table of Cases   xvii

1 Introduction   1

1.1 Public Order Act 1986   1.2 Public Order Act 1936   1.3 Background to the 1986 Act   1.4 Commencement of the Public Order Act 1986   1.5 Amendments to the Bill   1.6 No codification   1.7 Application of the Public Order Act 1986 to Scotland and Northern Ireland   1.8 Fine scales, penalties etc.

2 The new public order offences   6

2.1 Introduction   2.2 Riot   2.3 Violent disorder   2.4 Affray   2.5 Threatening behaviour etc. (fear or provocation of violence)   2.6 Disorderly conduct (harassment, alarm or distress)

3 Other public order offences   46

3.1 Carrying offensive weapons   3.2 Assault   3.3 Criminal damage   3.4 Contaminating or interfering with goods   3.5 Intimidation, including watching and besetting   3.6 Prohibition of uniforms and quasi-military organisations   3.7 Terrorist offences   3.8 Bomb hoaxes   3.9 Obstructing the police   3.10 Highway offences

4 Incitement to racial hatred   60

4.1 Introduction   4.2 The new racial hatred offences   4.3 The new offences: miscellaneous   4.4 Football exclusion orders: racial hatred

5 Police powers   73

5.1 Preventive powers: breach of the peace, binding over   5.2 Powers of arrest under the Police and Criminal Evidence Act 1984   5.3 Powers of arrest under the Public Order Act 1986   5.4 Information to be given on arrest   5.5 Arrest with warrant   5.6 Arrest by private person   5.7 Police road-blocks   5.8 No power to 'read the Riot Act'   5.9 Power to impose conditions on processions and assemblies and to prohibit processions   5.10 Bail conditions   5.11 Metropolitan Police Act 1839 and Town Police Clauses Act 1847 [5.12 Obstructing the police in the execution of their duty\

6   Use of the highway   88

6.1 Definition of 'highway'   6.2 Right of passage   6.3 Restrictions on the right to use the highway   6.4 By-laws 6.5 Obstruction of the highway 6.7 Police road-blocks   6.8 Picketing   6.9 Street offences 6.10 Litter   6.11 Street collections, leafleting etc.   6.12 Public nuisance

7   Law of trespass   115

7.1   Introduction   7.2 Civil law   7.3 Criminal law   7.4 The 'peace convoy'

8   New controls over processions and marches   132

8.1 Introduction   8.2 A right of assembly?   8.3 Meaning of 'procession' and 'public place'   8.4 Advance notice of processions   8.5 Police controls over public processions   8.6 Prohibiting public processions: bans   8.7 Judicial review

9   New controls over public assemblies   150

9.1 Introduction   9.2 A right of assembly?   9.3 Meaning of 'public assembly'   9.4 No advance notice requirement   9.5 Police controls on public assemblies   9.6 No power to prohibit assemblies   9.7 Judicial review

10   Public meetings   156

10.1 Introduction   10.2 Definition of 'public meeting'   10.3 Control of public meetings   10.4 Election meetings   10.5 Trafalgar Square and Hyde Park

11   Football matches: exclusion orders and alcohol-related offences   165

11.1 Introduction   11.2 Exclusion orders   11.3 Sporting Events (Control of Alcohol etc.) Act 1985: alcohol-related offences and licensing

Appendix 1   Public Order Act 1986   173

Appendix 2   **Public Order Act 1936**   201

Appendix 3   **Police and Criminal Evidence Act 1984, sections 24 to 26**
                 and schedule 2   215

Bibliography   219

Index   221

For Robert and Ruth

Preface

The object of this book is to provide a comprehensive, yet accessible, account of public order law. The need for a new work on this important subject arises from the passing of the Public Order Act 1986, the first major public order statute for 50 years. The Act is set out and discussed fully—the new criminal offences, the new police controls over processions and assemblies, the racial hatred provisions, criminal trespass and football exclusion orders. But because the Act is not a codifying statute its provisions cannot be read in isolation. It is necessary to consider the other outstanding features of public order law, in particular police powers at common law to control a breach of the peace, the recently created police powers of arrest under the Police and Criminal Evidence Act 1984, restrictions on the right to use the highway, the right of assembly, the law relating to public meetings, and other public order offences not included in the Public Order Act 1986. For reference purposes a number of other practical aspects of public order law are included.

I have therefore tried to write a complete working manual of public order law, designed for use by practitioners, students and those who are interested in the operation of rights and of restrictions on the freedom of assembly and the control of public disorder. If the emphasis lies inevitably with the criminal law, civil law aspects are not ignored. The law of trespass, in particular, has received much attention recently, and the decisions in *Thomas* v *National Union of Mineworkers (South Wales Area)* and *News Group Newspapers Ltd* v *Society of Graphical & Allied Trades 1982* show the increasing use of injunctions to restrain picketing and other assemblies.

I should like to thank friends and colleagues for their help and tolerance: in particular Marie Staunton, legal officer of the National Council for Civil Liberties, and Sue Dalal for their detailed comments on the manuscript, A.M. Strad for his technical assistance, and the publishers for their relaxed cooperation.

The law is stated, with best endeavours at accuracy, as at 23 December 1986.

Peter Thornton
1 Dr Johnson's Buildings
Temple, London EC4

Table of Statutes

Allotments Act 1922
  s 19 104
Ancient Monuments and Archaeological
    Areas Act 1979 123
  s 19 91
Bail Act 1976
  s 5 82
Burgh Police (Scotland) Act 1892 4
Cable and Broadcasting Act 1984 4, 67
Caravan Sites Act 1968 130
Caravan Sites and Control of Development
    Act 1960 93
  s 29(1) 124
City of London Police Act 1839
  s 35(13) 33
Civic Government (Scotland) Act 1982
  140
Commons Act 1899
  s 1 91
  s 10 91
Conspiracy and Protection of Property Act
    1875
  s 7 55, 80, 143, 153
Contempt of Court Act 1981
  s 12(1) 77
Control of Pollution Act 1974 112
  s 13(1A) 105
Countryside Act 1968
  s 41 91
Criminal Appeal Act 1968
  s 9 169
  s 50 169
Criminal Damage Act 1971 4, 50, 124
  s 1 51, 126
  s 1(2) 51
  s 1(3) 51
  s 2 12, 51
  s 3 38, 52, 126
  s 10(1) 52, 124
Criminal Justice Act 1967
  s 22 82
  s 91 41, 137
Criminal Justice Act 1982
  s 9(1) 77
  s 48 5
  s 60 82
Criminal Justice (Scotland) Act 1980 165,
  172

Criminal Justice (Scotland) Act 1980
  —continued
  Part V 3
Criminal Law Act 1967 31
  s 3 11, 22, 28, 38, 50, 159
  s 3(1) 16
  s 6(3) 17
  s 10(2) 19
Criminal Law Act 1977 33, 115, 123
  s 1 121
  s 1(1) 71, 114
  s 3 11
  s 5(8) 14, 21
  s 5(9) 14, 21
  s 6 121, 122, 126
  s 6(6) 79
  ss 6 to 9 128
  s 7 127
  s 7(11) 79
  s 8 49, 127
  s 8(4) 79
  s 9 127
  s 9(7) 79
  s 10 118
  s 10(3) 118
  s 10(5) 79
  s 12(1)(a) 127
  s 32 4
  s 51 58
Customs and Excise Management Act 1979
  s 86 48
  s 170 48
Disorderly Houses Act 1751 41
Employment Act 1980 99
Employment Act 1982 99
Explosive Substances Act 1883 58
  s 7 70
Explosives Act 1875
  s 77 128
Firearms Act 1968 72
  s 19 137
  s 20 127
Flags and Emblems Act 1954 4
Food Act 1984
  s 66 92
Forgery and Counterfeiting Act 1981 72
General Rate Act 1967
  s 26(4) 123

Glasgow Police Act 1866
  s 135(5)   41
Greater London Council (General Powers)
  Act 1968   86
Highways Act 1835
  s 5   88
Highways Act 1980
  s 35(6)   91
  s 137   90, 93, 111
  s 310   93
  s 328   88
House to House Collections Act 1939
  s 2(4)   106
  s 11(1)   109
Indecent Displays (Control) Act 1981   69
  s 1   137
Justices of the Peace Act 1361   76
Justices of the Peace Act 1968
  s 1(7)   78
Law Officers Act 1944
  s 1   90
Licensing Act 1872
  s 12   114
Litter Act 1983
  s 1   104
  s 5(9)   104
  s 5(10)   104
Local Government (Access to Information)
  Act 1985   158
Local Government Act 1972
  s 100A   156
  s 180   42
  s 222   104
  s 235   91
  s 237   92
  Sch 14   142
Local Government (Miscellaneous Provisions)
  Act 1982
  s 1   93
  s 3   92, 110
  Sch 4   92, 110
Magistrates' Courts Act 1980
  s 1   81
  s 24   4
  s 32   4
  s 34   5
  s 36   4
  s 63(2)   169
  s 75   5
  s 108   169
  s 115   78, 167
  s 115(3)   76
  s 116   78
  Sch 4   5
Magistrates' Courts (Appeal from Binding
  Over Orders 1956
  s 1   77
Metropolitan Police Act 1839   3
  s 52   82–3, 88, 90, 98, 142

Metropolitan Police Act 1839—*continued*
  s 54   35, 137
  s 54(13) 33
Misuse of Drugs Act 1971   72
  s 23   86
  s 23(3)   86
  s 28   65
National Parks and Access to the Countryside
  Act 1949
  s 90   91
Night Poaching Act 1828
  s 9   9
Obscene Publications Act 1959   64–5, 72, 112
  s 2(5)   65
Obscene Publications Act 1964
  s 1(3)   65
Offences against the Person Act 1861   14
  s 16   35
  s 18   49
  s 20   49
  s 42   49
  s 47   49
Official Secrets Act 1911   78
  s 8   70
Official Secrets Act 1920   78
Pedlars Act 1871   109, 110
  s 5   93
Police Act 1964   19
  s 5   86
  s 51   157
  s 51(1)   49, 84, 85
  s 51(3)   75, 84
Police and Criminal Evidence Act 1984   48,
  49, 73, 78, 85
  s 1   91
  s 4   96
  s 5(4)   40
  s 17(1)(c)   39
  s 24   16, 24, 30, 54, 78, 79, 80
  ss 24 to 26   78
  ss 24 to 26 (text)   215–17
  s 25   30, 44, 70, 79, 80, 86, 93, 102, 103,
  104, 130, 160, 161, 163
  s 25(3)(d)   93
  s 26   79, 93, 101
  s 27   79
  s 27(3)   79
  s 28   80
  s 61   79
  s 116   96
  Sch 2   78, 79, 101, 128
  Sch 2 (text)   217–18
Police, Factories, etc. (Miscellaneous
  Provisions) Act 1916
  s 5   106, 108
Powers of Criminal Courts Act 1973
  s 1(1)   78
  s 30   4
  s 31   5

Powers of Criminal Courts Act 1973
—*continued*
  s 31(3A) 5
Prevention of Corruption Act 1906
  s 2 70
Prevention of Crime Act 1953 4, 127
  s 1 46, 47, 48
  s 1(4) 137
Prevention of Terrorism (Temporary
    Provisions) Act 1984
  s 1 58
  s 2 57, 58
  s 10 58
  s 11 58
  s 12 79
  s 13 79
  s 14 58
  Sch 1 57
Prosecution of Offenders Act 1985
  s 25 70
Public Bodies (Admission to Meetings) Act
    1960 158
Public Health Act 1875
  s 171 142
Public Health Act 1936
  s 76 105
Public Health Act 1961
  s 75 91
Public Health Acts Amendment Act 1907
  s 81 137
Public Meeting Act 1908 137, 158, 163
  s 1 41, 156, 159, 160
Public Order Act 1936 1, 3, 4, 66, 82, 146,
    150
  s 1 57, 137, 159
  s 1(1) 158
  s 2 57, 159
  s 2(6) 159
  s 3 83, 132, 141, 142, 144
  s 3(1) 147, 149
  s 4 46
  s 5 3, 6, 19, 20, 26, 32, 33, 34, 36, 37, 38,
    40, 55, 62, 73, 75, 82, 130
  s 5A 60, 61, 63, 71
  s 5A(3) 65
  s 5A(6) 64
  s 7(1) 57
  s 7(2) 57
  s 7(3) 79
  s 9 136, 137, 157, 158
  s 9(1) 137
  text 207–14
Public Order Act 1986
  Part I 10, 45, 128
  Part II 10, 81, 89, 90, 132, 135, 150, 156
  Part III 3, 60, 61, 63, 65, 70, 72, 167
  Part IV 72
  s 1 6, 7, 8, 11, 14, 80
  s 1(1) 9

Public Order Act 1986—*continued*
  s 1(3) 12
  s 1(5) 10
  s 1(6) 18
  s 2 6, 19, 20, 23, 24, 39, 80
  s 2(1) 21
  s 2(2) 21
  s 2(4) 21
  s 2(5) 24, 25
  s 3 6, 11, 23, 25, 26, 27, 29, 30, 39
  s 3(1) 29
  s 3(2) 27
  s 3(3) 28, 29, 30
  s 3(4) 28
  s 3(5) 27
  s 3(6) 80
  s 3(7) 31
  s 4 6, 10, 20, 23, 25, 29, 30, 31, 32, 33, 36,
    38, 39, 41, 42, 43, 47, 55, 62, 70, 78, 106,
    107, 108, 124, 156, 157, 161
  s 4(2) 34
  s 4(3) 38, 80
  s 4(4) 39
  s 5 2, 10, 39, 40, 41, 43, 44, 55, 62, 78, 106,
    107, 108, 124, 156, 157, 161, 167
  s 5(3) 43, 44
  s 5(4) 44, 80
  s 5(5) 44
  s 5(6) 45
  s 6 14
  s 6(1) 14
  s 6(2) 29
  s 6(3) 38
  s 6(4) 43
  s 6(5) 15, 16
  s 6(6) 15
  s 7(1) 16
  s 7(2) 17, 24, 30, 39, 44
  s 7(3) 17, 25, 31, 39
  s 7(4) 25, 31
  s 8 10, 13, 22, 28, 38, 167
  s 9(1) 6, 7, 20, 25
  s 9(2) 6
  s 9(2)(d) 3, 32
  s 10(1) 19
  s 11 2, 80, 132, 140, 152
  s 11(1) 138
  s 11(2) 139
  s 11(3) 139
  s 11(4)(b) 140
  s 11(5b)(b) 140
  s 11(6) 140
  s 11(7) 140
  s 11(8) 141
  s 11(9) 141
  s 11(10) 140
  s 12 3, 56, 132, 141, 145, 148
  s 12(1) 142, 143, 153, 154
  s 12(2) 122

Public Order Act 1986—*continued*
s 12(2)(a)   143
s 12(2)(b)   143
s 12(3)   143
s 12(4)   144
s 12(5)   144
s 12(6)   144
s 12(7)   80, 144
s 12(9)   144
s 12(10)   144
s 13   3, 132, 141, 144, 155
s 13(1)   145, 146
s 13(2)   146
s 13(4)   145, 146
s 13(5)   146
s 13(6)   147
s 13(7)   147
s 13(8)   147
s 13(9)   147
s 13(10)   80, 147
s 13(11)   147
s 13(12)   147
s 13(13)   147
s 14   3, 56, 100, 135, 150, 152
s 14(1)   153, 154
s 14(2)   122
s 14(2)(a)   154
s 14(2)(b)   153
s 14(4)   154, 155
s 14(5)   155
s 14(6)   155
s 14(7)   80
s 14(8)   155
s 14(9)   155
s 14(10)   155
s 15   143, 148, 153
s 16   2, 10, 100, 136, 151, 156
s 17   63
ss 17 to 19   107, 108
ss 17 to 29   60, 61
s 18   60, 62, 72
ss 18 to 23   71
s 18(2)   62
s 18(3)   60, 62, 70, 80
s 18(4)   64
s 18(5)   65
s 18(6)   63
s 19   60, 64, 80
s 19(2)   65
s 19(3)   64
s 20   60, 65, 80
s 20(2)   66
s 20(4)   66
s 20(4)(c)   66
s 20(5)   66
s 21   60, 67, 72, 80
s 21(2)   67
s 21(3)   67
s 22   60, 67, 80

Public Order Act 1986—*continued*
s 22(3)   68
s 22(4)   68
s 22(5)   68
s 22(6)   68
s 22(7)   68
s 23   60, 68, 71, 72, 80
s 23(2)   69
s 23(3)   70
s 24(1)   72
s 24(2)   72
s 24(3)   72
s 24(4)   72
s 25(1)   72
s 25(2) to (4)   72
s 26(1)   71
s 26(2)   71
s 27(1)   69, 70
s 27(3)   62, 64, 71
s 28   71
s 29   63, 64, 67
s 30(1)   166
s 30(2)   167
s 30(3)   167
s 31   167
s 31(3)(c)   72
s 32   168
s 32(4)   80, 169
s 33   169
s 33(6)   169
s 34   168
s 34(1)   122
s 35   168
s 36   166
s 37   167
s 38   2, 46, 53, 55, 80
s 38(1)   53, 54
s 38(2)   53
s 38(3)   53
s 38(4)   55
s 38(5)   54
s 38(6)   54
s 39   115, 116, 122
s 39(1)   123
s 39(2)   125, 126
s 39(3)   80, 126, 128
s 39(4)   123, 125, 126
s 39(5)   122, 123, 124
s 40(1)   169
s 41   2
s 42(1)   3
s 42(2)   3
Sch 1   2, 165, 167, 169, 172
   Part III   3
Sch 2   46, 55
   para 1   55, 80
   para 2   47
   para 7   39
Sch 3   33, 46

Public Order Act 1986—*continued*
  text   173–206
Race Relations Act 1965   64
  s 6   61, 66
Race Relations Act 1976   63
  s 70   61
Refuse Disposal (Amenity) Act 1978
  ss 2 to 4   96
Representation of the People Act 1983   156,
  158
  s 95   161, 162
  s 96   161, 162
  s 97   163
  s 169   163
  Sch 8   159
Restriction of Offensive Weapons Act 1959
  48
Riot Act 1714   9, 19, 81
Riot (Damages) Act 1886
  s 63   19
  Sch 9   19
Road Traffic Act 1972   131
  s 5(2)   114
  s 95   169
  s 159   97
  s 196(1)   88
Road Traffic Regulation Act 1984
  s 14   131
  ss 99 to 104   96
Seditious Meetings Act 1817   6
Sexual Offences Act 1956
  s 10   70
  s 11   70
  s 13   103
  s 32   102
  s 37   70
  s 41   102
Sexual Offences Act 1967
  s 1   102
  s 7   103
Sexual Offences Act 1985
  s 1   103
  s 2   103
  s 4(1)   103
Sheriffs Act 1887
  s 8(2)   117
Shipping Offences Act 1793   6
Sporting Events (Control of Alcohol) Act
  1985   165
  s 1   171, 172
  s 1(2)   171
  s 1(4)   170
  s 1A   172
  s 2(1)   171
  s 2(2)   170
  s 2(3)   171

Sporting Events (Control of Alcohol) Act
  1985—*continued*
  s 2(A)   172
  s 3   171
  s 3(2)   171
  s 3(3)   166, 171
  s 3(10)   171
  s 5A   172
  s 5B   172
  s 5C   172
  s 6   171
  s 6(1)   171
  s 7(1)   171
  s 7(2)   171
  s 7(3)   171
  s 8   170, 171
  s 9(4)   171
  s 9(6)   170
Statutes of Forcible Entry 1381 to 1623   121
Street Offences Act 1959
  s 1   101, 137
  s 1(3)   79
  s 2   102
Supreme Court Act 1981
  s 48   169
  s 79   78, 169
  s 81   82
Theatres Act 1968
  s 5   60, 65, 66
  s 18(1)   66
Theft Act 1968
  s 9   123, 127
  s 10   49
  s 12   78
  s 25   78
Town and Country Planning Act 1971
  s 281(2)   73
Town Gardens Protection Act 1863
  s 1   104
  s 5   104
  s 7   104
Town Police Clauses Act 1847   3, 82, 90, 98
  s 21   83, 130, 142
  s 28   96, 105, 137
Trade Union and Labour Relations Act 1974
  s 15   56
  s 15(1)   98, 99, 100
Trading Representations (Disabled Persons)
  Amendment Act 1972   109
Treason Act 1351   7
Tumultuous Petitioning Act 1661   6
Unlawful Drilling Act 1819   57
Vagrancy Act 1824   44, 105, 106
  s 3   41, 102, 107, 110
  s 4   41, 46, 47, 110, 128
Wireless Telegraphy Act 1949   67

Table of Cases

9 Orpen Road, Stoke Newington, re [1971] 1
  WLR 166   *117*
Adler [1964] Crim LR 304   *96, 114*
Albert v Lavin [1982] AC 546   *75*
Allan [1965] 1QB 130   *27*
Allan and others v Ireland (1984) 79 Cr App
  R 206   *27, 35*
Ambrose (1973) 57 Cr App R 538
                                    32, 35-6, 52
American Cyanamid Co. v Ethicon Ltd
  [1975] AC 396   *119*
Anderson v Miller (1977) 64 Cr App R 178
                                          138
Annett and Moore (1980) 2 Cr App R (S)
  186   *31*
Arrowsmith v Jenkins [1963] 2 QB 561
                                    84, 94, 140
Asbury [1986] Crim LR 252   *28*
Ashmore [1974] Crim LR 375   *5*
Associated Provincial Picture Houses Ltd v
  Wednesbury Corporation [1948] 1 KB 223
                                        83, 148
Attorney-General v Stone (1895) 60 JP 168
                                          112
Attorney-General's Reference (No. 6 of
  1980) [1981] QB 715   *29, 50*
Attorney-General's Reference (No. 2 of
  1983) [1984] QB 456   *23*
Attorney-General's Reference (No. 3 of
  1983) [1985] 1 All ER 501   *26*
Aubrey-Fletcher (ex parte Thompson) [1969]
  2 All ER 846   *76*
Bailey v Williamson (1873) LR 8 QB 118
                                          164
Bates v Bulman (1979) 68 Cr App R 21   *47*
Beach and Morris (1909) 2 Cr App R 189   *14*
Beatty v Gillbanks (1882) 9 QB 308   *76*
Behrendt v Burridge [1976] 3 All ER 285
                                          102
Bennett v Bale [1986] Crim LR 404   *84*
Bentley v Brudzinski (1982) 75 Cr App R 217
                                           85
Betts v Stevens [1910] 1 KB 1   *85*
Bird [1985] 2 All ER 513   *22*
Bishop, *The Times*, 2 and 18 September 1986
                                           50
Bolton Justices (ex parte Graeme), *The
  Times*, 14 March 1986   *77*

Boyce v Paddington Borough Council [1903]
  1 Ch 109   *89*
Brazil v Chief Constable of Surrey [1983]
  Crim LR 483   *80*
Brennan, unreported, CA 17 December
  1985, ref. No. 753 B85   *18*
Britton [1967] 2 QB 51   *65*
Brooks and Breen v Nottinghamshire Police
  [1984] Crim LR 677   *77*
Broome v DPP [1974] AC 587   *94, 100*
Brown (1841) Car & M 314   *16*
Brown (1984) 79 Cr App R 115   *47*
Brown (24 October 1985) CA, ref. No. 1738
  B89, unreported   *74*
Brutus v Cozens [1973] AC 854   *34, 35, 36*
Bryan v Mott [1976] Crim LR 64   *48*
Bryan v Robinson [1960] 2 All ER 173   *35*
Buckingham (1975) 63 Cr App R 159   *126*
Burden v Rigler [1911] 1 KB 337   *158*
Burge v DPP [1962] 1 All ER 666   *102*
Burnley Borough Council v England and
  others (1977) 76 LGR 393   *92*
Burston Finance Ltd v Wilkins and Persons
  Unknown, *The Times*, 17 July 1975   *117*
Button v DPP [1966] AC 591   *26, 27*
Caird (1970) 54 Cr App R 499
                  7, 8, 12, 13, 18, 20, 23, 27, 28
Caldwell [1982] AC 341   *15, 52*
Cambridgeshire & Isle of Ely County Council
  v Rust [1972] 3 All ER 232   *94*
Campbell v Adair [1945] JC 29   *41*
Canterbury & St Augustine Justices (ex parte
  Klisiak) [1982] QB 398   *51*
Carasu Ltd v Smith [1968] 2 QB 383   *109*
Carr-Briant [1943] 2 All ER 156   *48*
Cawley v Frost [1976] 3 All ER 743   *138*
Central Criminal Court (ex parte Boulding)
  (1984) 79 Cr App R 100   *77*
Chief Constable of Devon & Cornwall (ex
  parte Central Electricity Generating
  Board) [1982] QB 458   *20, 73, 74*
Chief Constable of the Surrey Constabulary v
  Ridley and Steel [1985] Crim LR 725   *77*
Christians against Racism & Fascism v United
  Kingdom (1980) 21 DR 138   *135, 145*
Christie v Leachinsky [1947] AC 573   *80*
Clark (No. 2) [1964] 2 QB 315
                            89, 94, 114, 134

Clarkson (1971) 55 Cr App R 445   *13, 24, 27*
Collins [1972] 2 All ER 1105   *123*
Collins v Wilcock [1984] 3 All ER 374   *85*
Collinson (1931) 23 Cr App R 49   *137*
Commissioner of Police of the Metropolis (ex
    parte Blackburn) [1968] 2 QB 118   *75*
Coney (1882) 8 QBD 534   *13*
Conlan v Oxford (1984) 79 Cr App R 157   *77*
Connolly v Metropolitan Police
    Commissioner, *The Guardian*, 1 May 1980
                                                                   80
Cooper v Coles, *The Times*, 10 July 1986   *109*
Cooper v Metropolitan Police Commissioner
    (1986) 82 Cr App R 238   *94, 95*
Cooper v Shield [1971] 2 QB 334   *137*
Cox v Riley [1986] Crim LR 460   *52*
Crimlis [1976] Crim LR 693   *25*
Cugullere [1961] 2 All ER 343   *46*
Cunningham [1957] 2 QB 396   *14*
Dale v Smith [1967] 1 WLR 700   *102*
Daniel v Morrison (1980) 70 Cr App R 142
                                                              85, 97
Davies v Griffiths [1937] 2 All ER 671   *75*
Davis, re (1857) 2 H & N 149   *137*
Davis v Alexander (1970) 54 Cr App R 398
                                                                   47
Davis v Lisle [1936] 2 KB 434   *116, 157*
Despard v Wilcox (1910) 102 LT 103   *90*
Devlin v Armstrong [1971] NI 13   *13*
Dibble v Ingleton [1972] 1 QB 480   *85*
Dickinson v Ead (1914) 78 JP 326   *117*
Director of Public Prosecutions v Brooks
    [1974] 2 All ER 840   *69*
Director of Public Prosecutions v Roffey
    [1959] Crim LR 283   *152*
Director of Public Prosecutions v Whyte
    [1972] AC 849   *64*
Director of Public Prosecutions v Withers
    [1975] AC 842   *61*
Dixon v Attfield [1975] 1 WLR 1171   *94*
Donnelly v Jackman [1970] 1 WLR 562   *85*
Dubbins, *The Times*, 22 and 29 May 1986
                                                                   93
Duffy [1967] 1 QB 63   *16, 88*
Duncan v Jones [1936] 1 KB 218   *76, 134*
Dunn v Holt (1904) 73 LJ KB 341   *96*
Dwyer v Mansfield [1946] 2 All ER 247   *95*
Dwyer (J. W.) Ltd v Metropolitan Police
    District Receiver [1967] 2 QB 970   *10, 13*
Eaton v Cobb [1950] 1 All ER 1016   *84, 94*
Edgar (1913) 77 JP 356   *77*
Edmonds [1963] 2 QB 142   *46*
Edwards (1983) 5 Cr App R (S) 145
                                                              61, 63, 71
Edwards and Roberts (1978) 67 Cr App R 228
                                                                   136
Elkins v Cartlidge [1947] 1 All ER 829   *137*
Elliott v C [1983] 2 All ER 1055   *15*

Ettridge v Morrell, *The Times*, 5 May 1986
                                                                   162
Evans and others, *The Times*, 2 July 1969
                                                                   57
Evans v Hughes [1972] Crim LR 558   *48*
Evans v Wright [1964] Crim LR 466   *48*
Fabbri v Morris [1947] 1 All ER 315   *95*
Fagan v Metropolitan Police Commissioner
    [1969] 1 QB 439   *49*
Fairbanks, *The Times*, 3 July 1986   *17*
Faulkner v Talbot (1982) 74 Cr App R 1   *49*
Fegan [1972] NI 80   *23*
Fennell [1971] 1 QB 428   *85*
Field v Chapman, *The Times*, 9 October 1953
                                                                   102
Field v Receiver of Metropolitan Police
    [1907] 2 KB 853   *8, 12*
Fisher (1865) LR 1 CCR 7   *52*
Flockhart v Robinson [1950] 2 KB 498
                                                 136, 139, 141, 144
Flynn, *The Times*, 30 December 1985   *47*
Ford [1978] 1 All ER 1129   *102-3*
Ford v Receiver for the Metropolitan Police
    District [1921] 2 KB 344   *8*
Forde (James) (1985) 81 Cr App R 19   *87*
Foster v Attard [1986] Crim LR 627   *86*
Foy v Chief Constable of Kent (20 March
    1984) unreported   *97*
Frost and others, unreported, CA 5
    November 1985, ref. No. 4067 C85   *31*
Fursey (1833) 3 St Tr NS 543   *16*
G v Chief Superintendent of Police, Stroud,
    The Times, 29 November 1986   *74, 86, 148*
Gelberg v Miller [1961] 1 All ER 291   *97*
Gibson v Lawson [1891] 2 QB 545   *56, 153*
Gibson v Wales (1983) 76 Cr App R 60   *47*
Glynn v Simmonds [1952] 2 All ER 47   *138*
Graham and Burns (1888) 16 Cox CC 420
                                                              12, 13
Great Central Railway Co. v Bates [1921] 3
    KB 578   *157*
Greater London Council v Jenkins [1975] 1
    WLR 155   *118*
Green v Moore (1982) 74 Cr App R 250
                                                              84, 85
Grey (1982) 74 Cr App R 324   *103*
Grieve v Macleod [1967] Crim LR 424
                                                              47, 48
Gwynedd County Council v Jones, *The
    Times*, 28 July 1986   *63*
Hamilton [1986] Crim LR 187   *80*
Hampshire v Mace [1986] Crim LR 752   *103*
Hardman v Chief Constable of Avon &
    Somerset Constabulary [1986] Crim LR
    330   *52*
Harrison v Duke of Rutland [1893]
    1 QB 142   *89, 134*
Harrison v Thornton (1979) 68 App R 28   *47*

Harrow Justices (ex parte Osaseri) (1985) 81
  Cr App R 306   50
Hayes v Stevenson (1860) 25 JP 39   128
Hemmings v Stoke Poges Golf Club [1920] 1
  KB 720   121
Hickman v Maisey [1900] 1 QB 752
                                    89, 116, 134
Hills v Ellis [1983] 1 All ER 667   84
Hinchcliffe v Sheldon [1955] 1 WLR 1207 85
Hirst and Another v Chief Constable of West
  Yorkshire, The Times, 19 November 1986
                                95, 101, 111, 135
Hobday v Nicol [1944] 1 All ER 302   124
Holmes (1853) 3 Car & Kir 360   137
Homer v Cadman (1886) 55 LJ MC 110   95
Houghton [1982] Crim LR 112   47
Houghton v Chief Constable of Greater
  Manchester, The Times, 24 July 1986
                                          47, 48
Howell [1982] QB 416   38, 73, 74, 75, 98
Howley v Oxford (1985) 81 Cr App R 246   77
Hubbard v Pitt [1976] QB 142
          88, 94, 95, 99, 101, 116, 119, 133
Hughes (1830) 4 C & P 373   9, 13
Hunt (1820) 1 St Tr NS 171   13
Hunt v Broome [1974] AC 587   99
Inwood [1973] 2 All ER 645   80
Islington London Borough Council v Panico
  [1973] 1 WLR 1166   48
Iveagh v Martin [1961] 1 QB 232   89
Jacobs v London County Council [1950] AC
  361   112
John Lewis & Co. Ltd v Tims [1952] AC 676
                                           81
Johnson v Phillips [1975] 3 All ER 682
                                    85, 93, 97
Jones (1974) 59 Cr App R 120
                     9, 10, 21, 30, 56, 153
Jones and Mirless (1977) 65 Cr App R 250
                                           27
Jones; Smith [1976] 1 WLR 672   123
Jordan v Burgoyne [1963] 2 QB 744   36
Jordan and Tyndall [1963] Crim LR 124   57
Joy, re (1853) 22 LT Jo 80   128
Joyce v Hertfordshire Constabulary (1985) 80
  Cr App R 298   75
Kamara v DPP [1974] AC 104   10, 121
Kavanagh v Hiscock [1974] QB 600   100
Kay v Hibbert [1977] Crim LR 226   86
Keighley Justices (ex parte Stoyles) [1976]
  Crim LR 573   76
Kenlin v Gardiner [1967] 2 QB 510   85
Kent v Metropolitan Police Commissioner,
  The Times, 15 May 1981
                          134, 136, 145, 146, 148
Keys and Others, The Times, 22 November
  1986   31
Khan, unreported, CA, 14 January 1986, ref.

No. 5938 B85   31
King v Hodges [1974] Crim LR 424   86
Kingston Crown Court (ex parte Guarino)
  [1986] Crim LR 325   77
Knox v Anderton (1983) 76 Cr App R 156
                                          138
Lang v Hindhaugh, The Times, 25 March
  1986   88
Langford (1842) Car & M 602   13
Langrish v Archer (1882) 10 QBD 44   137
Lanham v Bernard; Lanham v Toye, The
  Times, 23 June 1986   76
Lawrence [1982] AC 510   15
Lewis (1881) 72 LT Jo 117   112
Lewis, ex parte (1888) 21 QBD 191
                                88, 156, 163
Lewis v Cattle [1938] 2 KB 454   85
Lewis v Cox (1985) 80 Cr App R 1   84
Liddle v Yorkshire (North Riding) County
  Council [1934] 2 KB 101   116
Liepins v Spearman [1986] RTR 24
                                86, 96, 131
Little and Dunning (ex parte Wise) (1910) 74
  JP 7   76
Lodwick v Sanders (1985) 80 Cr App R 304
                                       85, 97
Loudens v Keaveney [1903] 2 IR 82   89, 114
Lowe [1986] Crim LR 49   80
Lucas v Mason (1875) LR 10 Ex 251   159
Ludlow v Burgess (1982) 75 Cr App R 227
                                           85
Lyons (J.) & Sons v Wilkins [1899] 1 Ch 255
                                           56
McBean v Parker [1983] Crim LR 399   85, 86
M'Cusker v Smith [1918] 2 IR 432   56
McKenna and Vanner, unreported, CA, 11
  October 1985, ref. No. 4161 B85   53
McMahon v Dollard [1965] Crim LR 238   35
McPhail v Persons Unknown [1973] Ch 447
                                     118, 121
Madden (1975) 61 Cr App R 254   114
Malik [1968] 1 All ER 582   61, 71
Manchester Corporation v Connolly [1970]
  Ch 420, [1970] 1 All ER 961   119
Mandla v Dowell Lee [1983] 2 AC 548   63
Mansfield Justices (ex parte Sharkey and
  others), The Times, 13 October 1984   82
Mark and Mark [1961] Crim LR 173   85
Marsden (1868) LR 1 CCR 131   85
Marsh v Arscott (1982) 75 Cr App R 211
                                34, 37, 42, 138
Marshall v Tinnelly (1937) 81 SJ 902   157
Masterson v Holden [1986] 1 WLR 1017   36
Mathers v Penfold [1915] 1 KB 514   111
Maxwell and Clanchy (1909) 2 Cr App R 26
                                           85
Meaden v Wood [1985] Crim LR 678   108
Melser v Police [1967] NZ LR 437   42

Miller [1983] 2 AC 161   52
Morris-Lowe [1985] 1 All ER 400   102
Moss v McLachlan, *The Times*, 29 November
    1984   74, 97, 98
Moule [1964] Crim LR 303   96, 112
Muir and others *The Times*, 18 March 1986
                                           28, 29, 50
Munday v Metropolitan Police District
    Receiver [1949] 1 All ER 337   8
Murphy v Duke [1985] QB 905   109
Nagy v Weston [1966] 2 QB 561   94, 95
Neale v R.M.J.E. (1985) 80 Cr App R 20
                                              114
Newman v Francis (1953) 51 LGR 168   92
News Group Newspapers Ltd v Society of
    Graphical & Allied Trades 1982, *The Times*,
    1 August 1986   ix, 11, 28, 35, 55, 56,
                   98, 100, 114, 119, 134, 153, 154
Nicholson v Gage (1985) 80 Cr App R 40   38
Norbury [1978] Crim LR 435   114
North Curry (Inhabitants of) (1825) 4 B & C
    953   124
Oakwell [1978] 1 All ER 1223   35
O'Brien (1911) 6 Cr App R 108   8, 17
O'Brien v Friel [1974] NI 29   12
Ohlson v Hylton [1975] 2 All ER 490   46-7
O'Moran v DPP [1975] QB 864   57
Palgrave, *The Times*, 11 September 1986   53
Palmer v R (1971) 55 Cr App R 223   11, 22
Pankhurst v Jarvis (1910) 101 LT 946   90
Papworth v Coventry [1967] 2 All ER 41
                                           83, 90
Parkin v Norman [1983] QB 92
                              34, 36, 37, 38, 42
Patterson v Block, *The Times*, 21 June 1984
                                              47
Paul v Summerhayes (1878) 4 QBD 9   117
Pearce (1981) 72 Cr App R 295   71
Penwith District Council (ex parte May) (22
    November 1985, unreported, ref. No.
    CO/109/85)   110
Phillips (1842) 2 Mood CC 252   13
Piddington v Bates [1961] 1 WLR 162
                                          74, 100
Pigg (1982) 74 Cr App R 352   15
Pilgrim (1983) 5 Cr App R (S) 140   18
Pine (1934) 24 Cr App R 10   77
Pitcher v Lockett [1966] Crim LR 283   95
Pitchers v Surrey County Council [1923] 2 KB
    57   10
Pittard v Mahoney [1977] Crim LR 169   48
Pointon v Hill (1884) 12 QBD 306   111
Prebble (1858) 1 F & F 325   116, 157
Preece and Howells (1976) 63 Cr App R 28
                                              103
Randall v Tarrant [1955] 1 WLR 255   117
Rapier (1980) 70 Cr App R 17   47
Read, *The Times*, 7 January 1978   61, 64

Read v Jones [1983] Crim LR 809   37
Redbridge London Borough Council v
    Jaques [1970] 1 WLR 1604   94
Redford v Birley (1822) 1 St Tr (NS) 1071   7
Relf (1979) 1 Cr App R (S) 111   71
Rice v Connolly [1966] 2 QB 414   84, 85
Richards and Leeming (1985) 81 Cr App R
    125   86, 157
Ricketts v Cox (1982) 74 Cr App R 298   85
Ritchie v M'Phee (1882) 10 R (J) 9   74
Robson v Hallett [1967] 2 QB 939   86, 116
Roe v Kingeslee [1986] Crim LR 735   52
Rookes v Barnard [1964] AC 1129   56, 153
Russell [1985] Crim LR 231   46
S (Satnam) and S (Kewal) (1983) 78 Cr App R
    149   15
Salisbury Magistrates' Court (ex parte
    Mastin) [1986] Crim LR 545   20, 51, 98
Sandy v Martin [1974] Crim LR 258   137-8
Scott v Pilliner [1904] 2 KB 855   107
Senior [1899] 1 QB 283   84
Sewell v Taylor (1859) 7 CB(NS) 160   137
Sharp and Johnson [1957] 1 QB 552
                               12, 13, 25, 28, 78
Sharpe (1848) 3 Cox CC 288   14
Shaw v DPP [1962] AC 220   102
Shaw v Hamilton (1982) 75 Cr App R 288   77
Sheldon v Bromfield Justices [1964] 2 QB 573
                                              76
Simcock v Rhodes [1977] Crim LR 751
                                           34, 36
Simpson (1984) 78 Cr App R 115   47
Smith v Chief Superintendent of Woking
    Police Station (1983) 76 Cr App R 234   49
Smith v Hughes [1960] 2 All ER 859   102
Smith v Reynolds and others [1986] Crim LR
    559   20, 85, 93
Snodgrass v Topping (1952) 116 JP 332   104
Southampton Justices (ex parte Green)
    [1975] 2 All ER 1073   77
Spanner [1973] Crim LR 704   48
Steer [1986] Crim LR 619   51
Stewart [1896] 1 QB 300   92
Stunt v Boston [1972] RTR 435   86, 96, 131
Sudbury (1700) 1 Ld Raym 484   9
Summers (1972) 56 Cr App R 604   26
Swindon Crown Court (ex parte Pawittar
    Singh) (1984) 79 Cr App R 137   77
Swordheath Properties Ltd v Floydd [1978] 1
    WLR 550   118
Sykes v Holmes and Maw [1985] Crim LR 791
                                              114
Tacey (1821) Russ & Ry 452   52
Taylor v DPP [1973] AC 964   6, 27, 28, 29
Thomas (1983) 77 Cr App R 63   15
Thomas v National Union of Mineworkers
    (South Wales Area) [1985] 2 WLR 1081
                           ix, 55, 56, 100, 120, 153

Thomas v Sawkins [1935] 2 KB 249   *160*
Thompson [1974] Crim LR 720   *5*
Train (1862) 2 B & S 640   *112*
Trueman (1913) 77 JP 428   *77*
Tynan v Balmer [1967] 1 QB 91   *100*
Veater v G [1981] 1 WLR 567   *77*
Venna [1975] 3 All ER 788, [1976] QB 421
                                            12, 14
Vernon v Paddon [1973] 3 All ER 302   *34, 39*
Waite v Taylor (1985) 149 JP 551   *94, 95*
Walker (1934) 24 Cr App R 117   *84*
Waltham Forest London Borough Council v
     Mills [1980] Crim LR 243   *95*
Wandsworth County Court (ex parte
     London Borough of Wandsworth) [1975] 1
     WLR 1314   *117*
Ward v Holman [1964] 2 QB 580   *76*
Waters (1963) 47 Cr App R 149   *137*
Weight v Long [1986] Crim LR 746   *86*
Weiss v Monahan [1962] 1 All ER 664   *102*
Wellard (1884) 14 QBD 63   *137*
Wershof v Metropolitan Police
     Commissioner [1978] 3 All ER 540   *84, 86*
West Yorkshire Metropolitan Police v Teal
     and Bolloten (20 November 1981, Leeds
     Crown Court) unreported   *107, 110*
Westminster City Council v Monahan [1981]
     1 WLR 698   *117-18*
Wheeler, *The Times*, 17 December 1971
                                             114

Whitehouse v Gay News Ltd and Lemon
     (1979) 68 Cr App R 381   *61*
Whitton, *The Times*, 20 May 1986   *18*
Williams (G) (1984) 78 Cr App R 275   *49*
Williamson (1978) 67 Cr App R 35   *47*
Willmott v Atack [1977] QB 498   *84*
Wilson [1984] Crim LR 36   *17*
Wilson v Pringle [1986] 3 WLR 1   *50*
Wilson v Renton (1909) 47 SLR 209   *55*
Wilson v Skeock (1949) 113 JP 294   *76*
Wiltshire County Coucil v Frazer [1986] 1
     WLR 109   *118*
Wise v Dunning [1902] 1 KB 167   *76*
Witney v Cattanach [1979] Crim LR 461
                                             104
Woking Justices (ex parte Gossage)
     [1973] 1 QB 448   *76*
Wolverton Urban District Council v Willis
     [1962] 1 All ER 243   *95*
Wong Chang and others (1910)
     6 Cr App R 59   *8*
Wood (1984) 6 Cr App R (S) 2   *50*
Wood v Metropolitan Police Commissioner,
     The Times, 12 February 1986   *47*
Woodford v Smith [1970] 1 All ER 1091
                                         119, 157
Wooding v Oxley (1839) 9 C & P 1   *74, 161*
Woodrow (1959) 43 Cr App R 105   *30*
Woods v Lindsay 1910 SC (J) 88   *137*

1

Introduction

1.1 PUBLIC ORDER ACT 1986

The Public Order Act 1986 brings the most significant changes in public order law in England and Wales for 50 years. It abolishes a number of common law offences, including riot, unlawful assembly and affray, and replaces them with a wide range of statutory public order offences. The new offences are riot, violent disorder, affray, threatening behaviour etc. and disorderly conduct. The Public Order Act 1986 extends the existing controls over processions and creates for the first time controls over open-air assemblies. It also revises and expands the law against incitement to racial hatred and provides for the exclusion of certain offenders from sporting events, particularly association football matches. In the last stages of the Bill's passage through Parliament a power to direct trespassers to leave land was added as well as a new offence of contamination of or interference with goods.

1.2 PUBLIC ORDER ACT 1936

The Public Order Act 1936, the new Act's predecessor, which was born out of the fascist marches in the 1930s, prohibited quasi-military organisations and the wearing of uniforms for political objects. It developed police powers to keep the peace at processions by providing for the imposition of conditions, usually rerouting, where serious public disorder was apprehended, and, in exceptional circumstances, for banning processions altogether. The Public Order Act 1936 prohibited offensive conduct conducive to breaches of the peace and, by later amendment, created the offence of incitement to racial hatred.

1.3 BACKGROUND TO THE 1986 ACT

The Public Order Act 1986 represents the culmination of seven years' consideration of public order law. In June 1979 the Home Secretary announced to the House of Commons that he was instituting a review of the Public Order Act 1936 following the disturbances at Southall on 23 April. A Green Paper in 1980, *Review of the Public Order Act 1936 and Related Legislation* (Cmnd 7891), was followed by the government's proposals in a White Paper entitled *Review of Public Order Law* (Cmnd 9510) which was published in May 1985.

Other relevant reports include the report of the House of Commons Home Affairs Committee, *The Law Relating to Public Order* (HC (1979–80) 756 I and II, August 1980), the Law Commission's Working Paper No. 82, *Offences against Public Order*, and their subsequent report published in 1983 (Law Com. No. 123), both dealing with the common law offences, Lord Scarman's reports into the Red Lion Square disorders of 15 June 1974 (Cmnd 5919) and the Brixton disorders of 10–12 April 1981 (Cmnd 8427), and the Popplewell report, *Committee of Inquiry into Crowd Safety and Control at Sports Grounds: Final Report* (Cmnd 9710). The Public Order Bill was published on 5 December 1985.

1.4   COMMENCEMENT OF THE PUBLIC ORDER ACT 1986

The Public Order Act 1986 will come into force on a day or days to be appointed by the Home Secretary by statutory instrument (s. 41). Sections 11 and 38 and Schedule 1 will come into force on 1 January 1987. The remainder of the Act is expected to come into force on 1 April 1987. The 1986 Act will not affect any offence committed before the relevant provision of the Act comes into force (s. 41(2)).

1.5   AMENDMENTS TO THE BILL

A number of significant changes were made to the substance of the Bill during its consideration by the standing committee of the House of Commons and at subsequent stages of its passage through Parliament. The maximum term of imprisonment for the new offence of riot was reduced from life imprisonment to 10 years. The offence of harassment, alarm or distress (s. 5), commonly known as disorderly conduct, now requires, contrary to earlier drafts, a real victim present at the scene who is likely to have suffered actual alarm, distress or harassment. The definition of violence in Part I (new offences) has been redrafted along simpler lines.

The number of persons required to constitute an assembly (s. 16) was increased from three to 20—it had been described by one politician as 'Two's company, three's an assembly'. It is now envisaged that the giving of advance notice of processions may, in some circumstances, not be reasonably practicable, and therefore not required at all. The definition of a procession now excludes some everyday processions. An application by the police to ban a procession must now be based on a belief which is reasonable so that it is easier to apply for judicial review of the decision. Conditions imposed in advance of a proposed procession or assembly must be given in writing.

Incitement to racial hatred by words or gestures has been extended to private as well as public places and now carries a power of arrest. The Act also extends the criminal law to plays, videos and to a limited extent broadcasting, and a football exclusion order may be made on conviction of a racial hatred offence committed at or on the journey to or from a football match. A new law of criminal trespass to deal with the 'peace convoy' and other travellers was introduced at a late stage, as well as a new offence of contamination of or interference with goods.

1.6 NO CODIFICATION

The Public Order Act 1986 is not a codifying statute. There have been two major developments in recent years towards codification of the criminal law and allied subjects. The Police and Criminal Evidence Act 1984 is a 122-section-long statute which brings together the principal police powers of stop and search, entry, search and seizure, arrest and detention, and the questioning and treatment of suspects (as well as other important topics, including evidence in criminal proceedings and police complaints and discipline). The report to the Law Commission by a group of distinguished academic lawyers, entitled *Codification of the Criminal Law* (HC 270, 1985), includes a draft Criminal Code Bill and is a major step in the Law Commission's programme for reform of the criminal law. But the opportunity to codify the many and diverse powers which make up the law of public order has been passed by.

Many important aspects of public order law will not be found in the Public Order Act 1986, not least among them being the preventive common law power to arrest for a breach of the peace (see 5.1), which has survived the passage of the Police and Criminal Evidence Act 1984 and the Public Order Act 1986 and which remains at the heart of policing public disorder. Many other important provisions are also found elsewhere, including the unrepealed sections of the Public Order Act 1936. Other enactments deal with the use of the highway, the much-used police powers to give directions under the Metropolitan Police Act 1839 and the Town Police Clauses Act 1847, police road blocks, the obstruction of a police officer in the execution of his duty, certain aspects of picketing law, indoor public meetings and election meetings, and a number of public order offences including the carrying of offensive weapons.

The main argument for codification, namely, that clarification of public order laws makes them better known and understood was rejected in the White Paper. The government preferred the flexibility in the definition and control of common law powers by the courts and so decided to support the police view that there was no need for codification (Cmnd 9510, para. 6.13).

1.7 APPLICATION OF THE PUBLIC ORDER ACT 1986 TO SCOTLAND AND NORTHERN IRELAND

The Public Order Act 1986 extends principally to England and Wales only (s. 42(1)). Some sections, however, also extend to Scotland, notably the repeal of s. 5 of the Public Order Act 1936 (s. 9(2)(d)), conditions on public processions and assemblies (ss. 12 and 14) but not bans on public processions (s. 13), the whole of Part III (the racial hatred provisions) and the amendments to Part V of the Criminal Justice (Scotland) Act 1980 (the control of alcohol etc. at sporting events) (Sch. 1, Part II).

The provisions relating to Scotland are listed in Public Order Act 1986, s. 42(2). In Scotland, as in England and Wales, the combination of common law and statutory provisions applies. The common law offences of particular relevance to public order are assault, malicious mischief, mobbing and breach of the peace. The Criminal Damage Act 1971 does not apply in Scotland although the Public Order Act 1936 and the Prevention of Crime Act 1953 (offensive weapons) do. There are other statutory powers available to district and island councils under the Burgh Police (Scotland) Act 1892 as well as various local enactments which enable them to prohibit or regulate public processions in parts of their areas (see Cmnd 7891, para. 20).

Only a few provisions extend to Northern Ireland (s. 42(3)). They include the new offence of contaminating or interfering with goods (s. 38) and an amendment to the Cable and Broadcasting Act 1984. Proposals to repeal the Flags and Emblems Act 1954 (penalties for interfering with the flying of the Union flag) and, in a draft order in council published by the Secretary of State for Northern Ireland, to bring Ulster's public order laws closely into line with the Public Order Act 1986 are expected to become law by Easter 1987. In particular organisers of parades will be required to give the police seven days notice (instead of the current five), the police will have wide powers to impose conditions on processions and assemblies, and offences of incitement to racial or religious hatred will be extended.

1.8   FINE SCALES, PENALTIES ETC.

The penalties for the criminal offences referred to in this work are those prescribed at the time of going to print. In each case the length of imprisonment and the fine are the maximum penalties on conviction.

1.8.1   Fines

On conviction on *indictment* the Crown Court may impose a fine (Powers of Criminal Courts Act 1973, s. 30) of any amount (Criminal Law Act 1977, s. 32).

Fines for *summary offences* are subject to a standard scale of fines (Criminal Justice Act 1982, s. 37). The current amounts (set by the Criminal Penalties etc. (Increase) Order, SI 1984 No. 447) in the standard scale of maximum fines on adults are as follows:

Level	£
1	50
2	100
3	400
4	1,000
5	2,000

The statutory maximum fine on an adult on summary conviction for an *offence triable either way* (being the prescribed sum under Magistrates' Courts Act 1980, s. 32) is £2,000.

Juveniles. The maximum fine on summary conviction of a juvenile for an indictable or a summary offence is (Magistrates' Courts Act 1980, ss. 24 and 36):

		£
young person	(14–16)	400
child	(10–13)	100

The maximum fine on summary conviction where the statute has no expressed power to fine is £400 (Magistrates' Courts Act 1980, s. 34).

These fines are subject to alteration by the Home Secretary by statutory instrument (Criminal Justice Act 1982, s. 48).

A fine may not be ordered in addition to a probation order, a community service order, or an absolute or conditional discharge.

In fixing the amount of a fine the court must take into consideration the means of the defendant (see *R* v *Ashmore* [1974] Crim LR 375; *R* v *Thompson* [1974] Crim LR 720; Magistrates' Courts Act 1980, s. 35).

A defendant may be allowed time to pay a fine or to pay by instalments (Powers of Criminal Courts Act 1973, s. 31; Magistrates' Courts Act 1980, s. 75).

The court may impose a sentence of imprisonment in default of payment of a fine (the maximum periods applicable to the amounts imposed are set out in Powers of Criminal Courts Act 1973, s. 31(3A), and Magistrates' Courts Act 1980, Sch. 4).

2

The New Public Order Offences

This chapter deals with the new statutory public order offences of riot (Public Order Act 1986, s. 1), violent disorder (s. 2), affray (s. 3), threatening behaviour etc. (s. 4) and disorderly conduct (s. 5). It also contrasts the new offences with the repealed common law offences of riot, unlawful assembly and affray and with the repealed statutory offence of threatening behaviour etc. (Public Order Act 1936, s. 5).

2.1 INTRODUCTION

The Public Order Act 1986 abolishes (s. 9(1)) the common law offences of riot, rout, unlawful assembly and affray. It also abolishes (s. 9(2)) the offence of threatening behaviour etc. contrary to Public Order Act 1936, s. 5, and certain obsolete statutory offences under the Tumultuous Petitioning Act 1661, the Shipping Offences Act 1793 and the Seditious Meetings Act 1817 (prohibition of certain meetings within one mile of Westminster Hall when Parliament is sitting).

The Public Order Act 1986 replaces the abolished offences with a new expanded range of public order offences from riot with a maximum penalty of 10 years' imprisonment to the offence of disorderly conduct triable summarily only and punishable with a fine. The new offences are riot (s. 1), violent disorder (s. 2), affray (s. 3), threatening behaviour etc. (s. 4) and disorderly conduct (s. 5).

Despite the fact that the Public Order Act 1986 does not codify the whole of public order law—compare the Police and Criminal Evidence Act 1984 which generally codified police powers of stop, search, arrest etc.—this part of the Public Order Act 1986 exemplifies the gradual move towards codification of the criminal law (see *Codification of the Criminal Law*, Law Com. No. 143, 1985). This process now seems inevitable, although it has been argued that the common law provides greater flexibility in its approach to new circumstances. As Lord Reid observed in *Taylor* v *DPP* [1973] AC 964 at p. 990:

> I would not seek a rigid definition of a common law offence. . . . If a new point arises the question should always be whether it is within the mischief aimed at and within the principles established by the authorities.

On the other hand more rigid statutory offences may produce greater certainty in the application of the law by depriving judges of the power to bend and extend definitions of criminal offences to meet particular needs.

The obsolete and now abolished offence of rout, punishable by a fine or imprisonment, described conduct amounting to an embryonic riot. It was a disturbance of the peace by three or more persons who assembled together with an intention to do something which if executed would amount to a riot and who actually made a move towards the execution of their common purpose but did not complete it (*Redford* v *Birley* (1822) 1 St Tr NS 1071, 1211, 1214; *Russell on Crime*, 12th ed., vol. 1, p. 255; Hawk PC, bk 1, ch. 65, sect. 8).

2.2 RIOT

The Public Order Act 1986 repeals (s. 9(1)) the common law offence of riot and creates (s. 1) a new statutory offence of riot. The new offence penalises a person who uses violence where 12 or more persons present together use or threaten violence for a common purpose so as to cause a person of reasonable firmness to fear for his personal safety. The offence is triable only on indictment with a maximum penalty of 10 years' imprisonment.

2.2.1 Background

The offence of riot has been traditionally reserved for the most serious cases of public disorder, as reflected by the maximum penalty under the common law of life imprisonment. The justification for such a serious public order offence was explained by the Court of Appeal in *R* v *Caird* (1970) 54 Cr App R 499, the Cambridge Garden House Hotel case (at pp. 505 and 507):

> [Riot is] an offence which derives its great gravity from the simple fact that the persons concerned were acting in numbers and using those numbers to achieve their purpose. . . .
>
> The law of this country has always leant heavily against those who, to attain such a [common and unlawful] purpose, use the threat that lies in the power of numbers.

It is intended that the offence of riot will continue to be reserved only for very grave offences against public order involving large numbers, and it is expected that this charge will be the least frequently used of the new public order offences (Cmnd 9510, para. 3.16, Law Com. No. 123, paras. 2.10 and 2.11).

In the past some serious riots, such as the Sacheverell riots of 1709, led to prosecutions for *high treason* under the Treason Act 1351, an offence which even today carries the death penalty. The Chartists led by John Frost were convicted of high treason for their attack on Newport in 1839, but the sentences of death were commuted to transportation for life. A suggestion made by the Lord Chancellor in April 1986 that the capital offence of treason could be used as a legal remedy for acts of terrorism was later discounted by the Attorney-General who has responsibility for major State prosecutions. The 1351 Act, which was originally intended to deal with rival claims to the throne in the 14th century, was couched, he said, in such archaic language that not only would it be difficult to prove all the necessary ingredients but it would be difficult for a modern jury to come to grips with the terminology (*The Times*, 20 May 1986).

2.2.2   Riot at common law

At common law the offence of *riot* (otherwise known as *riotous assembly*) was defined in Hawk PC, bk 1, ch. 65, sect. 1, as

> a tumultuous disturbance of the peace, by three persons, or more, assembling together of their own authority, with an intent mutually to assist one another, against any who shall oppose them, in the execution of some enterprise of a private nature, and afterwards actually executing the same in a violent and turbulent manner, to the terror of the people, whether the act intended were of itself lawful or unlawful.

Five elements were generally considered necessary at common law in order to constitute the offence of riot:

(a)   the presence and participation of at least three persons,
(b)   a common purpose, lawful or unlawful,
(c)   the execution or inception of the common purpose,
(d)   an intent to help one another by force if necessary against any person who may oppose them in the execution of their common purpose, and
(e)   the use or threat of force or violence in and about the common purpose displayed in such a manner as to alarm or terrify at least one person of reasonable firmness.

(See *Field* v *Receiver of Metropolitan Police* [1907] 2 KB 853, 860; *R* v *Wong Chang and others* (1910) 6 Cr App R 59; *Ford* v *Receiver for the Metropolitan Police District* [1921] 2 KB 344; *Munday* v *Metropolitan Police District Receiver* [1949] 1 All ER 337; and see generally Archbold, 42nd ed., para. 25-13 et seq.).

Riot at common law was triable only on indictment. It was open to a jury trying a charge of riot to acquit of riot but convict of unlawful assembly or rout (*R* v *O'Brien* (1911) 6 Cr App R 108; *R* v *Caird* (1970) 54 Cr App R 499, 503–4).

The maximum penalty for riot at common law was life imprisonment.

2.2.3   The new offence of riot

The Public Order Act 1986, s. 1, provides that a person is guilty of riot if:

(a)   he is one of 12 or more persons who are present together in a public or a private place, and
(b)   they use or threaten unlawful violence, and
(c)   they do so for a common purpose, and
(d)   their conduct (taken together) is such as would cause a person of reasonable firmness present at the scene to fear for his safety, and
(e)   he actually uses unlawful violence for the common purpose.

These five elements show that the offence of riot continues to be a complex

offence. The new offence retains the difficult concept of common purpose and
the execution of the common purpose. It also preserves the concept of a person
of reasonable firmness who is required only hypothetically to be at the scene
(see below).

The new offence differs from the old offence in that:

(a)   the minimum number required is increased from three to 12,

(b)   each defendant must be proved to have used unlawful violence
(although those who encourage or assist the violence without actually using
violence will also be guilty—see below),

(c)   the necessary intent is altered: a person is guilty of riot only if he intends
to use violence or is aware that his conduct may be violent (see below), and
there is no need any more to prove an intention to help each other by force if
necessary, and

(d)   the maximum term of imprisonment is reduced from life to 10 years.

2.2.4   Elements of the new offence of riot

2.2.4.1   Twelve or more persons   The number of necessary participants is
increased by the Public Order Act 1986 from three to 12. The requirement of a
minimum of numbers—three for riot and also three for unlawful assembly at
common law—was unusual. No other major offence apart from conspiracy
depends for its definition upon proof of the commission of an offence by more
than one person (cf. the Night Poaching Act 1828, s. 9). The requirement of
numbers originated with Star Chamber and was confirmed by the courts of
common law in *R* v *Sudbury* (1700) 1 Ld Raym 484 (see also *R* v *Hughes* (1830)
4 C & P 373).

The figure of 12 (opposed in the Law Commission Working Paper No. 82,
para. 5.23, but proposed in the Law Commission's final report, Law Com. No.
123, para. 6.19, and described in both reports as necessarily arbitrary) reflects
the historical connection with the 'reading of the Riot Act' (the Riot Act 1714,
repealed in 1967, see 2.2.12) which provided that if 12 persons were still
assembled after the statutory hour they were guilty of a felony. Twelve is, of
course, still a magic number as the number of persons required for a jury in a
criminal trial.

2.2.4.2   Persons present together   The 12 or more persons must be present
together (Public Order Act 1986, s. 1(1)). This suggests that their presence
(and their activity) should be proximate in time and place. The prosecution
should not be allowed to frame a charge alleging that the riot took place over a
wide area or over a long period of time. Such a charge would be void for
duplicity. If separate incidents spring up over a period of time, for example
over a period of days during repeated inner city tension in one broad locality,
they should be charged as separate offences.

However, there is no doubt that riot can be a continuing offence. Section
1(2) specifically provides that it is immaterial whether or not the 12 or more use
or threaten violence simultaneously. In *R* v *Jones* (1974) 59 Cr App R 120, the
famous Shrewsbury picketing case, a charge of unlawful assembly, alleging that
the assembly had occurred on seven building sites in the county of Salop, was

held not to be bad for duplicity (see further below) because it described one activity although involving a number of acts at different places. Whether the decision in *Jones* would stand under the Public Order Act 1986 is doubtful, particularly in view of the further ruling in *Jones* that a similarly framed count of affray had to be quashed because it involved more than one activity. A charge alleging a number of incidents during the night on one housing estate may or may not therefore be bad for duplicity. It will be a question of fact in each case. Unless the prosecution can prove (at least on a prima facie basis) that the conduct is one continuous sequence of events in an unbroken chain, each separate activity should be separately charged.

The Law Commission Working Paper No. 82 (para. 5.28) suggested that the words 'present together' did not mean that the defendants must have been acting together or in concert with each other. Their acts might be unpremeditated and one individual might be scarcely aware in a general turmoil of precisely what others in the riot were doing. The essential factor was that together the participants formed a crowd, from which some might depart and others might join during the course of the conduct in question.

2.2.4.3 In a public or a private place Although most riots are committed in public places the offence of riot, as with all the new offences in the Public Order Act 1986, can also be committed in a private place (s. 1(5)). 'Private place' in this context is not restricted in any way, for example, by excluding dwellings (cf. offences contrary to Public Order Act 1986, ss. 4 and 5, below).

At common law a riot could take place anywhere on public or private property and even on enclosed premises (see, e.g., *Pitchers* v *Surrey County Council* [1923] 2 KB 57, in a military camp; *J.W. Dwyer Ltd* v *Metropolitan Police District Receiver* [1967] 2 QB 970, a robbery in a shop; *Kamara* v *DPP* [1974] AC 104, inside the High Commission of Sierra Leone).

Since no distinction is drawn in this Part of the Public Order Act 1986 (Part I, new offences) between public and private places, this aspect requires no close analysis. It should be noted that for the purposes of Part II of the Act (processions and assemblies) 'public place' is given a precise definition, meaning any highway, or any place to which the public or any section of the public has access, on payment or otherwise, as of right or by virtue of express or implied permission (s. 16; see 8.3 where this and other definitions of 'public place' are considered).

2.2.4.4 Use or threaten unlawful violence 'Violence' is interpreted in the Public Order Act 1986, s. 8, as meaning 'any violent conduct'. This is amplified in s. 8, more by illustration than definition, in two paragraphs:

(a) Violence includes (except in the context of affray) violent conduct towards property as well as violent conduct towards persons. The use of the word 'towards' makes it clear that neither injury to the person nor damage to property need occur. Violence obviously includes conduct which causes actual injury or damage, but the definition places the emphasis on the nature of the violent conduct rather than its consequences. The threat of injury or damage or an attempt to cause injury or damage is therefore enough. This point is reiterated in paragraph (b).

(b) 'Violence' is not restricted to conduct which actually causes or is even intended to cause injury to the person or damage to property but includes any other violent conduct. By way of example s. 8 refers to the throwing of missiles of a kind capable of causing injury—a bottle but not a paper dart—which fall short or miss their target (see also 3.1).

Violent conduct might also include wielding a lethal instrument or discharging a firearm in the direction of another (Law Com. No. 123, para. 5.33), running through the streets in a gang, heavy pushing at barriers or police cordons, and even a large number of pickets or demonstrators shouting threats to dissuade people from continuing to work, particularly where they are made in close proximity to their object. But mere 'abuse, swearing and shouting' by pickets or demonstrators, for the purpose of intimidation, does not amount to a threat of violence (*News Group Newspapers Ltd* v *Society of Graphical & Allied Trades 1982, The Times*, 1 August 1986, p.28 of the transcript), and should not therefore fall within the definition of violence in s. 8.

It should also be remembered that 'violence' is a strong word and is characterised in dictionary definitions by reference to extreme force, intensity, vehemence and severity. It should not be watered down.

The use of the word 'violence' replaces the more commonly used 'force', as in the use of reasonable force in self-defence (*Palmer* v *R* (1971) 55 Cr App R 223, 242), or reasonable force to prevent crime etc. (see Criminal Law Act 1977, s. 3). This change derives from the Law Commission's Report on Conspiracy and Criminal Law Reform (Law Com. No. 76 (1976) paras. 2.59 to 2.62), in which it was argued that 'force' had been too widely interpreted.

Unlawful violence. The violence must be unlawful, that is, not justified by law. This makes it clear that a person will only be penalised if his acts are done unlawfully. The common law defence of self-defence (see 2.3) and the provisions of the Criminal Law Act 1967, s. 3 (use of force in the prevention of crime or in making an arrest etc.), may exonerate a defendant in appropriate circumstances. It will therefore be a good defence for 12 or more to fight off a gang attacking a public house or its occupants or for a football club to use reasonable force to keep out swarms of angry fans unable to get into the ground after the gates have been closed. Once the defence has raised, for example, the issue of self-defence (the evidential burden), there can be no conviction unless the prosecution has disproved self-defence beyond reasonable doubt. See also, 2.3.3.4.

Use or threaten. Unlike the new offence of affray (s. 3) the words 'threaten violence' in the new offence of riot (s. 1) do not exclude the use of words. While mere altercations may not be prosecuted as an affray, threats which include words may be part of the incident which constitutes the offence of riot or violent disorder. In an early draft of the Public Order Bill references to 'words' were to include the distribution or display of any writing, sign or other visible representation, presumably such as leaflets, placards, banners, posters and even badges. But this reference to 'words' has been deleted from the final draft, therefore it must be given its ordinary meaning, which in this context ought to be no less than the spoken word or clearly visible written words. A riot may therefore be committed by one person using violence for the common purpose where the other 11 or more commit no violence at all but simply threaten to do so for a common purpose. In view of the definition of violence (above) this means that the new offence of riot could occur without any actual violence to persons or property taking place.

There is no known case at common law of riot by threat alone (see Law Commission Working Paper No. 82, para. 2.33), but at common law any person who actively encouraged or promoted a riot or an unlawful assembly, whether by words, by signs or by actions or by participating in it, was guilty of an offence (*R* v *Caird* (1970) 54 Cr App R 499). Also at common law, 'force or violence' (*Field* v *Receiver of Metropolitan Police* [1907] 2 KB 853) included threats of violence (see, e.g., *R* v *Sharp and Johnson* [1957] 1 QB 552). It should also be noted that the definition of assault (recommended for retention as one offence by the Law Commission's *Report on the Codification of the Criminal Law* (Law Com. No. 143)) includes the threat of assault (*R* v *Venna* [1976] QB 421, 428), just as the statutory definition of criminal damages includes the threat of damage (Criminal Damage Act 1971, s. 2, see 3.3).

2.2.4.5   For a common purpose   It was the element of 'common purpose' which prompted Lord Scarman to refer to the 'great forensic confusion' which prevailed when juries had the complex task of deciding whether the necessary elements of riot (and unlawful assembly) had been proved (Cmnd 8427, para. 7.39). There is no definition of 'common purpose' in the Public Order Act 1986 nor any clear definition elsewhere. The purpose may be either lawful or unlawful (*R* v *Graham and Burns* (1888) 16 Cox CC 420, 427, disturbances in Trafalgar Square at a meeting banned by the Metropolitan Police Commissioner which was held by the Metropolitan Radical Federation to demand the release of 'Irish patriots'), although any purpose which is executed with violence to the fear of others must arguably be unlawful.

However, the essential ingredient of this element of the offence of riot is the aggravated seriousness of violent behaviour when committed collectively by a crowd of like-minded persons whatever the role of the individual persons charged may be (see *R* v *Caird* (1970) 54 Cr App R 499). No proof of any prior plan or agreement is necessary (*O'Brien* v *Friel* [1974] NI 29, 42). For the avoidance of doubt the 'common purpose' may be inferred from conduct (s. 1(3)), but all 12 persons must share the purpose, and purpose should not be equated with motive (see also 2.2.5).

The Law Commission (Law Com. No. 123, para. 6.11 et seq.) rejected an earlier proposal that common purpose should be replaced by a concept of 'engaging in an unlawful course of violent conduct'. They preferred the retention of common purpose as more accurately reflecting the idea of concerted action on the part of a number of people. They believed that common purpose caught both the participants who had expressly or impliedly agreed to concerted action and the casual participant, the pure opportunist, who shared no purpose with anyone but joined in to achieve a common purpose such as an attack on the police. This reasoning is arguably wrong, in that it fails to distinguish between a shared common purpose and damage or injury caused by common acts which are committed for diverse purposes.

2.2.4.6   A person of reasonable firmness present at the scene   Despite the use of these words there is no need for a person of reasonable firmness to be actually present at the scene or even to be likely to be present at the scene (s. 1(4)). It is enough that a hypothetical person at the scene would have been put in fear.

In 1842 it was decided that it was sufficient if one person was put in fear (*R* v *Langford* (1842) Car & M 602). Later cases suggested that the objective test of putting a hypothetical bystander of reasonable firmness and courage in fear would suffice (*J.W. Dwyer Ltd* v *Metropolitan Police District Receiver* [1967] 2 QB 970; *Devlin* v *Armstrong* [1971] NI 13; *R* v *Sharp and Johnson* [1957] 1 QB 552, 560).

A 'person of reasonable firmness' is not defined. It is for the jury to decide what such a person is and whether that person would be put in fear for his personal safety in the circumstances. A judge might direct a jury that they should exclude children, elderly or infirm people from their considerations, unless these categories were actually present or might have been present as in the case of a disturbance at a holiday camp. Commonly, however, this element is proved by asking eyewitnesses or even victims what effect the disturbance had upon them. Police officers taking statements often invite witnesses to express their fear or alarm at the time.

It should be noted that the test is 'fear for personal safety', a lesser test than the common law requirement of terror (*R* v *Hughes* (1830) 4 C & P 373; *R* v *Graham and Burns* (1888) 16 Cox CC 420). As at common law (*R* v *Phillips* (1842) 2 Mood CC 252, the destruction of an old man's cottage) only one person need be put in fear.

2.2.4.7 Uses violence for the common purpose Whereas the 12 or more may *use or threaten* violence, the accused person must have actually *used* violence (as defined in s. 8) before he can be convicted of riot. This is intended to eliminate the danger of innocent bystanders being implicated in the offence (Law Com. No. 123, para. 6.22). But despite this safeguard prosecutors may attempt to prove the offence of riot against those who have not used violence themselves on the basis of participation in a joint enterprise.

A person who participates by encouraging or assisting others to use violence is guilty of riot (see *R* v *Caird* (1970) 54 Cr App R 499). Mere presence, as an innocent bystander or out of curiosity, would not be enough, although non-accidental presence, such as going to see what is happening, may be prima facie evidence (but no more) of encouragement of others (*R* v *Coney* (1882) 8 QBD 534; *R* v *Clarkson* (1971) 55 Cr App R 445). The headnote in the report (1 St Tr NS 171 at 173–4) of the Trial of Henry Hunt and others for riotous assembly prior to the St Peter's Field massacre in 1816 reads:

Persons who are present at a meeting with knowledge of such purpose, means, manner, and circumstances as render it unlawful, and who give their aid and countenance to the meeting, are guilty of unlawful assembling, but persons present without such knowledge or not giving such aid and countenance are not guilty.

If a riot follows from speeches at a meeting which incite violence, the speakers may be convicted of riot even though absent at the time of the riot (*R* v *Sharpe* (1848) 3 Cox CC 288).

Just as one person alone may be convicted of the crime of conspiracy (Criminal Law Act 1977, s. 5(8) and (9)), fewer than the specified number of 12 may be convicted of riot so long as it is proved that the required number, at least 12, took part (*R* v *Beach and Morris* (1909) 2 Cr App R 189, three defendants were charged with riot at common law, but only two convicted).

2.2.5   Mental element *(mens rea)*

A person is guilty of riot only if *he intends to use violence* or *is aware that his conduct may be violent* (s. 6(1)).

The mental element of each defendant must be proved in addition to the other elements set out in s. 1. Proof will be provided, as in other criminal offences, as a matter of inference from the conduct of the defendant, from prior planning or agreement, from behaviour at the scene, and from conduct subsequently, including any admissions of guilt. The common law intent to help one another by force if necessary against any person who may oppose the execution of the common purpose has been removed as adding nothing essential to the proper delimitations of the offence (Law Com. No. 123, para. 6.29).

2.2.5.1   Awareness   The alternative mental element of 'awareness' is a new word in the criminal law. It originates from a number of Law Commission reports, including the Report on the Mental Element in Crime (Law Com. No. 89), the Report on Offences Relating to Public Order (Law Com. No. 123), and the Report on the Codification of the Criminal Law (Law Com. No. 143, see draft cl. 22 at pp. 63 et seq. and 183).

The new awareness test, however, is only a modified form of an existing concept, namely recklessness. It takes its meaning from the various offences, mostly assaults, in the Offences against the Person Act 1861. The word used to describe the mental element for those offences is 'maliciously', which means either (a) an actual intention to do the particular kind of harm that was in fact done, or (b) recklessness as to whether such harm should occur or not (*R* v *Cunningham* [1957] 2 QB 396). 'Recklessness' has the same meaning in the common law offences of assault and battery (*R* v *Venna* [1976] QB 421, 428–9; and see 3.2).

'Awareness' in the Public Order Act 1986, s. 6, means just that kind of recklessness. The defendant foresees that the particular kind of harm may be done (assaults) or violence may occur (riot) and yet he goes on to take the risk of it. For example, a person is guilty of assault if he deliberately punches another person or if (recklessly) he flails his arms vigorously in a crowd knowing that somebody may get hurt. In riot the same approach applies. It must be proved that the defendant used violence, for example by throwing a bottle, and it must be proved that either (a) he intended to use violence—he deliberately threw the bottle at a police officer, it did not slip out of his hand by accident—or (b) he was aware that his conduct might be violent—he tossed the bottle in the general direction of the police not caring whether the bottle fell short or not but knowing that there was some risk of injury.

The concept of recklessness, however, has developed with some awkwardness in recent times (see *R* v *Caldwell* [1982] AC 341 and *Elliott* v *C* [1983] 2 All ER 1055, arson cases; *R* v *Lawrence* [1982] AC 510, reckless driving; and the rape cases: *R* v *Pigg* (1982) 74 Cr App R 352, *R* v *Thomas* (1983) 77 Cr App R 63, *R* v *Satnam S and Kewal S* (1983) 78 Cr App R 149). Broadly speaking, recklessness in criminal damage is an objective test, recklessness in rape cases is a subjective test. In relation to criminal damage, for example, a person is reckless if he does an act which in fact creates an obvious risk that property will be destroyed or damaged and when he does the act he either has not given any thought to the possibility of there being any such risk or has recognised that there was some risk involved and has none the less gone on to do it (*R* v *Caldwell*). This test is both strict in its definition—some critics say almost to the point of creating an absolute offence—and almost impossible to apply. Judges have difficulty explaining it to juries in simple terms (particularly in arson cases where alternative charges may be laid) and juries no doubt have difficulty understanding it.

The awareness test has a narrower definition than the *Caldwell* test of recklessness and one which is more favourable to the defendant. It covers the case where the actor recognizes that there is some risk involved (is aware) and nevertheless goes on to do the act which creates the risk, but it does not cover the case where a risk is obvious but the actor has not given any thought to the possibility of there being any such risk (see generally Law Com. No. 143, para 8.18 et seq.). Awareness—it may still be called recklessness—provides a subjective test of conscious risk-taking as the preferred minimum fault element for the new offence of riot (and also for the new offences of violent disorder and affray).

One possible result of introducing this test for three new offences only (riot, violent disorder and affray) will be that a court may have to consider two tests of recklessness arising out of one set of facts. If a defendant were charged in the same indictment, for example, with riot (or violent disorder or affray) and causing criminal damage (see 3.3), the minimum required mental element would be awareness for the offence of riot but the *Caldwell* test of recklessness for the offence of criminal damage.

The end result, nevertheless, is a mental element for riot which is wider than the principal common law offence against public order in the criminal law of the Republic of South Africa which consists in 'the unlawful and *intentional* commission by a number of people acting in concert of acts of sufficiently serious dimensions which are intended forcibly to disturb the public peace or security or to invade the rights of others' (see Law Com. No. 123, p. 132).

2.2.5.2 Intoxication (s. 6(5), (6))   A defendant who claims that his awareness is impaired by intoxication has no special defence if the intoxication was self-induced (s. 6(5)). He will be treated as if he was unimpaired. Intoxication means any intoxication whether caused by drink, drugs or other means (presumably including glue sniffing), or by a combination of means (s. 6(6)). The drunken football rioter will therefore be treated as if he were sober.

If on the other hand the intoxication was not self-induced, for example where drinks have been laced without the defendant's knowledge, or it was caused solely by the taking or administration of a substance in the course of medical treatment, the defendant's awareness may be genuinely impaired (s. 6(5)), in which case the burden of proving this allegation on a balance of probabilities rests upon the defendant (s. 6(5)).

2.2.6   Power of arrest

Riot is an arrestable offence under Police and Criminal Evidence Act 1984, s. 24, because on conviction a person may be sentenced to a term of imprisonment in excess of five years (the maximum penalty is 10 years, see 2.2.11). Accordingly, any person (a police officer or other citizen) may arrest without warrant anyone whom he reasonably suspects to have committed or to be in the act of committing the offence of riot (see 5.2).

There is a power of arrest at common law for breach of the peace which is widely used to prevent or disperse riots (see 5.1) as well as the right that every person has to use such force as is reasonable in the circumstances in the prevention of crime (Criminal Law Act 1967, s. 3(1)).

The police may also use reasonable force to suppress a riot (*R* v *Fursey* (1833) 3 St Tr NS 543, which concerned a public meeting advertised to be held to adopt preparatory measures for holding a national convention 'as the only means of obtaining the rights of the people' and declared by the Secretary of State to be 'dangerous to the public peace and illegal'—the jury returned a verdict of not guilty). If the force is unreasonable or it is used against innocent persons a civil action for trespass to the person will lie against the police. The use of a team carrying short shields and batons to 'incapacitate missile throwers and ringleaders by striking in a controlled manner with batons about the arms and legs or torso' and the use of mounted police to disperse a crowd 'using impetus and weight to create fear and a scatter effect' by advancing into the crowd at a canter—just two of the riot tactics in a secret manual drawn up by the Association of Chief Police Officers—may go beyond the scope of reasonable force, but modern police tactics are undoubtedly more militaristic in style. In his report for 1985 the Metropolitan Police Commissioner said that he would be prepared to use water cannon and to fire plastic bullets (baton rounds) if necessary.

If requested, ordinary citizens are obliged to assist the police and if they refuse they commit a criminal offence unless they have a lawful excuse or it is physically impossible for them to assist (*R* v *Brown* (1841) Car & M 314). Also there is 'a general liberty even as between strangers to prevent a felony', to intervene in circumstances of necessity 'with the sole object of restoring the peace by rescuing a person being attacked' (*R* v *Duffy* [1967] 1 QB 63 at 67–8).

2.2.7   Prosecution: DPP's consent

A prosecution for an offence of riot or incitement to riot can only be instituted by, or with the consent of the Director of Public Prosecutions (s. 7(1)).

The offence of riot has been charged relatively sparingly in recent years. Charges have been brought against, amongst others, inner city rioters, football hooligans, Hell's Angels, and striking miners. Many prosecutions have been unsuccessful, notably the Bristol riot trial of 1981 (for a full account see Kettle and Hodges, *Uprising!*) and the 1985 miners' cases (both of riot and unlawful assembly), often displaying the difficulty of proving a common purpose. By October 1985, 440 men had been charged with riot or unlawful assembly arising out of incidents in the miners' strike in Nottinghamshire and South Yorkshire and no jury had returned a verdict of guilty (although a few cases were still pending). But riot has a long history of acquittals, including Ben Tillett for incitement to riot in the 1893 dock dispute, the Penrhyn quarry dispute case in 1901 and Oswald Mosley for riotous assembly in Worthing in 1934 (see Williams, *Keeping the Peace*, pp. 240–1).

2.2.8   The charge: duplicity

A charge of riot which alleges that 12 or more persons were 'using *or* threatening' unlawful violence will not be bad for duplicity and therefore invalid. The Public Order Act 1986, s. 7(2), specifically provides that the wording of the definition of riot creates only one offence (s. 7(2)). This avoids the difficulty which has arisen over the application of r. 7 of the Indictment Rules 1971 which permits the framing of a charge in the alternative where the enactment creating the offence puts the doing of acts or different intentions in the alternative.

2.2.9   Mode of trial

The offence of riot is triable on indictment only (s. 1(6)).

2.2.10   Alternative verdicts

The Public Order Act 1986 does not provide a special alternative verdict in the case of riot (although it does so in the case of violent disorder and affray: s. 7(3), and see 2.3.9 and 2.4.10). At common law the alternative verdicts available where a jury entered a verdict of not guilty of riot were guilty to an offence of unlawful assembly (or rout) or of common assault (*R* v *O'Brien* (1911) 6 Cr App R 108, in which the wording of the charge contained all the words necessary to constitute a charge of common assault).

Under the provisions of the Criminal Law Act 1967, s. 6(3), which permits a jury to acquit of the offence specifically charged in the indictment but to convict of an alternative offence where the allegations in the indictment amount to or include an allegation of another offence triable by that court, the jury could technically convict the defendant of either violent disorder or affray, as long as the necessary ingredients of the lesser offences (including, for example, violence towards persons, not property, in affray) were proved (see *R* v *Wilson* [1984] Crim LR 36). It is submitted, however, that the better practice would be to set out the alternative charges in the indictment in cases where the prosecution wish to put their case in the alternative. On this footing the jury would always be able to turn to the indictment to see the necessary ingredients and particulars of each charge laid against the defendant.

In practice the trial judge is only obliged to leave to the jury all the lesser alternative verdicts theoretically comprised in the charge if that is necessary in the interests of justice. It is wrong to leave lesser alternatives to the jury if they do not arise on the issues presented at the trial and it is wrong to fail to leave them when they do so arise (*R* v *Fairbanks, The Times*, 3 July 1986). If the judge is minded to leave to the jury an alternative not dealt with by counsel he should warn counsel before speeches (*R* v *Brennan*, unreported, CA 17 December 1985, ref. 753 B85).

2.2.11   Penalty

The maximum penalty for riot is 10 years' imprisonment and/or a fine (s. 1(6)).

When convictions have been obtained, substantial terms of imprisonment have been imposed. A Chelsea football fan who was sentenced to life imprisonment at the Central Criminal Court in November 1985 had his sentence reduced to three years for riot, but made to run consecutively to a seven-year sentence for wounding with a beer glass (*R* v *Whitton, The Times*, 20 May 1986). Undergraduate students of good character received custodial sentences (12 months' imprisonment and Borstal training) for their part in the Cambridge Garden House Hotel case (*R* v *Caird* (1970) 54 Cr App R 499) in which Sachs LJ said (at p. 506):

> When there is wanton and vicious violence of gross degree the court is not concerned with whether it originates from gang rivalry or from political motives. It is the degree of mob violence that matters and the extent to which the public peace is being broken. It makes no difference whether the mob has attacked a first-class hotel in Cambridge or some dance-hall frequented by the less well-circumstanced.

In 1981 an 18-year-old man was sentenced at Nottingham to three years' imprisonment for incitement to riot after posting leaflets headed 'Burn Babylon burn', urging people to have bigger and better riots and to destroy the system (*Daily Telegraph*, 21 October 1981). In *R* v *Pilgrim* (1983) 5 Cr App R (S) 140 sentences of eight, five and three years' imprisonment were passed for a serious attack by 100 youths on a rival group inside a public house, one of them being killed.

The Law Commission Working Paper No. 82 (para. 5.51) favoured a maximum penalty of 14 years for riot. The Law Commission's final report (Law Com. No. 123, para. 6.32) proposed a maximum of 10 years. They suggested that the penalty should not only reflect the gravity of the defendant's conduct but also that it would not be necessary to prove that the defendant had injured another or damaged property. The government accepted the Law Commission's 10-year penalty in its White Paper (Cmnd 9510, May 1985) but increased it to life imprisonment in the Public Order Bill, apparently to keep in line with the sentence imposed in the Chelsea football case, but reduced it to 10 years after the appeal hearing (see *R* v *Whitton*, above). Even 10 years' imprisonment is generally very much longer than other common law or post common law countries: for example, Canada—two years, Australia (most States)—three years, New Zealand—two years, and in India, where the law of public order has remained the same since Lord Macaulay drafted the Indian Penal Code in 1860—two years.

2.2.12   'Reading the Riot Act'

The provision of 'reading the Riot Act' no longer applies. It had long been in disuse when it was repealed by the Criminal Law Act 1967, s. 10(2). The Riot Act 1714 had provided that if 12 persons assembled unlawfully to the disturbance of the peace and failed to disperse within one hour after proclamation by a justice of the peace, sheriff, under-sheriff, or mayor they were guilty of a felony.

2.2.13   Compensation for riot damage

The Riot (Damages) Act 1886 provides for compensation to be paid out of the local police fund for damage or loss relating to houses, shops or buildings, or their contents, provided the damage was done by 'persons riotously and tumultuously assembled together'. This provision is retained by the Public Order Act 1986 and 'riotously' is to be construed in accordance with the new s. 1 definition of riot (s. 10(1)). Since the definition of riot (see 2.2.3) is more restricted, for example in terms of numbers, claims for compensation will be similarly restricted.

Claims must be made in writing within 14 days (this period may be extended) to the compensation authority (the local authority or in London the Metropolitan Police Receiver). Compensation must be 'just'. If the claimant is dissatisfied he can bring an action against the compensation authority for recovery of his loss. See generally the Riot (Damages) Act 1886, s. 63 and Sch. 9; Police Act 1964 and *Halsbury's Laws of England*, 4th ed., vol 36, paras. 241 et seq.

2.3   VIOLENT DISORDER

The Public Order Act 1986, s. 2, creates a brand new offence of violent disorder. There was no offence of violent disorder at common law, but in effect the new offence replaces the common law offence of unlawful assembly. The offence of violent disorder is intended for use as the normal charge for serious outbreaks of public disorder. It penalises a person who uses or threatens violence where three or more persons present together use or threaten violence so as to cause a person of reasonable firmness to fear for his personal safety. The offence is triable either way with a maximum penalty on indictment of five years' imprisonment.

2.3.1   Background

The offence of violent disorder was introduced as a flexible offence particularly suitable for dealing with group violence. It will probably also be used for some cases previously charged as riot (Cmnd 9510, para. 3.13). It is designed for application over a wide spectrum of situations ranging from major public disorder to minor group disturbances involving some violence, such as those commonly associated with football hooliganism.

The Law Commission had proposed (Law Com. No. 123, para. 5.23) that unlawful assembly should be replaced by two new offences, the offence of violent disorder and an extended Public Order Act 1936, s. 5, offence described as conduct intended or likely to cause fear or provoke violence. But the White Paper (and the subsequent Public Order Bill) preferred to merge the second proposed offence with the existing Public Order Act 1936, s. 5, offence and create a new offence of threatening behaviour etc. (Public Order Act 1986, s. 4).

The common law offence of *unlawful assembly*, now abolished (Public Order Act 1986, s. 9(1)) and replaced by the new offence of violent disorder, was elusive in definition. Modern authorities tended to include the following elements (see Archbold, 42nd ed., para. 25–2):

(a) an assembly of three or more persons,
(b) with intent to commit a crime by open force, or
(c) with intent to carry out any common purpose, lawful or unlawful,
(d) in such a manner as to endanger the public peace, or to give firm and courageous persons in the neighbourhood of such assembly reasonable grounds to apprehend a breach of the peace in consequence of it.

But there were differing views as to the precise nature of an unlawful assembly (see for example *R* v *Chief Constable of Devon & Cornwall (ex parte Central Electricity Generating Board)* [1982] QB 458, 471, cf. 473–4) and the distinction between a riot and an unlawful assembly was not always easily drawn. Generally an unlawful assembly was an incipient or inchoate riot, the preparation for a riot which lacked the execution of the common intended purpose, and which 'became riotous at latest when alarming force or violence begins to be used' (*R* v *Caird* (1970) 54 Cr App R 499, 504–5).

As with riot the offence of unlawful assembly has been used in recent times against football hooligans, rival gangs of Hell's Angels, large numbers of pickets and rampaging students. Indictments charging riot often pleaded unlawful assembly in the alternative as a lesser charge. In 1985 the occupants of some 30 vehicles, part of the 'peace convoy' (see generally 7.4), were charged with unlawful assembly for driving round in a bean field and destroying the crop. The charges were later dropped and replaced with individual charges of criminal damage (see *R* v *Salisbury Magistrates' Court (ex parte Mastin)* [1986] Crim LR 545, see 3.3) and obstruction of the police (see *Smith* v *Reynolds and others* [1986] Crim LR 559, see 5.12).

2.3.2 The new offence of violent disorder

The Public Order Act 1986, s. 2, provides that a person is guilty of violent disorder if:

(a) he is one of three or more persons present together in a public or a private place, and
(b) they use or threaten unlawful violence, and
(c) their conduct (taken together) is such as would cause a person of reasonable firmness present at the scene to fear for his safety, and
(d) he actually uses or threatens unlawful violence.

This definition is broadly similar to the new definition of riot (see 2.2.3). In common with the offence of riot, violent disorder contains the elements of:

(a)   persons who are present together,
(b)   use or threat of unlawful violence,
(c)   a person of reasonable firmness present at the scene.

Violent disorder differs from riot in that:

(a)   The required number of persons present for riot is 12, but only three for violent disorder (as with the repealed common law offence of unlawful assembly).
(b)   There is no requirement in violent disorder for a common purpose.
(c)   Whereas for riot a person is only guilty if he *uses* violence, in violent disorder a person is guilty of the offence if he *uses or threatens* violence.

2.3.3   Elements of the new offence of violent disorder

2.3.3.1   Three or more persons   An offence of violent disorder is not committed unless at least three persons participate using or threatening violence (s. 2(1)). The number of three persons is retained from the number required for the old offence of unlawful assembly (now repealed). Just as one person alone may be convicted of the crime of conspiracy (Criminal Law Act 1977, s. 5(8) and (9)) so too may any number less than three persons be convicted of this offence so long as it is proved that the required number, at least three, took part.

2.3.3.2   Persons present together   The three or more persons must be present together (s. 2(1)). This suggests that their presence (and their activity) should be proximate in time and place. The prosecution should not be allowed to frame a charge alleging that the offence took place over a wide area or over a long period of time. Such a charge would be void for duplicity. If separate incidents spring up over a period of time, for example during repeated inner city tension in one broad locality, they should be charged as separate charges.
However, there is no doubt that as with the offence of riot (see 2.3.3.2) violent disorder can be a continuing offence. Section 2(2) specifically provides that it is immaterial whether or not the three or more use or threaten violence simultaneously. In *R* v *Jones* (1974) 59 Cr App R 120, the famous Shrewsbury picketing case, a charge of unlawful assembly alleging that the assembly had occurred on seven building sites in the county of Salop was held not to be bad for duplicity, because it described one activity although involving a number of acts at different places. But the decision in *Jones* is of dubious validity in the context of the new offence of violent disorder, particularly since in *Jones* a similarly framed count of affray was quashed on appeal for duplicity on the ground that it did involve more than one activity.

2.3.3.3   In a public or a private place   Violent disorder may be committed in *private* as well as in *public* places (s. 2(4)), in common with all the new offences in this Part of the Public Order Act 1986. As with affray this will often mean fights in private clubs or at private functions held in village halls and other places closed to the public. But since violent disorder, unlike affray, is not limited to violence to the person (see 2.3.3.4) it will also include damage and destruction caused by youths on the rampage in holiday camps, youth clubs and sports clubs, colleges and other institutions which are private and not open to all members of the public.

2.3.3.4   Use or threaten unlawful violence   'Violence' is interpreted in the Public Order Act 1986, s. 8, as meaning 'any violent conduct'. This is amplified in s. 8, more by illustration than definition, in two paragraphs:

(a)   Violence includes (except in the context of affray) violent conduct towards property as well as violent conduct towards persons. The use of the word 'towards' makes it clear that neither injury to the person nor damage to property need occur. Violence obviously includes conduct which causes actual injury or damage, but the definition places the emphasis on the nature of the violent conduct rather than its consequences. The threat of injury or damage or an attempt to cause injury or damage is therefore enough. This point is reiterated in paragraph (b).

(b)   'Violence' is not restricted to conduct which actually causes or is even intended to cause injury to the person or damage to property but includes any other violent conduct. By way of example s. 8 refers to the throwing of missiles of a kind capable of causing injury—a bottle but not a paper dart—which fall short or miss their target (see also 3.1).

It should also be remembered that 'violence' is a strong word and is characterised in dictionary definitions by reference to extreme force, intensity, vehemence and severity. It should not be watered down.

For further discussion of violence see 2.2.4.4.

Unlawful violence.   The violence must be unlawful, that is, not justified by law. This makes it clear that a person will only be penalised if his acts are done unlawfully. The common law defence of self-defence and the provisions of the Criminal Law Act 1967, s. 3 (use of force in the prevention of crime or in making an arrest etc.), may exonerate a defendant in appropriate circumstances. Group defence by a group of football supporters under attack from a rival group might be a legitimate excuse for violence as long as the violence remains within reasonable bounds in the circumstances and does not develop from self-defence into retaliation.

A person defending himself cannot weigh to a nicety the exact measure of his necessary defensive action. If the jury thought that in a moment of unexpected anguish a person attacked had only done what he honestly and instinctively thought was necessary, that would be most potent evidence that only reasonable defensive action had been taken. (*Palmer* v *R* (1971) 55 Cr App R 223, 242.)

In the law of self-defence there is no longer a rule that a person attacked must retreat, but failure to do so would be a factor to be considered in deciding whether the conduct was reasonable (*R* v *Bird* [1985] 2 All ER 513). Even a petrol bomb may be possessed lawfully by way of self-defence if the defendant's object is to protect himself or his family or his property against imminent apprehended attack by means which he believes are no more than reasonably necessary to meet the force used by the attackers (*Attorney-General's Reference (No. 2 of 1983)* [1984] QB 456, following *R* v *Fegan* [1972] NI 80 in which a Roman Catholic who had married a Protestant woman lawfully armed himself with a revolver after being subjected to threats and beatings). Once the defence has raised the issue of self-defence (the evidential burden), the burden of disproving self-defence beyond reasonable doubt rests upon the prosecution.

Use or threaten.   The three or more participants need only threaten violence for the offence of violent disorder to be complete. Unlike the new offence of affray (s. 3) the words 'threaten violence' in the new offence of violent disorder (s. 2) do not exclude the use of words. Therefore while mere altercations may not be prosecuted as an affray, threats by words alone may be a part or the whole of the incident which constitutes the offence of violent disorder. Although the offence of violent disorder may be technically complete on threats of violence alone, that is, without any actual violence taking place, it was not envisaged that this offence should be used in those circumstances. The offence of threatening behaviour etc. (s. 4) is a more appropriate charge. For further discussion see 2.2.4.4.2.

2.3.3.5   A person of reasonable firmness present at the scene   Despite the use of these words there is no need for the prosecution to prove that either there were any people (other than the defendants) at the scene or that any of them feared for their personal safety (s. 2(3)). It is enough that a hypothetical person at the scene would have been put in fear.

   The objective test of putting a hypothetical innocent bystander of reasonable firmness and courage at the scene has long since been established, although it is good practice for the prosecution to ask eyewitnesses or victims what effect the conduct complained of had upon them at the time. Generally, see 2.2.4.6.

2.3.3.6   Uses or threatens violence   For the offence of violent disorder to be made out the three or more must have used or threatened violence and in addition the defendant must be proved to have used *or* threatened violence. This provides a combination of alternatives for the commission of the offence. At its highest the offence is committed when the defendant is one of three or more persons who use violence and the defendant actually uses violence. At its lowest the offence is committed without any violence by either the defendant or the others who are present, threats alone being sufficient. Or there could be a combination of the use of violence and threats of violence.

   The definition of violent disorder differs therefore from riot in that the participant may be found guilty if he uses *or threatens* violence. As with riot (but not affray) the words 'threaten violence' do not exclude the use of *words* as sufficient conduct to prove this ingredient of the offence of violent disorder. See generally, 2.2.4.4.2.

   A defendant who does not use or even threaten violence may be convicted of the offence of violent disorder if he participates by encouraging or assisting others to use or threaten violence (see *R* v *Caird* (1970) 54 Cr App R 499 and 2.2.4.4.2). Verbal encouragement or waving others on may be enough. Mere presence, as an innocent bystander or out of curiosity, would not be enough, although non-accidental presence, such as going to see what is happening, may be prima facie evidence (but no more) of the encouragement of others (*R* v *Coney* (1882) 8 QBD 534; *R* v *Clarkson* (1971) 55 Cr App R 445).

2.3.4   Mental element *(mens rea)*

A person is guilty of violent disorder only if *he intends to use or threaten violence* or *is aware that his conduct may be violent or threaten violence* (s. 6(2)).

The mental element must be proved in addition to the other elements set out in s. 2. Proof will be provided, as with other criminal offences, from the conduct of the defendant, from prior planning or agreement, from behaviour at the scene, and from conduct subsequently including any admissions of guilt. For further details of the mental element, the new concept of awareness and the issue of intoxication (which apply to violent disorder), see 2.2.5.

2.3.5   Power of arrest

Violent disorder is an arrestable offence because the maximum penalty is five years' imprisonment (Police and Criminal Evidence Act 1984, s. 24). There is therefore no need for a specific arrest power in Public Order Act 1986, s. 2. For additional arrest powers available in circumstances of public disorder and police powers to disperse crowds, see 2.2.6 and chapter 5.

2.3.6   Prosecution

The DPP's consent is not required (cf. 2.2.7).

2.3.7   The charge: duplicity

In order to avoid the possibility that a charge of violent disorder might be judged bad for duplicity, s. 7(2) specifically provides that s. 2 creates just one offence. Prosecutors therefore will be able to charge a person with 'using violence' or 'threatening violence' or both. A single charge containing the words 'using or threatening violence' will not be invalid for duplicity. This provision in s. 7(2) applies to all the new public order offences. It avoids the difficulty which has arisen over the application of r. 7 of the Indictment Rules 1971 which permits the framing of a charge in the alternative where the enactment creating the offence puts the doing of acts or different intentions in the alternative.

2.3.8   Mode of trial

The offence of violent disorder (like the new offence of affray) is triable either way (s. 2(5)), that is, either on indictment in the Crown Court or summarily in the magistrates' court. The defendant can elect to be tried on indictment by a jury if he so wishes.

It has been suggested that the expeditious disposal in the magistrates' court of less serious cases of violent disorder (and affray) may often be the most effective means of quelling further disturbances (Law Com. No. 123, para. 5.37), although the retention of the defendant's right to elect trial by jury and the delay in proceeding swiftly with cases involving large numbers of defendants may thwart this particular notion.

2.3.9 Alternative verdicts

When a charge of violent disorder (or affray) is tried *on indictment* the jury may acquit the defendant of violent disorder but convict him of an offence of threatening behaviour etc. contrary to Public Order Act 1986, s. 4 (s. 7(3)). This is permitted despite the fact that an offence under s. 4 is not triable on indictment and cannot therefore be set out as a separate charge in the indictment. In the event of a conviction on indictment of an offence contrary to s. 4 the penalty will be no greater than if the offence had been tried summarily (s. 7(4), and see 2.5). For further provision for alternative verdicts under the Criminal Law Act 1967 and the circumstances in which trial judges should and should not leave alternative verdicts to the jury, see 2.2.10.

2.3.10 Penalty

On indictment the maximum penalty for violent disorder is five years' imprisonment and/or a fine. On summary conviction in the magistrates' court the maximum penalty is six months' imprisonment and/or a fine not to exceed the current statutory maximum of £2,000 (s. 2(5)).

2.4 AFFRAY

The Public Order Act 1986 repeals (s. 9(1)) the common law offence of affray and creates (s. 3) a new statutory offence of affray. The new offence penalises a person who uses or threatens violence towards another so as to cause a person of reasonable firmness to fear for his personal safety. The offence is triable either way with a maximum penalty on indictment of three years' imprisonment.

2.4.1 Background

The most common form of affray at common law was a fight between two men or two groups, which terrified innocent bystanders. The word 'affray' and the French word '*effrayer*', to frighten, are of common origin. The new offence is intended to be the normal charge brought in cases of fights outside pubs and clubs. It is designed to cover street fights whereas violent disorder is designed for group or mob violence.

Affray was charged, before the Public Order Act 1986, more frequently than the other common law offences of riot and unlawful assembly (about 1,000 people a year were charged with affray), despite the fact that it was for many years considered to be obsolete as an offence—but not as an activity—until its modern revival in *R v Sharp and Johnson* [1957] 1 QB 552, the first reported case for over 100 years. In recent times the courts have encouraged prosecutors to think hard before charging affray, suggesting that 'a great deal of time and money' should not be wasted by charging affray which should be 'reserved for serious cases which were not far short of a riot' (*R v Crimlis* (1976) Crim LR 693: a fight between a small number of persons outside a public house in which two men were knocked unconscious). This approach may in future be superseded by using the new offence of violent disorder for minor riots.

In practice, although some minor fights have been charged as threatening behaviour etc. under the Public Order Act 1936, s. 5, or as specific cases of assault, affray has often been charged, not according to the gravity of the fight, but where the individual roles of the participants have been difficult to identify, and specific charges of assault, criminal damage or carrying offensive weapons could not be brought. This approach was specifically endorsed by the House of Lords in *Button* v *DPP* [1966] AC 591. On other occasions, unnecessary, lengthy trials have taken place when specific charges have been clearly identified and would have reflected the criminality of the conduct complained of.

2.4.2   Affray at common law

At common law an affray was defined as a violent breach of the peace by one or more persons which took place in such a manner as to terrify a person of reasonable firmness (*R* v *Summers* (1972) 56 Cr App R 604; *Taylor* v *DPP* [1973] AC 964). The penalty was imprisonment and/or a fine without limit.

In order to establish the offence of affray in a public place the prosecution had to prove:

(a)   unlawful fighting or unlawful violence used by at least one person against at least one other, *or*
(b)   an unlawful display of force by at least one person without actual violence, such that
(c)   a bystander of reasonable firmness and courage (whether or not present or likely to be present) might reasonably be expected to be terrified (*Attorney-General's Reference (No. 3 of 1983)* [1985] 1 All ER 501).

An affray could also be committed in private as the House of Lords decided in *Button* v *DPP* [1966] AC 591, reversing a view held since about 1820 but considered to be in accord with earlier authorities.

The Law Commission, however, concluded that the common law offence of affray needed some clarification and narrowing of its elements (Law Com. No. 123, para. 3.1).

2.4.3   The new offence of affray

The Public Order Act 1986, s. 3, provides that a person is guilty of affray if:

(a)   he uses or threatens unlawful violence towards another, and
(b)   his conduct is such as would cause a person of reasonable firmness present at the scene to fear for his personal safety.

This new definition differs from the old common law offence in that:

(a)   The rather uncertain element of a display of force (alternative to actual fighting or violence) is replaced with 'threatens violence'.
(b)   The element of terror is replaced by fear for personal safety.

(c)   No person of reasonable firmness need be present where the affray is in private (there was doubt about this at common law).

(d)   The penalty (see 2.4.11) is reduced to a maximum of three years.

(e)   A new alternative verdict is provided in trial on indictment (see 2.4.10).

2.4.4   Elements of the new offence of affray

2.4.4.1   Numbers and participation   There is no requirement of numbers as in riot (12 or more) or violent disorder (three or more). At common law a display of force by one man alone might be enough (*Taylor* v *DPP* [1973] AC 964). The new offence of affray under Public Order Act 1986, s. 3, preserves that position. One person may be guilty of affray if he makes a violent, unlawful attack on another whether that person defends himself (and is therefore not fighting unlawfully) or merely submits; there need be no reciprocity of violence (see Law Com. No. 123, para. 3.19). The offence therefore covers both the acts of the single person and the acts of two or more persons using or reciprocating in violence or threats of violence.

Thus one person alone can be convicted of affray whether or not other persons are taking part in the affray and whether or not other persons are charged. Although if two or more persons are involved, the conduct of each person charged will be judged not by the person's own conduct but by the conduct of the group (s. 3(2)). In other words, a person may be guilty of affray without actually using or threatening violence. He is guilty of affray if he is a willing participant in a group whose overall conduct amounts to the use or threat of unlawful violence (and see *R* v *Caird* (1970) 54 Cr App R 499, 2.2.4.7).

Mere presence at an affray does not make a person a party to it, unless there is evidence at the very least of encouragement of the participants in some way (*R* v *Allan* [1965] 1 QB 130). If someone stands by and watches a fight as it progresses and does nothing to stop it, he is not guilty of affray even if he harbours a secret intention to help one side if necessary; to hold otherwise would be to convict a man on his thoughts (*R* v *Allan*). Presence which is not accidental at an affray is no more than evidence of possible encouragement (*R* v *Clarkson* (1971) 55 Cr App R 445; *R* v *Jones and Mirless* (1977) 65 Cr App R 250). Physical proximity to the fight which does in fact encourage the fight is not enough unless there is also an intention to encourage the fight (*R* v *Jones and Mirless*). But if someone actively encourages the activity or joins in, for example by shouting encouragement or waving others on or running with the crowd, some of whom are throwing stones at a rival group, he is probably as guilty of affray as those who threw stones (see *Allan and others* v *Ireland* (1984) 79 Cr App R 206, a threatening behaviour case).

2.4.4.2   Public or private place   An affray may be committed in private as well as in public (s. 3(5)). This retains the position at common law (see *Button* v *DPP* [1966] AC 591, an affray during a dance in a scout hall hired by the local darts league in which tickets were distributed only to certain classes of person, and non-ticket holders were not admitted).

2.4.4.3   Uses or threatens unlawful violence   'Violence' is interpreted in the

Public Order Act 1986, s. 8, as meaning 'any violent conduct'. In the case of affray it includes violent conduct towards persons, but not violent conduct towards property. Throwing stones at an empty car or breaking the windows of a derelict building cannot amount to affray, although it would be different if people were known to be inside. The use of the word 'towards' makes it clear that injury to the person need not actually occur. Violence is not restricted to conduct which actually causes or is even intended to cause injury to the person. It includes other violent conduct such as the throwing of missiles which fall short or miss their target (s. 8). See generally, 2.2.4.4.

Unlawful violence.   The violence must be unlawful, that is, not justified by law. The common law defence of self-defence and the provisions of the Criminal Law Act 1967, s. 3 (the use of force in the prevention of crime or in making an arrest etc.) may exonerate the defendant in appropriate circumstances. See generally, 2.2.4.4.1 and 2.3.3.4.1.
    In *R* v *Sharp and Johnson* [1957] 1 QB 552 the use of a razor by a cripple in self-defence in a fight on the Highway at Wapping was described by the Court of Appeal as 'extravagant' but the issue should have been left to the jury to decide (see also *Taylor* v *DPP* [1973] AC 964, 986–7). Defendants charged with maliciously inflicting grievous bodily harm were entitled to have put to the jury their defence that they were engaged in rough and undisciplined horseplay, that they had not intended any harm and that they had thought that the victims were consenting to what occurred (*R* v *Muir and others, The Times*, 18 March 1986), and see *R* v *Asbury* [1986] Crim LR 252, and below).

Threatens violence.   In the offence of affray only, the threat of violence cannot be made by the use of words alone (s. 3(3)). The threat must therefore be a physical threat. A physical gesture, such as a clenched fist waved in the air, may be sufficient, but a verbal gesture or verbal abuse, however violent in content, will not be sufficient unless accompanied by a physical threat. In a civil case concerned with mass picketing at Wapping (*News Group Newspapers Ltd* v *Society of Graphical & Allied Trades 1982, The Times*, 1 August 1986) it was held that 'abuse, swearing and shouting' by demonstrators did not amount to a threat of violence (transcript, p. 28). Similarly, 'If a threat is little more than idle abuse and is not to be taken seriously, then it would not be sufficient to found an action for intimidation' (transcript, p. 29). However, a verbal threat accompanied by a menacing gesture or even physical presence proximate to the threatened person may be sufficient proof of this ingredient.
    A defendant who does not use or even threaten violence may be convicted of the offence of affray if he participates by encouraging or assisting others to use or threaten violence (see *R* v *Caird* (1970) 54 Cr App R 499, a riot case, see 2.2.4.4.2).

2.4.4.4   A person of reasonable firmness present at the scene   Despite the use of these words there is no need for the prosecution to prove either that there were people (other than the defendants) present at the scene or that they were put in fear of their personal safety (s. 3(4)). It is enough that a hypothetical person at the scene would have been put in fear. There need not be 'reciprocal violence' (*Taylor* v *DPP* [1973] AC 964, 989).

Commonly, however, this ingredient is proved by asking eyewitnesses what effect the fighting had upon them. If they were afraid, this element is proved. If, on the other hand, the eyewitnesses were not put in fear, for example because the fight was very minor or short-lived or a long way off, the prosecution would have difficulty in proving the offence despite the objective hypothetical test and a submission of no case to answer might, exceptionally, succeed.

It should be noted that the test under the Public Order Act 1986, s. 3(1), is that of conduct causing a person to *fear for his personal safety*, a lesser test than the common law requirement of *terror* (see *Taylor* v *DPP* [1973] AC 964, 987). If there is no element of fear the conduct complained of may constitute a lesser offence such as threatening behaviour etc. contrary to the Public Order Act 1986, s. 4 (see 2.5).

The statutory offence of affray envisages therefore the following sort of conduct. Fighting by one or more persons, usually in public (on the streets, for example after public house closing time or at or outside football matches) but also in private (at clubs, discothèques or village halls or anywhere on private property whether inside or in the open air), which puts bystanders or victims in fear or would put them in fear if they were present. The fighting can be hand-to-hand fighting or fighting with weapons (anything from knives and machetes brought specially for the fight to items picked up at the scene like glasses or bottles, stones or lumps of wood). Even conduct falling short of actual fighting can amount to an affray. Threatening to fight or to injure somebody or to damage something, for example by brandishing weapons or by charging in a group towards other people, could be an affray (although better charged under the Public Order Act 1986, s. 4). And although affray is usually charged against a number of persons who have fought or threatened to fight together, one person alone, fighting or even threatening to fight, can be convicted of affray. Fighting even by consent, as the old prize-fighting cases showed (and see more recently *Attorney-General's Reference (No. 6 of 1980)* [1981] QB 715), is an assault and a victim cannot normally consent to being fought or even assaulted (cf. *R* v *Muir and others, The Times*, 18 March 1986).

2.4.5 Mental element *(mens rea)*

A person is guilty of affray (as with violent disorder, see 2.3.4) only if *he intends to use or threaten violence* or *is aware that his conduct may be violent or threaten violence* (s. 6(2)). The mental element must be proved in addition to the other elements set out in s. 3. For proof of the mental element generally, including the new test of awareness and also intoxication, see 2.2.5.

A person will therefore not be guilty of affray if his conduct is unintentional, that is, accidental (accident is a general defence under the criminal law), for example if he tripped and fell striking somebody, or the conduct was otherwise not intended, for example if a fight was brewing and he threw away a bottle which could have been used as a weapon. Nor, for example, will he be guilty of threatening violence if the threats (which must be more than words: s. 3(3)) are empty threats or are made as a joke. But under the awareness test (s. 6(2) and see 2.2.5.1) half-hearted behaviour may be sufficient if a person is aware that there is some risk of the conduct being violent and he goes on to do the thing that creates the risk. If one of a group of youths who are shouting abuse at another group (this in itself may be an offence under s. 4, but words alone do not constitute an affray: s. 3(3)) half-heartedly lobs a stone towards the other group without intending to injure anyone he may be guilty of affray.

2.4.6   Power of arrest

Section 3(6) provides a specific power of arrest without warrant to a constable who reasonably suspects anyone of *committing* affray. The power of arrest is provided in s. 6 because the maximum penalty for the offence of affray is less than five years' imprisonment. This precludes affray from being an arrestable offence under the Police and Criminal Evidence Act 1984, s. 24.

The arrest power, it should be noted, is restricted to a person reasonably suspected of committing an offence. It does not extend to a person reasonably suspected of having committed the offence or of being about to commit the offence (see discussion of breach of the peace and arrest powers, chapter 5). The Police and Criminal Evidence Act 1984, s. 25, does, however, permit a constable, who has reasonable grounds for suspecting that an offence which is not an arrestable offence (including affray, a s. 4 offence and disorderly conduct) has been committed or attempted or is being committed or attempted, to make an arrest to prevent the person from causing injury or damage.

2.4.7   Prosecution

The DPP's consent to bring a prosecution is not required. A prosecution can be brought by the police through the Crown Prosecution Service or by an individual in a private prosecution.

2.4.8   The charge: duplicity

In order to avoid the possibility that a charge of affray might be judged bad for duplicity, s. 7(2) specifically provides that s. 3 creates just one offence. A charge of affray may accuse a person of 'using unlawful violence', of 'threatening unlawful violence' or both. A charge of 'using or threatening unlawful violence' will therefore not be bad for duplicity (and therefore invalid as a charge).

An affray is a continuous offence which may continue over 'divers streets from 8.30 p.m. to 12.30 a.m. as long as the fight or display of force continues (*R* v *Woodrow* (1959) 43 Cr App R 105), but where the affray starts afresh at a different place and is therefore a separate offence one count alone will be bad for duplicity (*R* v *Jones* (1974) 59 Cr App R 120, and see 2.2.4.2).

2.4.9   Mode of trial

The offence of affray (like the offence of violent disorder) is triable either way (on indictment or summarily in the magistrates' court). The defendant may elect trial on indictment (trial by jury).

2.4.10   Alternative verdicts

On the trial on indictment of a charge of affray the jury may acquit of affray but convict of an offence under s. 4, even though the offence under s. 4 is triable only summarily and cannot therefore be charged in the indictment (s. 7(3)). In the event of a conviction under s. 4 as an alternative to a conviction for affray, the penalty for the s. 4 offence will be the same as in the magistrates' court (s. 7(4), and see 2.5). For further provision for alternative verdicts under the Criminal Law Act 1967 and the circumstances in which trial judges should and should not leave alternative verdicts to the jury, see 2.2.10.

2.4.11 Penalty

On indictment in the Crown Court the maximum penalty is three years' imprisonment and/or a fine. On summary conviction the maximum penalty is six months' imprisonment and/or a fine not to exceed the statutory limit (Public Order Act 1986, s. 3(7)).

Serious affrays have in the past attracted severe sentences of imprisonment, although the penalty should reflect the distinction between the planned affray of a serious nature and the spontaneous outbreak of fighting (see *R* v *Annett and Moore* (1980) 2 Cr App R (S) 186). A Chelsea football supporter convicted of taking part in an affray in a public house after Chelsea's defeat by Manchester United was sentenced to four years' imprisonment (*The Times*, 14 October 1986). In *R* v *Keys and Others, The Times*, 22 November 1986 the Court of Appeal gave guidance on sentencing in cases of affray at common law. The crime of affray might range from the comparatively trivial rowdy scene spontaneously arising to the sort of lengthy pitched battle going on for hours which took place at Broadwater Farm, Tottenham, North London, with scores of casualties, arson and looting. In the case of a very serious affray, where it was clear that there was at least some measure of preparation, organisation and central direction, the organisers and ringleaders, if they were detected—which would seldom be the case—could expect sentences in the range of seven years and upwards. At the other end of the scale came the people who had been on the edges of the affray. But where there had been a major affray and also a prolonged and vicious attack upon the police, any participant, however slight his involvement, could expect a sentence of at least 18 months to 2 years. The carrying of weapons, the throwing of missiles and so on, ought to be reflected in an increase in that minimum. The court reduced sentences of five years to three and a half years, and of seven years to four and a half years.

More commonly, however, affrays are punished by short terms of imprisonment or youth custody (or detention centre) often between six and eighteen months. In *R* v *Khan* (CA, 14 January 1986, ref. 5938 B85) the court upheld a sentence of 12 months' youth custody for the 16-year-old member of a gang which had ambushed a rival school's basketball team causing injuries. In *R* v *Frost and others* (CA, 5 November 1985, ref. 4067 C85) the court said that deterrent sentences for street fighting were appropriate, but reduced sentences of five years' imprisonment and four and three years' youth custody to 15 months' imprisonment and 12 months' youth custody in cases where no weapons had been used.

A Birmingham man who took part in an incident which led to the Handsworth riots in 1985 was sentenced to 12 months' imprisonment suspended for two years after being convicted by a jury of affray and possessing an offensive weapon, a pool cue. The judge accepted that he had been horrified by the consequences of the riot and had shown remorse by helping to stop the disturbances (*The Times*, 19 August 1986).

2.5   THREATENING BEHAVIOUR ETC. (FEAR OR PROVOCATION OF VIOLENCE)

The Public Order Act 1986 abolishes (s. 9(2)(d)) the offence of threatening behaviour (conduct conducive to breaches of the peace) under the Public Order Act 1936, s. 5, and replaces it with a revised and extended offence of threatening behaviour etc. (described in the 1986 Act's marginal note as fear or provocation of violence)—hereafter called a s. 4 offence. The new offence retains the familiar words of threatening, abusive or insulting words or behaviour but jettisons the equally familiar concept of a breach of the peace. It extends the prohibition of conduct from public places or public meetings to private places except dwellings.

2.5.1   Background

The Law Commission (Law Com. No. 123, para. 5.40 et seq.) had proposed a different (and much simpler) offence which would have been triable either way, but the s. 4 offence is triable summarily only. The new offence has been defined with some difficulty. The original version in the first draft of the Bill was withdrawn and replaced, the difficulties arising out of the nature of the conduct to be penalised, the effect of the conduct and the mental element.

The repealed Public Order Act 1936, s. 5, offence (for full wording see appendix 2) had been the most frequently used of all public order offences. As one academic lawyer described it, the offence in the Public Order Act 1936, s. 5, was used 'as a form of dragnet provision against those whose behaviour is considered by the police and the courts to be worthy of punishment' (A. Dickey [1971] Crim LR 265). In the miners' strike of 1984–5 the charge was laid against some 4,000 striking miners, sometimes only for shouting 'scab'.

It is an offence which has been frequently criticised. In submissions made by the National Council for Civil Liberties on the 1936 Public Order Bill the precursor to the s. 5 offence was attacked:

> The Council's experience is that a strained interpretation is frequently put on this offence by magistrates. For example, an unemployed man was fined some years ago for using the words: 'Give us bread'. The Council considers, therefore, that any extension of this vague and elastic offence is dangerous and they would, indeed, welcome its total repeal.

As the lowest-level public order offence it was used in many contexts (see Williams, *Keeping the Peace*), often beyond the scope of its original intentions. In *R* v *Ambrose* (1973) 57 Cr App R 538 Lawton LJ said (at p. 540):

> It is important that section 5 of the Public Order Act [1936] should not be misused. It is clear from the long title to that Act ['and to make further provision for the preservation of public order on the occasion of public processions and meetings and in public places'] why it was passed and the

Court notices with regret that in recent years there has been a tendency to use the provisions of section 5 for purposes which were not within the intention of Parliament.

2.5.2 The repealed offence

The Public Order Act 1936, s. 5 (for full wording see appendix 2) penalised:

(a)   the use of words or behaviour, or
(b)   the distribution or display of any writing, sign or visible representation,
(c)   which was threatening, abusive or insulting,
(d)   with the intent to provoke a breach of the peace or whereby a breach of the peace was likely to be occasioned.

The offence was confined to public places and public meetings, was triable summarily only (although it had been triable on indictment between 1963 (Public Order Act 1963) and 1978 (Criminal Law Act 1977)), and carried a maximum penalty of six months' imprisonment and/or a fine up to level 5.

Many local Acts and by-laws contain similar provisions to the Public Order Act 1936, s. 5, offence. Two such offences in London statutes—Metropolitan Police Act 1839, s. 54(13), and City of London Police Act 1839, s. 35(13)—are specifically repealed by the Public Order Act 1986, Sch. 3.

All cases cited below refer to charges brought under the Public Order Act 1936, s. 5.

2.5.3 The new offence

A person is guilty of a s. 4 offence if:

(a)   he uses towards another person threatening, abusive or insulting words or behaviour, or
(b)   he distributes or displays to another person any writing, sign or other visible representation which is threatening, abusive or insulting, and
(c)   he intends that person to believe that immediate unlawful violence will be used against him or anyone else by him or by anyone else, or
(d)   he intends to provoke the immediate use of unlawful violence by that person or anyone else, or
(e)   whereby that person is likely to believe that such violence will be used, or
(f)   whereby it is likely that such violence will be provoked.

The principal differences between the repealed Public Order Act 1936, s. 5, and the new Public Order Act 1986, s. 4, are:

(a)   The new offence can be committed in private as well as in public places (see 2.5.4.1).
(b)   The concept of a breach of the peace is replaced by the concept of fear or provocation of violence.
(c)   The possible effect of the threatening behaviour is extended to cover situations where there is unlikely to be any violence as a result of the conduct

because the victim, for example, a policeman or an elderly lady, is unlikely to be provoked into violence by the defendant's behaviour. This overrules the important decisions in *Marsh* v *Arscott* (1982) 75 Cr App R 211 and *Parkin* v *Norman* [1983] QB 92 (see 2.5.4.4).

2.5.4 Elements of the new offence

2.5.4.1 Public and private places   The offence may be committed in either a *public place* (not defined in this part of the Act—see 7.3) or a *private place*, but not in a dwelling unless the words or behaviour take effect outside the dwelling (s. 4(2)). In other words abuse from the window of a private house directed at a person in the street or a missile thrown from private land on to the highway or threats made inside someone's garden all fall within the s. 4 offence. But insults during the course of a domestic dispute inside (but not outside) a house, even from one house to another, are outside the scope of the offence.

For the purposes of the Public Order Act 1986 a *dwelling* means any structure or part of a structure which is occupied as a person's home or as other living accommodation (whether separate or shared), and includes a tent, caravan, vehicle, vessel or other temporary or movable structure (s. 8). It does not include an office or factory or other place of work, or any other building not lived in, or land attached to or adjacent to a dwelling—these are private places where the behaviour specified in s. 4 will be an offence.

This element was proposed in the White Paper (Cmnd 9510, para. 3.8) to deal particularly with the acquittal of miners charged with threatening words or behaviour under the Public Order Act 1936, s. 5, where the defendants were able to say that they were on National Coal Board or other private property while the victims of the threats were on the public highway.

2.5.4.2 Threatening, abusive or insulting   The words or behaviour (or writing, sign etc.) need not be threatening, abusive *and* insulting. One or more of the three elements must be proved. An information alleging threatening *and* insulting words and behaviour is not bad for duplicity (*Vernon* v *Paddon* [1973] 3 All ER 302; and see 2.5.6). Where a defendant is charged with using threatening, abusive or insulting words or behaviour he is guilty if the conduct is proved to fall under one of the three headings (*Simcock* v *Rhodes* [1977] Crim LR 751). If the words or behaviour are neither threatening, abusive nor insulting, no offence will be committed even if it provokes others to unlawful behaviour.

The words 'threatening' etc. are to be given their ordinary meaning; whether the words or behaviour are threatening etc. is a question of fact for the magistrates:

> Vigorous and it may be distasteful or unmannerly speech or behaviour is permitted so long as it does not go beyond any of these limits. It must not be threatening. It must not be abusive. It must not be insulting. I see no reason why any of these should be construed as having a specially wide or a specially narrow meaning. They are limits easily recognisable by the ordinary man. (Lord Reid in *Brutus* v *Cozens* [1973] AC 854, 862.)

The words or behaviour (or writing, sign etc.) must be threatening, abusive or insulting and not merely calculated to cause annoyance (*Bryan* v *Robinson* [1960] 2 All ER 173, a decision under the similarly worded offence in the Metropolitan Police Act 1839, s. 54, now repealed).

Threatening.   Threatening words or behaviour covers both threats in the ordinary sense of the word and violence itself (*R* v *Oakwell* [1978] 1 All ER 1223). A wide range of conduct is included, such as intimidation at football matches (even running on to the pitch), encouragement to others to fight, physical behaviour on the streets including running in groups or occupying the pavement in a hostile manner, physical intimidation on picket lines where threats are shouted or vehicles are banged, throwing missiles, and swearing at somebody where it amounts to more than mere abuse. In the context of alleged intimidatory picketing outside newspaper premises in Wapping (*News Group Newspapers Ltd* v *Society of Graphical & Allied Trades 1982, The Times*, 1 August 1986), it was held that mere 'abuse, swearing and shouting' did not amount to a threat of violence (transcript, p. 28). Two protesters who ran on to a cricket pitch in Birmingham during a test match—one of whom put a set of bails down her trousers—to protest against the deportation of a Jamaican man were acquitted of using threatening words or behaviour when the prosecution offered no evidence (*The Times*, 9 September 1986). A threat to kill is a separate offence contrary to the Offences against the Person Act 1861, s. 16, carrying a maximum penalty of ten years' imprisonment.

    Group action may make all the participants in the group guilty of the offence even though there is no proof that an individual has used threatening words or behaviour. In *McMahon* v *Dollard* [1965] Crim LR 238 it was held that a group of youths dressed in leather jackets who took up the whole pavement and chanted 'Down with the mods' particularly when motor scooters drove by was guilty of the offence. In *Allan* v *Ireland* (1984) 79 Cr App R 206 the defendants were 11 members of a group of some 250 football supporters who emerged out of Euston station and proceeded down the road chanting, shouting and disturbing traffic. The first 10 to be tried were not identified individually nor was there any evidence of their acts of threatening behaviour. The magistrate rejected a submission of no case to answer being of the opinion that the group was a homogeneous one and that members of the public felt threatened by their conduct. The Divisional Court upheld the magistrate's decision on the basis that there was at least a prima facie case of identification, because the defendants had been arrested, charged and bailed as part of a group of persons who were alleged to have used threatening behaviour and they had appeared at the court to answer to their names in relation to the incident.

Abusive.   The word must be given its ordinary meaning (see *Brutus* v *Cozens* [1973] AC 854). Mere abuse, for example, by swearing, may be insufficient. It must be seen in its context and not in isolation from the effect elements of the offence.

Insulting.   The word must be given its ordinary meaning; 'insulting means insulting and nothing else' (*Brutus* v *Cozens* [1973] AC 854). Rude or offensive words or behaviour are not necessarily insulting (*R* v *Ambrose* (1973) 57 Cr

App R 538), although telling a constable to 'fuck off' when he had told a noisy group of youths emerging from a dance hall at night to be quiet and go home was insulting within the Public Order Act 1936, s. 5 (*Simcock* v *Rhodes* [1977] Crim LR 751).

Insult means 'hit by words' (*Jordan* v *Burgoyne* [1963] 2 QB 744). In this context a speaker must take his audience as he finds them (*Jordan* v *Burgoyne*, in which an audience which included Jews was 'insulted' by the assertion that Nazi policies had been correct). In *Brutus* v *Cozens* a sit-down protest during a tennis match at Wimbledon to protest at apartheid in South Africa was not inevitably insulting to the spectators. It was a question of fact for the magistrates. Conduct which showed a disrespect for the rights of others so that they were likely to resent the behaviour or protest against it (as the Divisional Court had held) was not necessarily insulting.

Some slogans or chants during demonstrations have been held to be insulting and there have been successful prosecutions for insulting heckling at public meetings and the distribution of insulting leaflets. An overt display of homosexual conduct—kissing, cuddling and fondling genitals over clothing at a bus stop in Oxford Street, London at 1.55 a.m.—was capable of amounting to insulting behaviour even though the conduct was not aimed at a particular person or persons (*Masterson* v *Holden* [1986] 1 WLR 1017):

> Overt homosexual conduct in a public street, indeed overt heterosexual conduct, may well be considered by many persons to be objectionable and may well be regarded by another person, particularly by a young woman, as conduct which insults her by suggesting that she is somebody who would find such conduct in public acceptable herself (per Glidewell LJ at p. 1024).

Other, not dissimilar cases, however, have resulted in acquittals.

There is no need for a person to be insulted, so long as the insult is directed at a person or group of persons and is capable of being perceived as an insult (*Parkin* v *Norman* [1983] QB 92). But this does not mean that the words or behaviour have to be actually directed by one person at another. They are insulting if there is a human target which they strike, whether they are intended to strike that target or not (*Masterson* v *Holden*, attempting to reconcile *Brutus* v *Cozens* [1973] AC 854, 865–6, and *Parkin* v *Norman* [1983] QB 92, 99).

2.5.4.3 'With intent' clauses   The s. 4 offence is in two halves. The first half requires that the words or behaviour (or writing, sign etc.) are threatening, abusive or insulting. The second half of the offence may be committed in one of four ways; two of those ways require an intention (the 'with intent' clauses), two do not (the 'whereby' clauses—see 2.5.4.4).

The two 'with intent' clauses are:

(a)   with intent to cause the person threatened etc. to believe that immediate unlawful violence will be used against him or against another person by the person threatening etc. or by anyone else, or

(b)   with intent to provoke the immediate use of unlawful violence by the person threatened etc. or by anyone else.

The intent clause (a) is a new clause. The intent clause (b) reflects the wording of the repealed Public Order Act 1936, s. 5, 'with intent to provoke a breach of the peace'.

The distinction between (a) and (b) is that in (b) a violent reaction is intended whereas in (a) the reaction intended is not one of violence but of fear that something will happen. Note that the reaction in both cases need not in fact occur. The offence is committed if the actor, for example, with the necessary intent, threatens to strike the victim or the victim's elderly father ((a)) or threatens to strike them unless they agree to fight ((b)), even though the victim and his father treat the threat as a joke and have no intention of fighting. Note too the use of the word 'immediate'. The offence will not be committed if the actor threatens to strike the victim some time in the future ((a)) or threatens him with a challenge to fight at some future date ((b)).

In addition to proving either intent clause (a) or intent clause (b) the prosecution must also prove that the accused intended his words or behaviour to be threatening etc. or that he was aware that they might be threatening etc. (see 2.5.5).

2.5.4.4 'Whereby' clauses The two 'whereby' clauses, which will be used more often than the two 'intent' clauses (see 2.5.4.3) because they will be easier to prove, are:

(a) whereby the person threatened etc. is likely to believe that unlawful violence will be used, or
(b) whereby it is likely that unlawful violence will be provoked.

Clause (a) is a new clause. Clause (b) reflects the wording of the Public Order Act 1936, s. 5, 'whereby a breach of the peace is likely to be occasioned'. Where either of the 'whereby' clauses is proved no specific intent on the part of the defendant need be proved other than the general mental element (see 2.5.5).

Clause (a) makes it clear that there is no need for proof of the likelihood of a violent reaction to the threatening etc. words or behaviour. All that is required is a likelihood of the victim fearing that violence (even the threat of violence—see 2.5.4.5) will occur. Thus the offence will be committed even if there is no possibility that the victim will react with violence, for example, if the victim is old and frail, or the victim is a police officer who is not expected to resort to violence, or any other law-abiding citizen likely to ignore the threat, abuse or insult.

Clause (a) therefore overrules a number of important decisions under the repealed Public Order Act 1936, s. 5, which decided that no offence was committed where the victims were police officers even though the conduct complained of was itself a breach of the peace. In *Marsh* v *Arscott* (1982) 75 Cr App R 211 (followed in *Read* v *Jones* [1983] Crim LR 809) the defendant used threatening and insulting words and behaviour to police officers in the car park of a shop late at night. No offence was committed under the Public Order Act 1936, s. 5, because the car park was not a public place (see 2.5.4.1) and because the only people present were police officers whose duty it was to keep the peace. In *Parkin* v *Norman* [1983] QB 92 the defendant's conviction for insulting behaviour in a public lavatory was quashed because, although his homosexual advance was capable of amounting to insulting behaviour, the only person present was a plain-clothes police officer who was unlikely to break the peace. A similar decision was reached in *Nicholson* v *Gage* (1985) 80 Cr App R 40, a case of a peeping tom in a public lavatory.

Clause (b), although similar to the Public Order Act 1936, s. 5, wording of 'whereby a breach of the peace is likely to be occasioned', deliberately turns away from the concept of a breach of the peace which was considered by the Law Commission to be too uncertain of meaning (despite the decision in *R* v *Howell* [1982] QB 416, see 5.1) to be retained (Law Com. No. 123, para. 5.14). It therefore substitutes the test of 'likely that violence will be provoked'.

2.5.4.5   Unlawful violence.   'Violence' is interpreted in the Public Order Act 1986, s. 8, as meaning 'any violent conduct'. Violence in s. 8 includes violent conduct towards property as well as violent conduct towards persons. The wording of s. 4 suggests that in the context of a s. 4 offence violence will normally be violence toward persons not property. Nevertheless an offence would be committed if a threat were made to a person, for example, to damage that person's car, and that person believed that the damage would be done. The use of the word 'towards' makes it clear that neither injury to the person nor damage to property need occur. Section 8 specifically refers to other violent conduct such as the throwing of missiles capable of causing injury which fall short or miss their target.

For further discussion of violence, see 2.2.4.4.

The violence must be *unlawful*, that is, not justified by law (s. 4(1)). The common law defence of self-defence and the provisions of the Criminal Law Act 1967, s. 3 (use of force in the prevention of crime or in making an arrest etc.), may justify violence and make it lawful in appropriate circumstances. See 2.2.4.4.1 and 2.3.3.4.1.

2.5.5   Mental element *(mens rea)*

A person is guilty of a s. 4 offence only if he *intends his words or behaviour or the writing or sign or other visible representation to be* or *is aware that his words etc. may be, threatening, abusive or insulting* (Public Order Act 1986, s. 6(3)). This is in effect the same position as under the Public Order Act 1936, s. 5 (see *Parkin* v *Norman* [1983] QB 92).

This mental element must be proved in addition to the other elements of the offence, namely, that the words or behaviour were threatening, abusive or insulting, and also one of the four 'with intent' or 'whereby' clauses (see 2.5.4.3 and 2.5.4.4). Where the prosecution seek to prove one of the two intent clauses (see 2.5.4.3) they must therefore also prove the general intent (or awareness) element in relation to the words or behaviour.

For proof of the mental element generally and the new concept of awareness and intoxication which also apply to this offence, see 2.2.5.

2.5.6   Power of arrest

The Public Order Act 1986, s. 4(3), provides a specific power of arrest without warrant for a constable who reasonably suspects anyone to be committing a s. 4

offence. A constable in uniform may enter and search any premises for the purpose of arresting a person for a s. 4 offence (Police and Criminal Evidence Act 1984, s. 17(1)(c) as amended by Public Order Act 1986, Sch. 2, para. 7). For further discussion of arrest powers see 2.4.6 and chapter 5.

2.5.7   Prosecution

The DPP's consent to bring a prosecution is not required. A prosecution can be brought by the police through the Crown Prosecution Service or by an individual in a private prosecution.

2.5.8   The charge: duplicity

For the avoidance of doubt it is declared in the Public Order Act 1986, s. 7(2) that s. 4 of the Act creates one offence. This means that a charge that a defendant has acted contrary to s. 4 is not void for duplicity (and therefore invalid) if it charges, for example, 'threatening, abusive or insulting words or behaviour' (and see *Vernon* v *Paddon* [1973] 3 All ER 302, see 2.5.4.2).

2.5.9   Mode of trial

This offence is triable summarily only, although note that an alternative verdict of guilty of a s. 4 offence may be brought in on the trial on indictment of a charge of violent disorder (s. 2) or affray (s. 3)—s. 7(3), see 2.5.10.

2.5.10   Alternative verdicts

The special provisions of the Public Order Act 1986 do not apply so as to permit the magistrates to find a defendant not guilty of an offence contrary to s. 4 but guilty of some lesser offence such as disorderly conduct. On a charge under s. 4 the defendant must be found guilty or not guilty as charged and nothing more. Note, however, that a defendant charged on indictment with violent disorder (s. 2) or affray (s. 3) may be found not guilty as charged but guilty of a s. 4 offence, even though a s. 4 offence is triable summarily only (Public Order Act 1986, s. 7(3)). On conviction of a s. 4 offence by a jury, the penalty is no greater than the maximum on summary conviction (see 2.5.11).

2.5.11   Penalty

The penalty for a s. 4 offence on summary conviction is imprisonment not exceeding six months and/or a fine not exceeding level 5 (Public Order Act 1986, s. 4(4))—for fine scales see 1.8.1).

2.6   DISORDERLY CONDUCT (HARASSMENT, ALARM OR DISTRESS)

The Public Order Act 1986, s. 5, creates a new offence of disorderly conduct (described in the Act's marginal note as harassment, alarm or distress). The offence is the lowest-level offence for use in a public order context. It penalises threatening, abusive or insulting words or behaviour or disorderly behaviour within the hearing or sight of a person likely to be caused harassment, alarm or distress.

2.6.1   Background

The new offence contrary to the Public Order Act 1986, s. 5, commonly (and hereafter) known as disorderly conduct, was the most controversial of the new statutory offences in the Public Order Act 1986 both before and during the passage of the Bill. Whereas the repealed Public Order Act 1936, s. 5, offence (now replaced by the Public Order Act 1986, s. 4) was the lowest-level public order offence before the passing of the Public Order Act 1986, the new Public Order Act 1986, s. 5, offence is more widely drawn and embraces behaviour which formerly would generally not have been punishable as a crime. In particular it covers behaviour which falls short of violence or the threat or fear of violence.

The conduct aimed at has been described as 'minor acts of hooliganism' and in particular behaviour directed at the elderly and others who may feel especially vulnerable, including members of ethnic minority communities (Cmnd 9510, para. 3.22). Instances of such behaviour were given as hooligans on housing estates causing disturbances in the common parts of blocks of flats, blockading entrances, throwing things down the stairs, banging on doors, peering in at windows and knocking over dustbins; groups of youths persistently shouting abuse and obscenities or pestering people waiting to catch public transport or to enter a hall or cinema; someone turning out the lights in a crowded dance hall, in a way likely to cause panic; rowdy behaviour in the streets late at night which alarms local residents. Many of these examples would be caught by the definition of the more serious, but not substantially more serious, s. 4 offence. It remains to be seen how this offence will be used in practice.

The clause was controversial (and much amended) during the course of the Bill because it extends the criminal law into areas of annoyance, disturbance and inconvenience hitherto unpunished as crime. The Green Paper (Cmnd 7891) made no proposal for such an offence and the White Paper (Cmnd 9510) only put one forward 'tentatively', suggesting (para. 3.26) that:

> It is not easy to define the offence in a manner which conforms with the normally precise definitions of the criminal law, but which at the same time is sufficiently general to catch the variety of the conduct aimed at. The Government recognises that there would be justifiable objections to a wide extension of the criminal law which might catch conduct not deserving of criminal sanctions.

The White Paper's tentative proposal, therefore, contained certain safeguards or limitations on the offence of disorderly conduct. It suggested that a power of arrest would be unnecessary. But the Act, surprisingly in view of the arrest powers under the Police and Criminal Evidence Act 1984 (see chapter 5), creates an unusual two-stage power of arrest (s. 5(4)). The White Paper also suggested that the behaviour should actually cause someone to feel harassed, alarmed or distressed (not that it was merely likely to do so) and that the degree of harassment, alarm or distress should be substantial. But these proposals are absent from the new s. 5 offence.

2.6.2 The new offence

A person is guilty of the offence of disorderly conduct if:

(a) he uses threatening, abusive or insulting words or behaviour, or
(b) he uses disorderly behaviour, or
(c) he displays any writing, sign or other visible representation which is threatening, abusive or insulting, and
(d) he does so within the hearing or sight of a person likely to be caused harassment, alarm or distress by the above conduct.

The principal differences between the s. 4 offence and the s. 5 offence are:

(a) The s. 5 offence includes the new concept of disorderly behaviour.
(b) The s. 5 offence contains no intent clauses, and there is no requirement for the behaviour to cause or provoke violence or the fear of violence.
(c) It need only be proved that harassment, alarm or distress are likely.
(d) Section 5 contains three specific defences, a special power of arrest and the offence is not punishable with imprisonment.

2.6.3 Elements of the new offence

2.6.3.1 Public and private places   As with the s. 4 offence the s. 5 offence of disorderly conduct may be committed in either a *public place* (not defined in this part of the Act—see 8.3) or a *private place*, but not in a dwelling unless the effect of the words or behaviour take effect outside the dwelling (Public Order Act 1986, s. 5(2)). For further details, including the meaning of dwelling, see 2.5.4.1.

2.6.3.2 Threatening, abusive or insulting   For a full discussion of these words see 2.5.4.2. Note that the words or behaviour do not have to be directed 'towards another person' (as required with a s. 4 offence).

2.6.3.3 Disorderly behaviour   These words are not defined in the Public Order Act 1986. Nor are they defined elsewhere, although they appear—as does the word disorderly—in a number of different contexts. Disorderly behaviour will therefore be given its ordinary meaning. Dictionary definitions show that disorderly behaviour is characterised as unruly, turbulent, tumultuous, even riotous, or as constituting a public nuisance (see 6.12).

The phrase is most commonly observed in drunk and disorderly behaviour (Criminal Justice Act 1967, s. 91). Acting at a public meeting in a disorderly manner may amount to an offence (Public Meeting Act 1908, s. 1) and disorderly persons may be removed (see 10.3). Sections 3 and 4 of the Vagrancy Act 1824 set out a catalogue of idle and disorderly persons. Keeping a disorderly inn or a disorderly house has long been punished both at common law and under statute (see, for example, the Disorderly Houses Act 1751).

In Scotland riotous, disorderly or indecent behaviour is an offence contrary to the Glasgow Police Act 1866, s. 135(5). In *Campbell* v *Adair* 1945 JC 29, the conviction of an omnibus inspector for disorderly behaviour was upheld. He had adopted a high-handed attitude towards a passenger who was in a state of advanced pregnancy, had spoken loudly to her and bullied her by accusing her of attempting to board the bus whilst it was in motion. Lord Moncrieff said (at p. 33) that disorderly was 'a word which indicates less aggressive conduct than would be required to constitute a breach of the peace'.

In a New Zealand case, *Melser* v *Police* [1967] NZLR 437, Turner J said (at p. 444):

> Disorderly conduct is conduct which is disorderly; it is conduct which, while sufficiently ill-mannered, or in bad taste, to meet with the disapproval of well-conducted and reasonable men and women, is also something more—it must, in my opinion, tend to annoy or insult such persons as are faced with it—and sufficiently deeply or seriously to warrant the interference of the criminal law.

In the same case McCarthy J said (at p. 446):

> I agree that an offence against good manners, a failure of good taste, a breach of morality, even though these may be contrary to the general order of public opinion, is not enough to establish this offence. There must be conduct which not only can fairly be characterised as disorderly, but also is likely to cause a disturbance or to annoy others considerably.

2.6.3.4   Within the hearing or sight of a person likely to be caused harassment, alarm or distress   The person must be present. A hypothetical person (as with the offences of riot, violent disorder and affray) is not enough. But the person, the victim of this offence, does not have to give evidence that they were actually caused harassment, alarm or distress. The victim does not have to give evidence at all, nor does he have to be identified by name. It would be sufficient for a police officer to give evidence that there was a victim and that in all the circumstances the victim was likely to be caused harassment, alarm or distress.

The conduct complained of must be within the hearing or sight of the victim. If there is no victim there is no offence. If the victim is out of sight and cannot see the disorderly behaviour, even if it is just over the fence, or the victim cannot hear the abusive words, for example, because he is deaf, even though the actor is very close, there will be no offence.

No offence will be committed if the person is not likely to be caused harassment, alarm or distress. A police officer should not be distressed by mere abuse or insulting behaviour. If therefore there is no one else within hearing or sight other than a police officer it will be arguable, depending on the facts of the case, that no offence has been committed. The decisions in *Marsh* v *Arscott* (1982) 75 Cr App R 211 and *Parkin* v *Norman* [1983] QB 92 should therefore apply to the s. 5 offence of disorderly conduct but not to the s. 4 offence of threatening behaviour etc. (see 2.5.4.4).

The words 'harassment, alarm or distress' are not defined in the Public Order Act 1986. They must be given their ordinary meaning. The proposal in the White Paper (Cmnd 9510, para. 3.26) that the harassment, alarm or distress should be substantial has not been followed. The words suggest something less than fear of violence and something more than mere annoyance or disturbance.

It is submitted that they are all strong words whose value should not be watered down in the interpretation of this section.

2.6.4 Mental element *(mens rea)*

A person is guilty of a s. 5 offence only if he *intends his words or behaviour (or the writing, sign etc.) to be threatening, abusive or insulting* or *is aware that it may be threatening, abusive or insulting* or if he *intends his behaviour to be, or is aware that it may be, disorderly* (Public Order Act 1986, s. 6(4)).

The mental element must be proved in addition to the other elements of the offence, namely, that the words or behaviour were threatening, abusive or insulting or the behaviour was disorderly, and that it was likely to cause harassment, alarm or distress to a person within hearing or sight.

For proof of the mental element generally and the new concept of awareness and intoxication which also apply to this offence, see 2.2.5.

2.6.5 Three specific defences

The Public Order Act 1986, s. 5(3), provides three specific defences to a charge of disorderly conduct. In each defence the burden will rest on the defendant to prove the defence on a balance of probabilities. In other defences of general application, such as accident or self-defence or lack of intent, the burden does not rest on the defendant. It rests on the prosecution to disprove the defence beyond reasonable doubt.

The three specific defences are:

(a)   It is a defence for the defendant to prove that he had no reason to believe that there was any person within hearing or sight who was likely to be caused harassment, alarm or distress (s. 5(3)(a)).

It would be a defence to an allegation of swearing at a cat (the abuse does not have to be directed towards a person—cf. the s. 4 offence) that the defendant did not know that there was somebody on the other side of the fence who was likely to be distressed. It might be no defence where the defendant knew that that person often took a seat behind that particular fence. It would be a defence to an allegation of insulting behaviour by urinating in the street at night if the defendant could show that he had no reason to believe that there was a person peeking from behind the curtains at No. 16. It might be no defence where the defendant failed to look about him. In each case the defendant's belief must be a reasonable one before the defence can succeed. Reasonableness is an objective test.

(b)   It is a defence for the defendant to prove that he was inside a dwelling and he had no reason to believe that the words or behaviour would be heard or seen by a person outside (s. 5(3)(b)).

The defendant's belief must be reasonable before the defence can succeed. Reasonableness sets an objective test. The person outside must be outside 'that or any other dwelling' (s. 5(3)(b)). This means that the defendant's belief must be related to persons either outside in the open air in a public place or to persons who are in another building which is not a dwelling, such as an office or factory or unoccupied house (for the definition of dwelling, see 2.5.4.1).

(c)   It is a defence for the defendant to prove that his conduct was reasonable (s. 5(3)(c)). It might be reasonable, for example, to shout abuse at another person in order to try to stop that person committing a crime, such as an assault or theft. Running full pelt along a busy pavement might be disorderly conduct, but it might also be reasonable in hot pursuit of a suspected criminal.

2.6.6 Power of arrest

The Public Order Act 1986, s. 5(4), provides a specific two-stage power of arrest. A constable may arrest a person without warrant if:

(a)   he engages in offensive conduct which the constable warns him to stop, and
(b)   he engages in further offensive conduct immediately or shortly after the warning.

'Offensive conduct' means conduct which the constable reasonably suspects to constitute the offence (s. 5(5)), that is, threatening etc. words or behaviour or disorderly behaviour. But a constable cannot arrest for threatening etc. words or behaviour alone or disorderly behaviour; the conduct must also be within the sight of a person likely to be caused harassment, alarm or distress. Otherwise the arrest may be unlawful. It is not enough that a person bangs on dustbins or peers in at windows. There must also be a victim before the arrest power can be exercised.

The conduct in the two stages need not be of the same nature (s. 5(5)). If in stage one the constable warns the person to stop jostling people at a bus stop, and in stage two the person stops jostling but swears at passers-by, the arrest power can operate, as long as the conduct in stage two takes place 'immediately or shortly after the warning'. A gap of a few minutes, but not half an hour or an hour or more, will probably permit an arrest, but it will be a question of fact in each case.

Even if the two-stage power of arrest (often compared to the two-stage power of arrest for 'sus', the repealed offence of being a suspected person under the Vagrancy Act 1824) cannot operate, for example, if the person stops the offensive conduct after the constable's warning, the police officer can still make an arrest under the Police and Criminal Evidence Act 1984, s. 25, if it appears to him that service of a summons is impracticable or inappropriate because any of the general arrest conditions apply (see 5.2).

2.6.7 Prosecution

The DPP's consent to bring a prosecution is not required. A prosecution can be brought by the police through the Crown Prosecution Service or by an individual in a private prosecution.

2.6.8 The charge: duplicity

For the avoidance of doubt it is declared by the Public Order Act 1986, s. 7(2), that s. 5 of the Act creates one offence. This means that a charge that a defendant has acted contrary to s. 5 is not void for duplicity (and therefore invalid) if it charges, for example, 'threatening, abusive or insulting words or behaviour'.

2.6.9 Mode of trial

This offence is triable summarily only.

2.6.10 Penalty

The maximum penalty for a s. 5 offence is a fine not exceeding level 3 (Public Order Act 1986, s. 5(6)—for fine scales see 1.8.1). This is the only offence of the five new public order offences in Part I of the Public Order Act 1986 which is not imprisonable.

3

Other Public Order Offences

This chapter deals with a number of commonly used public order offences, including the carrying of offensive weapons, assault and criminal damage. It also deals with some less frequently charged offences such as intimidation, which is usually associated with unlawful picketing, offences prohibiting uniforms and quasi-military organisations, terrorist offences, bomb hoaxes and the new offence of contaminating or interfering with goods (Public Order Act 1986, s. 38). Apart from the contamination of goods offence, none of these offences appear in the Public Order Act 1986, except by way of amendment or modification to their existing definition in other statutes.

3.1 CARRYING OFFENSIVE WEAPONS

The Public Order Act 1986 schs. 2 and 3, rationalises the law relating to offensive weapons by repealing the Public Order Act 1936, s. 4 (prohibition of offensive weapons at public meetings and processions), by repealing that part of the Vagrancy Act 1824, s. 4, which penalises the possession of an offensive weapon, and by making a minor amendment to the Prevention of Crime Act 1953, s. 1, which remains the principal enactment on the subject.

3.1.1 The offence

The Prevention of Crime Act 1953, s. 1, provides that a person is guilty of an offence if:

    (a)   he has with him an offensive weapon,
    (b)   in a public place,
    (c)   without lawful authority or reasonable excuse.

3.1.1.1 He has with him The Prevention of Crime Act 1953, s. 1, contemplates not the use but the premeditated carrying of the article for the prohibited purposes. The prosecution must prove knowledge (*R* v *Cugullere* [1961] 2 All ER 343—three pickaxe handles in the back of a stolen van) or, where two or more are charged, that each knew of weapons that another had with him and that there was a common purpose (*R* v *Edmonds* [1963] 2 QB 142). It is a defence if the defendant did not know or had forgotten that the weapon was there (*R* v *Russell* [1985] Crim LR 231—cosh under the car seat). The defendant does not have the weapon with him for the purposes of the Act if he suddenly uses an article which he was innocently carrying (*Ohlson* v *Hylton*

[1975] 2 All ER 490—carpenter taking hammer from his bag; cf., under the Firearms Act 1968, *R* v *Houghton* [1982] Crim LR 112) or which somebody else was innocently carrying (*Bates* v *Bulman* (1979) 68 Cr App R 21). Picking up a stone and throwing it would therefore probably not be an offence under the Prevention of Crime Act 1953 (despite the decision in *Harrison* v *Thornton* (1979) 68 Cr App R 28), although it would be an offence under the Public Order Act 1986, s. 4.

3.1.1.2   Any offensive weapon   For an article to be an offensive weapon it must fall into one of the three following categories (Prevention of Crime Act 1953, s. 1(4)):

(a)   an article *made* for causing injury to the person, such as a knuckleduster, a dagger or a flick-knife (*Gibson* v *Wales* (1983) 76 Cr App R 60); *R* v *Simpson* (1984) 78 Cr App R 115), or even a police truncheon (*Houghton* v *Chief Constable of Greater Manchester, The Times*, 24 July 1986), but not necessarily a lock knife (see *Patterson* v *Block, The Times*, 21 June 1984) or a sheath-knife (*R* v *Williamson* (1978) 67 Cr App R 35); *or*

(b)   an article *adapted* for use for causing injury to the person, such as a bottle broken to cause a jagged edge or rubber hose filled with metal (see *Grieve* v *Macleod* [1967] Crim LR 424); *or*

(c)   an article *intended* by the person having it with him for use by him (or by some other person: Public Order Act 1986, sch. 2, para. 2) for causing injury to the person, such as a kitchen knife or a spanner.

Categories (a) and (b) are often referred to as *offensive weapons per se*, although this term does not appear in the Act. If the article falls into either category (a) or (b) there is no need to prove an intention to injure (*Davis* v *Alexander* (1970) 54 Cr App R 398—waving a sword-stick in the street). If the article falls within category (c), i.e., is not made or adapted for use, it is for the prosecution to prove the necessary intention to cause injury. If proved, only then will the question of lawful authority or reasonable excuse arise. An intention to frighten or intimidate is not sufficient unless it is capable of causing injury by shock (*R* v *Rapier* (1980) 70 Cr App R 17—threatening doormen at a night-club with a knife after being refused admission).

It is for the jury to decide which of the three categories is appropriate to the article in question (*R* v *Williamson* (1978) 67 Cr App R 35—a sheath-knife). Two or more counts should not be put into the indictment to cover the alternative possibilities (*R* v *Flynn, The Times*, 30 December 1985; see also *R* v *Brown* (1984) 79 Cr App R 115).

3.1.1.3   In a public place   'Public place' is defined as including any highway and any other premises or place to which at the material time the public have or are permitted to have access, whether on payment or otherwise (Prevention of Crime Act 1953, s. 1(4)). For a full discussion of the different definitions of public place, see 8.3. (See also *Wood* v *Metropolitan Police Commissioner, The Times*, 12 February 1986, a case under the now repealed provisions of the Vagrancy Act 1824, s. 4.)

3.1.1.4 Without lawful authority or reasonable excuse The issue of lawful authority or reasonable excuse only arises if the article is proved to be an offensive weapon within one of the above three categories. The burden is on the defendant to prove that he had the article with him with lawful authority or reasonable excuse (Prevention of Crime Act 1953, s. 1(1)). The standard of proof is on a balance of probabilities, as it is in all criminal cases where the defendant bears a burden of proof (*R v Carr-Briant* [1943] 2 All ER 156; *Islington London Borough Council v Panico* [1973] 1 WLR 1166) and in all civil cases. Lawful authority would include a police officer carrying a weapon as a court exhibit. Carrying a weapon for self-defence may be a reasonable excuse if in fear of immediate attack (*Evans v Hughes* [1972] Crim LR 558—one or two days after an attack might cause sufficient fear, but eight days later was borderline; cf. *Pittard v Mahoney* [1977] Crim LR 169—ball and chain carried four weeks after attack). But the Prevention of Crime Act 1953 was never intended to sanction the permanent carrying of weapons (*Grieve v Macleod* [1967] Crim LR 424—taxi driver carrying adapted rubber hose to defend himself against violent passengers). The carrying of a knuckleduster and a truncheon while collecting wages might provide a defence, but not in between wage collections (*Evans v Wright* [1964] Crim LR 466). The carrying of truncheons by security guards at a dance hall as 'a deterrent' or 'part of the uniform' is no lawful authority or reasonable excuse (*R v Spanner* [1973] Crim LR 704). Nor is it a reasonable excuse to have a weapon for the purpose of committing suicide (*Bryan v Mott* [1976] Crim LR 64). But the carrying of a police truncheon, an offensive weapon *per se*, as part of a fancy dress outfit, is a reasonable excuse (*Houghton v Chief Constable of Greater Manchester, The Times*, 24 July 1986).

3.1.2 Penalty

On indictment the maximum penalty is two years' imprisonment and/or a fine. On summary conviction the maximum penalty is three months' imprisonment and/or a fine up to level 5 (Prevention of Crime Act 1953, s. 1(1)).

3.1.3 Power of arrest

The arrest power in the Prevention of Crime Act 1953, s. 1(3), has been repealed and replaced by the Police and Criminal Evidence Act 1984 arrest powers so that the general arrest conditions (see 5.2) apply.

3.1.4 Other provisions concerning weapons

Other relevant provisions prohibiting weapons include:

(a) Criminal Damage Act 1971, s. 3—the offence of possessing anything with intent to destroy or damage property (see 3.3).

(b) Restriction of Offensive Weapons Act 1959 and Customs and Excise Management Act 1979, s. 170—penalties for manufacture, sale, hire etc. and illegal importation of dangerous weapons.

(c) Customs and Excise Management Act 1979, s. 86—smuggling while armed with an offensive weapon.

(d)   Criminal Law Act 1977, s. 8—trespassing with a weapon of offence in a building or on land ancillary to a building (see 7.3).

(e)   Theft Act 1968, s. 10—aggravated burglary with a weapon of offence, or firearm or explosive (see 7.3.7.3).

3.2   ASSAULT

A full range of assault charges is available to cover situations of public disorder, including common assault (Offences against the Person Act 1861, s. 42), assault occasioning actual bodily harm (Offences against the Person Act 1861, s. 47), causing or inflicting grievous bodily harm and wounding with and without intent (Offences against the Person Act 1861, ss. 18 and 20), manslaughter and murder. There is also the often used statutory offence of assaulting a constable in the execution of his duty contrary to the Police Act 1964, s. 51(1), punishable on summary conviction with a maximum penalty of six months' imprisonment and/or a fine not exceeding level 5 (see also the offence of obstructing a constable in the execution of his duty, 5.12). For full details of all these offences see *Stone's Justices' Manual 1986*, Archbold, 42nd ed., Smith and Hogan, *Criminal Law*, 5th ed., and other standard works on criminal law.

Assault includes (a) assault and (b) battery, although strictly speaking they are two offences.

An *assault* is any act which intentionally or recklessly (*R* v *Venna* [1976] QB 421—lashing out with feet but not intending to kick police officer) causes another person to apprehend immediate and unlawful personal violence (*Fagan* v *Metropolitan Police Commissioner* [1969] 1 QB 439, 440—driving a car on to a constable's foot and leaving it there). In an indecent assault case an assault was defined as any intentional touching of another person without the consent of that person and without lawful excuse. It need not necessarily be hostile or rude or aggressive, as some of the cases seemed to indicate (*Faulkner* v *Talbot* (1982) 74 Cr App R 1). It is an assault (without a battery) to throw a stone or other missile at somebody even if it misses; to ride or drive at somebody; to point a gun at somebody; or to advance in a threatening manner. It is even an assault to frighten somebody by staring at them through a window (*Smith* v *Chief Superintendent of Woking Police Station* (1983) 76 Cr App R 234, the victim need not give evidence of violence if it can be inferred from the circumstances). Unlawful imprisonment by the police or by store detectives is an assault, so is an unlawful search of the person (see the Police and Criminal Evidence Act 1984). But mere words alone are not an assault (Hawk PC, bk 1, ch 62, sect. 1).

A *battery* is an act by which a person intentionally or recklessly applies unlawful force to the complainant (*R* v *Williams (G)* (1984) 78 Cr App R 275, 279). It is a battery to strike, hit, push, spit at, throw something (which connects) at, or fire something at somebody. It is not a battery to touch somebody merely to attract their attention (in this respect police officers have no extra powers over ordinary citizens—see chapter 5). The force (note the replacement in the Public Order Act 1986 of the word 'force' by the word 'violence', see 2.2.4.4) must be unlawful. Therefore the common law defence of self-defence and defence of property and the provisions of the Criminal Law Act 1967, s. 3 (the use of force in the prevention of crime or in making an arrest etc.) apply. But it is no defence to say, minor scuffles apart, that two parties consented to fight in a public place, for example, to settle a difference (*Attorney-General's Reference (No. 6 of 1980)* [1981] QB 715; cf. *R v Muir, The Times*, 18 March 1986, 2.4.4.3). An intention to injure was not essential to a civil action in battery; it was necessary to prove only an intentional hostile touching of the plaintiff by the defendant (*Wilson v Pringle* [1986] 3 WLR 1).

Before 1828 all common assaults were triable only on indictment. Now they are triable summarily only and should not be charged contrary to the Offences against the Person Act 1861, s. 42 (*R v Harrow Justices (ex parte Osaseri)* (1985) 81 Cr App R 306).

Violence at or in the vicinity of football grounds is likely to be punished with deterrent sentences: unless there are exceptional mitigating circumstances, youths between 17 and 21 convicted of any offence of violence towards a police officer or steward, or to spectators who are not involved in the violence, should receive a custodial sentence, usually a short detention centre order, but a youth custody order would be appropriate where a weapon was used, a disabling injury caused or the offender was 'addicted to the use of violence' (*R v Wood* (1984) 6 Cr App R (S) 2).

Violence on the pitch may also be punished severely. A football player in a non-league match who lost his temper when a free kick was awarded against his team and punched the referee unconscious and jumped on his back was imprisoned for 28 days for the offence of assault occasioning actual bodily harm (*The Times*, 2 August 1986). A Welsh rugby union international who had knocked out an opponent with a punch in a local match received a sentence of 28 days' imprisonment which was reduced by the Court of Appeal to a suspended sentence of 12 months (*R v Bishop, The Times*, 2 and 18 September 1986). A policeman was sentenced to six months' imprisonment (later upheld on appeal) for biting off part of the ear of a rival officer during a Welsh inter-force rugby match (*The Times*, 26 September 1986). Two football supporters were imprisoned for three months and eight weeks respectively for insulting language and behaviour at a match in Bradford at which a fish-and-chip van was burnt out (*The Times*, 14 October 1986). A Dundee United footballer was fined £100 in Scotland for spitting and making signs at rival fans (*The Times*, 26 October 1986). Two Portsmouth football players were ejected by the police from their own ground for swearing at a linesman (*The Times*, 28 October 1986). See Home Office Research Study No. 89, *Personal Violence* by Roy Walmsley (1986), for much information on offences of personal violence, including football hooliganism.

3.3   CRIMINAL DAMAGE

A full range of criminal damage charges is available under the Criminal Damage Act 1971 to cover situations of public disorder, including damage or destruction of property, threats to damage or destroy property, arson, and damage or destruction of property with intent to endanger life or being reckless whether life would be endangered.

In summary the offences of criminal damage and their penalties are as follows:

(a)   *Destroying or damaging property* (Criminal Damage Act 1971, s. 1). It is an offence if a person:

(i)   destroys or damages property belonging to another,
(ii)   without lawful excuse,
(iii) intending to destroy or damage the property, or
(iv)   being reckless as to whether the property would be destroyed or damaged.

This offence is triable either way except where it appears to the court that the value of the property damaged or destroyed does not exceed £400 in which case the offence is triable summarily only (Magistrates' Courts Act 1980, s. 22). The figure of £400 is likely to be increased to £2,000 in 1987 (see Criminal Justice Bill, cl. 24, 13 November 1986). In *R* v *Salisbury Magistrates' Court (ex parte Mastin)* [1986] Crim LR 545 it was held that where a number of motor vehicles belonging to the 'peace convoy' had damaged the crop in a bean field to the total value of £5,800 the prosecution were entitled to charge drivers with sums of damage ranging for individual defendants between £16 and £117 and so deprive the defendants of their right to trial by jury, even though (as the defence argued) it was essentially a joint enterprise and the prosecution's calculations in the circumstances were wholly artificial. The court suggested that in some cases it is desirable for the prosecution to specify the limited value in the charge. (See also *R* v *Canterbury & St Augustine Justices (ex parte Klisiak)* [1982] QB 398.)

The penalty on indictment is imprisonment not exceeding 10 years and on summary conviction six months' imprisonment and/or a fine not exceeding the statutory maximum (for fine scales see 1.8.1) except where the value of the damage is £400 or less when the maximum penalty on summary conviction is three months' imprisonment and/or a fine up to £1,000.

(b)   *Arson* (Criminal Damage Act 1971, s. 1(3)). Arson is the above offence committed by fire. The offence is triable either way (subject to the £400 limit, see above) and punishable on indictment with a maximum of life imprisonment and summarily with six months' imprisonment and/or a fine not exceeding the statutory maximum.

(c)   *Endangering life* (Criminal Damage Act 1971, s. 1 (2)). The offences under (a) and (b) above are aggravated if in addition it is proved that the person intended by the destruction or damage to endanger life or was reckless as to whether the life of another would be thereby endangered. There must be a causal link between the damage to property and the danger to life (*R* v *Steer* [1986] Crim LR 619).

This offence is triable on indictment only and punishable with a maximum penalty of life imprisonment.

(d)   *Threats to destroy or damage property* (Criminal Damage Act 1971, s. 2). It is an offence if a person:

(i)   makes a threat to another person to destroy or damage property belonging to that person or to someone else,

(ii)   without lawful excuse, and

(iii)   intending that the other person would fear that the threat would be carried out.

This offence is triable either way and punishable on indictment with a maximum penalty of 10 years' imprisonment and summarily with a maximum of six months' imprisonment and/or a fine not to exceed the statutory maximum.

(e)   It is also an offence to *possess anything* with intent to destroy or damage property (Criminal Damage Act 1971, s. 3, see 3.1.4), punishable on indictment with a maximum penalty of 10 years' imprisonment or summarily with a maximum penalty of six months' imprisonment and/or a fine not to exceed the statutory maximum.

'Damage' is not defined in the Criminal Damage Act 1981. In some old cases 'damage' included the dismantling of machinery without injuring individual parts (*R* v *Tacey* (1821) Russ & Ry 452; *R* v *Fisher* (1865) LR 1 CCR 7). Damage need not be permanent. CND graffiti on the 40th anniversary of the bombing of Hiroshima, mixed with solvents designed to wash the paint away, nevertheless caused damage (*Hardman* v *Chief Constable of Avon & Somerset Constabulary* [1986] Crim LR 330, Bristol Crown Court), although the decision might have been different if the local authority had not suffered expense and inconvenience in cleaning off the graffiti before the rain washed it away. What constitutes damage is a matter of fact and degree. Damage need not be permanent to constitute criminal damage, but the application of graffiti to a structure will not necessarily amount to causing criminal damage (*Roe* v *Kingeslee* [1986] Crim LR 735, smearing mud graffiti on a police cell wall was criminal damage). In *R* v *Ambrose* (1973) 57 Cr App R 538, 540, in which count 7 in the indictment charged criminal damage for carving 'Peter loves Joy' on a police cell door, Lawton LJ said that 'the court wished it to be clearly understood that those who draft indictments should use common sense and should not put into indictments charges which are of such a trivial nature'. Erasure of a programme from a computer circuit card was criminal damage (*Cox* v *Riley* [1986] Crim LR 460).

'Property' is defined in the Criminal Damage Act 1981, s. 10(1), as meaning property of a tangible nature, whether real or personal, including money. For the full definition, see 7.3.3.4.

Note that the test of *recklessness* (see *R* v *Caldwell* [1982] AC 341) for criminal damage is wider than the test of awareness for the new statutory offences in the Public Order Act 1986 (see 2.2.5.1). A defendant who awoke to find his mattress smouldering, but did nothing to extinguish it, and merely moved to another room, was guilty of reckless arson (*R* v *Miller* [1983] 2 AC 161).

Minor damage is often punished with a fine, and with a compensation order to pay for the damage if the offender has the means to pay. Compensation orders will often be greater than the fine, for example, where one of a number of youths who have been drinking deliberately or recklessly pushes another through a plate-glass window. It would be reckless to push somebody with some force outside a shop window without actually intending to break the window. In cases of football hooliganism deterrent custodial sentences can be expected, even for persons of good character (*R v McKenna and Vanner*, CA, 11 October 1985, ref. 4161 B85). Serious cases of damage in the course of a riot will be heavily punished. In *R v Palgrave* (*The Times*, 11 September 1986) the defendant was sentenced to five years' imprisonment for arson and possessing a petrol bomb during the 1985 Handsworth riots.

3.4   CONTAMINATING OR INTERFERING WITH GOODS

The Public Order Act 1986, s. 38, creates a new offence of contaminating or interfering with goods with the intention of causing public alarm or anxiety, injury or loss. This section creates a number of detailed offences under this heading. It was introduced at a late stage during the passage through Parliament of the Public Order Act and is designed to penalise the increasing use of contamination or threats to contaminate goods, usually foodstuffs which are on sale throughout the country, with the purpose of publicising a cause, causing economic loss or extorting money as a form of blackmail. The charge is a serious one and carries a maximum penalty of 10 years' imprisonment.

3.4.1   The new offences

The Public Order Act 1986, s. 38, creates three groups of offences:

(a)   Contamination of or interference with goods (s. 38(1)).
(b)   Threatening to contaminate or interfere with goods (s. 38(2)).
(c)   Possession of articles (s. 38(3)).

3.4.2   Contamination of or interference with goods

It is an offence for a person (with the necessary intention—see below):

(a)   to contaminate or interfere with goods, or
(b)   to make it appear that goods have been contaminated or interfered with, or
(c)   to place goods which have been contaminated or interfered with, or which appear to have been contaminated or interfered with, in a place where goods of that description are consumed, used, sold or otherwise supplied.

The words 'contaminated or interfered with' are not defined in the Public Order Act 1986. They will therefore have their ordinary meaning. It can be seen from the section as a whole that the contamination or interference need be minimal, and under s. 38(2) (see 3.4.3) there need be no contamination or interference at all so long as there is a claim that there has been. It is therefore not necessary that there should be any poison or drug inserted into the goods for the offence to be made out, although if this has in fact happened and shoppers are put at risk of injury the offence will be aggravated in terms of penalty (see below).

'Goods' are defined as including substances whether natural or manufactured and whether or not incorporated in or mixed with other goods (Public Order Act 1986, s. 38(5)).

The necessary intention is:

(a)   to cause public alarm or anxiety, or
(b)   to cause injury to members of the public consuming or using the goods, or
(c)   to cause economic loss to any person by reason of the goods being shunned by members of the public, or
(d)   to cause economic loss to any person by reason of steps taken to avoid any such alarm or anxiety, injury or loss.

3.4.3   Threats to contaminate or interfere with goods

It is an offence for a person (with the necessary intention—see below):

(a)   to threaten that he or another will do any of the acts mentioned in s. 38(1) (see 3.4.2), or
(b)   to claim that he or another has done any of the acts mentioned in s. 38(1).

A claim that another has done any such acts is not an offence where a person in good faith reports or warns that such acts have been, or appear to have been, committed (s. 38(6)).

The necessary intention is:

(a)   to cause public alarm or anxiety, or
(b)   to cause economic loss to any person by reason of the goods being shunned by members of the public, or
(c)   to cause economic loss to any person by reason of steps taken to avoid any such alarm or anxiety, injury or loss.

3.4.4   Possession of articles

It is an offence for a person to be in possession of the following articles with a view to the commission of the offence of contamination or interference with goods contrary to s. 38(1):

(a)   materials to be used for contaminating or interfering with goods or making it appear that goods have been contaminated or interfered with, or
(b)   goods which have been contaminated or interfered with, or which appear to have been contaminated or interfered with.

3.4.5   Power of arrest

The offences defined in the Public Order Act 1986, s. 38, are arrestable offences because the maximum penalty (see 3.4.7) is in excess of five years' imprisonment (Police and Criminal Evidence Act 1984, s. 24). There is therefore no need for a specific arrest power in the Public Order Act 1986, s. 38. For a full discussion of arrest powers see chapter 5.

3.4.6 Mode of trial

All the offences defined in the Public Order Act 1986, s. 38, are triable either way, that is either on indictment in the Crown Court or summarily in the magistrates' court (s. 38(4)). The defendant can elect to be tried on indictment by a jury if he so wishes.

3.4.7 Penalty

A person guilty of any of the offences defined in the Public Order Act 1986, s. 38, is liable on conviction on indictment to a maximum penalty of 10 years' imprisonment and/or a fine without limit, or on, summary conviction to a maximum penalty of six months' imprisonment and/or a fine not exceeding the statutory maximum (for fine scales, see 1.8) (s. 38(4)).

3.5 INTIMIDATION, INCLUDING WATCHING AND BESETTING

3.5.1 Introduction

The offence of intimidation, including watching and besetting, contrary to the Conspiracy and Protection of Property Act 1875, s. 7, was more or less defunct until it enjoyed a modest revival during the miners' strike of 1984–5 (for example, out of 7,658 arrests made between 13 March and 8 November 1984 during the strike 226 were for alleged offences under s. 7). Some benches of justices had refused to entertain s. 7 charges, taking the view that the conduct complained of should be charged under the Public Order Act 1936, s. 5, or not at all.

In [1985] Crim LR 64 F. Bennion argued that although it was virtually obsolete it should be preserved to punish 'illegal mass picketing'. The government appears to have answered this appeal and has specifically retained the offence and approved of its use by providing a power of arrest and increasing the penalty (Public Order Act 1986, sch. 2). However, the wording of the offence (or offences) is archaic, difficult to understand and inconsistent with the pattern of the new statutory offences in the Public Order Act 1986. It may therefore be better practice to prosecute alleged illegal activity by reference to the new offences defined in the Public Order Act 1986, particularly s. 4 (threatening behaviour etc.) and s. 5 (disorderly conduct) or to use the civil law to restrain tortious conduct (see *Thomas* v *National Union of Mineworkers (South Wales Area)* [1985] 2 WLR 1081, and *News Group Newspapers Ltd* v *Society of Graphical & Allied Trades 1982*, *The Times*, 1 August 1986, 7.2).

3.5.2 The offence

The Conspiracy and Protection of Property Act 1875, s. 7, sets out five separate criminal offences (although in Scotland they are considered to be one offence: *Wilson* v *Renton* (1909) 47 SLR 209) including watching and besetting. These offences are triable summarily and the Public Order Act 1986 has increased the maximum penalty from three months' imprisonment to six months and from a fine on level 2 to a fine up to level 5 (Public Order Act 1986, sch. 2, para. 1).

3.5.3   Ingredients of the offence

It is an offence if a person, with a view to compelling another to abstain from
doing, or to do, an act which that other person has a legal right to do or abstain
from doing, wrongfully and without legal authority:

   (a)   uses violence to or intimidates such other person or his wife or children,
or injures his property, or
   (b)   persistently follows such other persons about from place to place, or
   (c)   hides any tools, clothes or other property owned or used by such other
person, or deprives him of or hinders him in the use thereof, or
   (d)   watches or besets the house or other place where such other resides, or
works, or carries on business, or happens to be, or the approach to such house
or place, or
   (e)   follows such other person with two or more other persons in a
disorderly manner in or through any street or road.

The language of 'compelling' etc. has been borrowed and reformulated for the
test of intimidation in the control of processions and assemblies (Public Order
Act 1986, ss. 12 and 14, and for a discussion of intimidation in civil cases
concerned with picketing see *Thomas* v *National Union of Mineworkers (South
Wales Area)* [1985] 2 WLR 1081; *News Group Newspapers Ltd* v *Society of
Graphical & Allied Trades 1982, The Times*, 1 August 1986; and 6.8, 7.2 and
9.5).
   The words 'wrongfully and without legal authority' have caused some
difficulty. Bennion [1985] Crim LR 64 suggests that 'wrongfully' should be
equated with unlawfully, although Scott J in *Thomas* v *National Union of
Mineworkers (South Wales Area)* found that 'unlawful picketing' was an
unhelpful and misleading term. In *J. Lyons & Sons* v *Wilkins* [1899] 1 Ch 255,
272, it was said that the words 'wrongfully and without lawful authority' were
inserted to provide for any unforeseen case in which evidence of the overt acts
may possibly shew some lawful excuse or justification.
   'Intimidation' includes putting a person in fear by the exhibition of force or
violence or the threat of force or violence, and there is no limitation restricting
the meaning of 'intimidation' to cases of violence or threats of violence to the
person (*R* v *Jones* (1974) 59 Cr App R 120). It also includes threats of breaches
of contract (*Rookes* v *Barnard* [1964] AC 1129). 'Intimidate' is not a term of
art; it must be given 'a reasonable and sensible interpretation' (*Gibson* v
Lawson [1891] 2 QB 545). See also, 6.8 and 9.5.
   Watching and besetting is subject to the defence that peaceful picketing at
one's place of work within the meaning of the Trade Union and Labour
Relations Act 1974, s. 15 (see 6.8) is not unlawful (see *Thomas* v *National
Union of Mineworkers (South Wales Area)* [1985] 2 WLR 1081, 1105), although
s. 15 does not confer a right to enter upon private property against the will of
the owner for the purpose of peaceful picketing (*M'Cusker* v *Smith* [1918] 2 IR
432). Picketing by only two persons may fall within this wording (*J. Lyons &
Sons* v *Wilkins*). In practice this offence is usually only charged in respect of
'watching and besetting' private residences.

3.6 PROHIBITION OF UNIFORMS AND QUASI-MILITARY ORGANISATIONS

The following two offences are unaffected by the Public Order Act 1986:

(a) Public Order Act 1936, s. 1, *prohibits the wearing of a uniform* signifying association with any political organisation or with the promotion of any political object in any public place or at any public meeting. The maximum penalty on summary conviction is three months' imprisonment and/or a fine not exceeding level 4 (Public Order Act 1936, s. 7(2)).

Uniforms were commonly worn, for example, black shirts by the British Union of Fascists and the Imperial Fascist League, blue shirts by the Kensington Fascists, and grey by the United Empire Fascist Party (see *Brownlie's Law of Public Order and National Security*, 2nd ed., pp. 181–2). In *O'Moran* v *DPP* [1975] QB 864 a black beret, dark glasses, black pullover and other dark clothing was held to be a uniform (even the wearing of a black beret alone), but not the wearing of a badge. The Prevention of Terrorism (Temporary Provisions) Act 1984, s. 2, prohibits the wearing of any item of dress or the wearing, carrying or display of any article, in a public place, in such a way or in such circumstances as to arouse reasonable apprehension of membership or support of a proscribed organisation, at present restricted to the Irish Republican Army and the Irish National Liberation Army (Prevention of Terrorism (Temporary Provisions) Act 1984, sch. 1).

(b) Public Order Act 1936, s. 2, *prohibits the formation of military or semi-military organisations* and the organising, training or equipping of members or adherents of an association for the purpose of (i) usurping the functions of the police or the armed forces, or (ii) using or displaying physical force in promoting any political object. The maximum penalty on indictment is two years' imprisonment and/or a fine and on summary conviction six months' imprisonment and/or a fine not exceeding the statutory maximum (Public Order Act 1936, s. 7(1)).

Illegal training and drilling in the use of arms is prohibited by the Unlawful Drilling Act 1819.

These offences contrary to ss. 1 and 2 of the Public Order Act 1936, which were created to deal with the growth of fascist political organisations in the 1930s, have not been repealed by the Public Order Act 1986. They both require the *consent of the Attorney-General* to proceedings. Very few prosecutions are brought under either section; for examples of successful prosecutions see *R* v *Jordan and Tyndall* [1963] Crim LR 124 in which Jordan received nine months' and Tyndall six months' imprisonment for taking part in a Nazi organisation called Spearhead (see also 4.3.4), and *R* v *Evans and others, The Times*, 2 July 1969, a Free Wales Army case in which two defendants received sentences of 15 months' and a third was sentenced to nine months' imprisonment.

3.7 TERRORIST OFFENCES

The Prevention of Terrorism (Temporary Provisions) Act 1984, like its forerunners the 1974 Act (passed in a night after the Birmingham public house bombings) and the 1976 Act, contains Draconian 'temporary' powers to exclude persons, notably residents of Northern Ireland, from Great Britain (s. 4), to exclude persons from the United Kingdom (s. 6), and to arrest and detain for questioning without charge for up to five days (s. 12).

It also contains powers to prohibit a wide range of activity connected with terrorism, including membership etc. of a proscribed organisation (s. 1, and see 3.6), display of support for a proscribed organisation (s. 2), financial contribution towards acts of terrorism (s. 10) and failure to disclose information about acts of terrorism (s. 11).

'Terrorism' is defined in wide terms as meaning the use of violence for political ends, and includes any use of violence for the purpose of putting the public or any section of the public in fear (s. 14).

Only 185 out of 6,291 people detained under the Prevention of Terrorism Act since it was introduced in 1974 have been charged with offences under the legislation, according to Home Office figures released in July 1986.

For further information on the issues of the Prevention of Terrorism (Temporary Provisions) Act 1984 see the report of Lord Shackleton, *Review of the Operation of the Prevention of Terrorism (Temporary Provisions) Acts 1974 and 1976* (Cmnd 7324, 1978), the report of Lord Jellicoe, *Review of the Operation of the Prevention of Terrorism (Temporary Provisions) Act 1976* (Cmnd 8803, 1983) and NCCL, *The New Prevention of Terrorism Act: The Case for Repeal*. See also the Prevention of Terrorism (Supplemental Temporary Provisions) Order 1984 (SI 1984 No. 418) and the Suppression of Terrorism Act 1978 which gives effect to the European Convention on the Suppression of Terrorism.

3.8   BOMB HOAXES

The Criminal Law Act 1977, s. 51, makes it an offence (a) to place any article in any place whatsoever, or (b) to dispatch any article by post, rail or other means, or (c) to communicate any false information, with the intention of inducing the belief that the article or a bomb is likely to explode or ignite.

This offence is triable either way. The maximum penalty on indictment is five years' imprisonment and on summary trial three months' imprisonment and/or a fine not exceeding the statutory maximum. Without aggravating features sentences are usually in the range of six to 12 months' imprisonment, although suspended sentences and occasionally fines are imposed (see £50 fine for hoax bomb alert at the South African Airways desk at Heathrow Airport, *The Times*, 25 May 1986). Before this offence was created a bomb hoax was charged as a public nuisance (see 6.12). The real thing is more serious and is dealt with under the Explosive Substances Act 1883.

3.9   OBSTRUCTING THE POLICE

The frequently used offence of obstructing a constable in the execution of his duty is dealt with in 5.12.

3.10   HIGHWAY OFFENCES

Chapter 6 deals with offences of obstruction of the highway, street offences, public nuisance etc.

4

Incitement to Racial Hatred

This chapter deals with the six new offences of racial hatred and consequential provisions which are set out in Part III of the Public Order Act 1986. These offences replace the offence of incitement to racial hatred contrary to the Public Order Act 1936, s. 5A, and the offence of incitement to racial hatred in the theatre contrary to the Theatres Act 1968, s. 5, and extend the law against racial hatred to recordings, some broadcasts and cable programmes.

4.1 INTRODUCTION

4.1.1 Summary of changes made by the Public Order Act 1986

Part III of the Public Order Act 1986 provides controls on the stirring up of racial hatred (ss. 17–29). It replaces the single offence of incitement to racial hatred contrary to the now repealed Public Order Act 1936, s. 5A, and extends this area of public order law in the following ways:

(a) by dividing the old s. 5A offence into two separate offences of publishing or distributing written material (Public Order Act 1986, s. 19) and the use of words or behaviour (s. 18);

(b) by creating a further offence of possessing racially inflammatory matter (s. 23);

(c) by replacing the offence of incitement to racial hatred by public performance of a play contrary to the Theatres Act 1968, s. 5, with a new offence (s. 20);

(d) by creating offences to punish the stirring up of racial hatred by means of recordings (s. 21) and broadcasts and cable programmes (s. 22), except those transmitted by the British Broadcasting Corporation or the Independent Broadcasting Authority;

(e) by adding to the test of 'racial hatred is likely to be stirred up' an alternative test of 'intends to stir up racial hatred';

(f) by removing s. 5A's exemption for material circulated privately to members of an association; and

(g) by creating a power of arrest for the offence of using words or behaviour to stir up racial hatred (s. 18(3)).

The new offences have similar penalties to the repealed s. 5A and similarly require the Attorney-General's consent to prosecution. Additional powers of entry, search and forfeiture are also provided.

4.1.2 Race Relations Act 1965, s. 6

The first offence of incitement to racial hatred was created by the Race Relations Act 1965, s. 6. Before then such conduct was penalised, albeit rarely, under the common law offences of seditious libel, criminal libel or public mischief, all of which offences have survived the passage of time (except conspiracy to effect a public mischief: *DPP* v *Withers* [1975] AC 842) but are rarely used (cf. the newspaper prosecution for blasphemous libel in *Whitehouse* v *Gay News Ltd and Lemon* (1979) 68 Cr App R 381). In *R* v *Edwards* (1983) 5 Cr App R (S) 145 Lawton LJ emphasised (at p. 148) the seriousness of the offence of incitement to racial hatred by equating it to the common law offence of sedition (see 4.3.4).

There were few prosecutions under the 1965 Act and many were brought against black people, the most notable being the trial of Michael X for addressing a Black Power meeting in Reading (*R* v *Malik* [1968] 1 All ER 582). Many prosecutions failed, principally because the offence required proof of intent to stir up racial hatred. In the prosecution of John Kingsley Read, the leader of the British Movement, an Old Bailey jury acquitted Read of the offence (*R* v *Read, The Times*, 7 January 1978). He was alleged to have addressed his supporters, after an Asian youth was killed in Southall, with the words 'One down, a million to go', and also to have referred to 'niggers, wogs and coons'. His defence was that the words were intended as a joke. Presumably the prosecution failed to prove the specific intent to stir up racial hatred as the 1965 Act required. Lord Scarman (*The Red Lion Square Disorders*, Cmnd 5919, para. 125) observed: 'Section 6 of the Race Relations Act is merely an embarrassment to the police. Hedged about with restrictions (proof of intent, requirement of the Attorney-General's consent) it is useless to a policeman on the street.' For further background see Lester and Bindman, *Race and Law*.

4.1.3 Public Order Act 1936, s. 5A

The 1965 Act offence was replaced by the Public Order Act 1936, s. 5A (see Appendix 2). Section 5A was inserted into the 1936 Act by the Race Relations Act 1976, s. 70. The 1976 amendment removed proof of intent and replaced it with the requirement to prove that hatred would, having regard to all the circumstances, be likely to be stirred up against any racial group in Great Britain. Prosecutions were still few in number and many failed. If Read (see 4.1.2) had been prosecuted under the 1976 amendment (s. 5A) he might well have been acquitted on the basis that there was no likelihood of his own supporters being stirred to racial hatred by his words.

4.1.4 Public Order Act 1986, Part III

Part III of the Public Order Act 1986 (ss. 17–29) is an attempt to cure these defects. It creates a number of new offences and combines from the previous legislation the two tests of intent to stir up racial hatred and the likelihood of racial hatred being stirred up. But legal and other restraints on prosecution remain. The Attorney-General must still give his consent to a prosecution, and successive Attorneys-General have publicly expressed their reluctance to prosecute. They say that unsuccessful prosecutions do more harm than good to racial equality. It remains to be seen whether the creation of new offences will increase the prosecution rate in the light of these continuing restraints and whether it will convince the police that these offences should be part of their everyday armoury of public order powers.

4.2   THE NEW RACIAL HATRED OFFENCES

The Public Order Act 1986 creates six separate offences.

4.2.1   Use of words or gestures

Under the Public Order Act 1986, s. 18, a person is guilty of an offence if:

(a)   he uses threatening, abusive or insulting words or behaviour, or
(b)   he displays any written material which is threatening, abusive or insulting, and
(c)   *either* he intends thereby to stir up racial hatred, *or*
(d)   having regard to all the circumstances racial hatred is likely to be stirred up thereby, and he intended his words or behaviour or the written material to be, or was aware that they might be, threatening, abusive or insulting.

As with all the new offences under this Part of the Public Order Act 1986 this offence is triable either way. The maximum penalty on conviction on indictment is two years' imprisonment and/or a fine of unlimited amount, or on conviction summarily six months' imprisonment and/or a fine not exceeding the statutory maximum (s. 27(3)). For fine scales see 1.8. A constable (not necessarily in uniform) may arrest without warrant anyone he reasonably suspects to be committing this offence (s. 18(3)).

4.2.1.1   Public or private place   The s. 18 offence can be committed in a public or a private place, except that no offence is committed where the words or behaviour are used, or the written material is displayed, by a person inside a dwelling and are not heard or seen except by other persons in that or another dwelling (s. 18(2)). The extension of this offence to some private places is similar to the provisions in the s. 4 offence of threatening behaviour etc. (see 2.5).

4.2.1.2   Threatening, abusive or insulting words or behaviour   These words must be interpreted on the same basis as in ss. 4 and 5 of the Public Order Act 1986 (and the repealed Public Order Act 1936, s. 5), see 2.5 and 2.6.

Section 18 extends this aspect of incitement to racial hatred from words to words or behaviour, a phrase used in the wording in ss. 4 and 5 of the Public Order Act 1986. The word 'gestures', which was used in the original draft of the Public Order Bill, would have been narrower than 'behaviour' and included obvious racist gestures such as a Nazi salute and other gestures which are racist in context. Gestures alone are now unlikely to be sufficient except where the context is obvious. Offensive gestures by white people clearly directed at black people in the street would be an offence under ss. 4 and 5 but might not be an offence under s. 18 unless it can be shown that racial hatred was likely to be stirred up, for example, amongst other white bystanders. Even then it could be argued that hatred—on any basis a strong word—was neither intended nor likely, and that the real object was something less than hatred, say resentment or disapproval or dislike. These examples suggest that these new offences, although a strengthening of the previous law in the Public Order Act 1936, s. 5A, will still face difficulties of proof in the courts.

4.2.1.3 Written material Written material includes any sign or other visible representation (s. 29). It includes presumably placards, banners and even badges as well as books, pamphlets and leaflets. It clearly includes the use of pictorial matter as well as the use of words. It is intended to include illustrations, symbols and signs, such as swastikas or the depiction in cartoon form of assaults on black people (see House of Commons Standing Committee G debate 20 March 1986).

This section does not apply to material for use in a broadcast or cable programme (s. 18(6)). For the offence relating to broadcasts and cable programmes see 4.2.5.

4.2.1.4 Racial hatred In Part III of the Public Order Act 1986, 'racial hatred' means hatred against a group of persons in Great Britain defined by reference to colour, race, nationality (including citizenship) or ethnic or national origins (s. 17). This definition does not include religion, although a group identified through religion may bear other characteristics within the definition. Broadly speaking the difference between a racial group and a religious (or political) group is that membership of the former is inherited and membership of the latter involves personal choice.

Some have argued that the definition protects Jews from racial but not religious prosecution, although in practice this has not caused legal difficulties (see *R* v *Edwards* (1983) 5 Cr App R (S) 145, see 4.3.5), and in *Mandla* v *Dowell Lee* [1983] 2 AC 548 a case concerning the education of a Sikh boy, Lord Fraser of Tullybelton (at p. 562) found that an ethnic group must have two essential characteristics: a long shared history, of which the group is conscious as distinguishing it from other groups, and a cultural tradition of its own including family and social customs and manners, often but not necessarily associated with religious observance.

The Commission for Racial Equality takes the view that as a result of the decision in *Mandla* v *Dowell Lee* gypsies are included in the definition of 'racial group' for the purposes of civil proceedings but are excluded for the purposes of the new incitement to racial hatred provisions, despite being a frequent target for abuse. In *Gwynedd County Council* v *Jones, The Times*, 28 July 1986, it was held that there was nothing in the decision in *Mandla* v *Dowell Lee* and the other cases to indicate that language (the Welsh language) was a significant factor in the characteristics which distinguish a racial group for the purposes of the discrimination provisions of the Race Relations Act 1976.

The group must be in Great Britain. It is not unlawful to foment racial hatred against people outside this country, although in practice this form of incitement directed at people outside the country will usually affect members of the same group who are inside Great Britain.

4.2.1.5 '*Intends to stir up hatred*' '*racial hatred is likely to be stirred up*' These alternatives combine the two tests of the Race Relations Act 1965 and the 1976 amendment. Penalising conduct which is intended to stir up racial hatred even though it may not be possible to prove that it is likely to do so arises where those confronted with the conduct either agree with it (as in *R* v *Read*, see 4.1.2) or are so implacably opposed to it that there is no chance of their being influenced by it.

Where it is alleged that the defendant did not intend to stir up hatred, but that in all the circumstances it was likely that hatred would be stirred up, the prosecution must also prove that the defendant intended his conduct to be threatening, abusive or insulting, or that he was aware that it might be. The new test of awareness is a form of recklessness—see 2.2.5.

4.2.1.6 Specific defence It is a defence for the defendant to prove (on a balance of probabilities) that:

(a)   he was inside a dwelling (defined in s. 29), and
(b)   he had no reason to believe that the words or behaviour or written material would be heard or seen by a person outside that dwelling or any other dwelling (s. 18(4)).

4.2.2   Publishing or distributing written material

Under the Public Order Act 1986, s. 19, a person is guilty of an offence if:

(a)   he publishes or distributes written material, and
(b)   the written matter is threatening, abusive or insulting, and
(c)   *either* he intends thereby to stir up racial hatred *or* having regard to all the circumstances racial hatred is likely to be stirred up thereby.

The offence is punishable on conviction on indictment with a maximum penalty of two years' imprisonment and/or a fine. On summary conviction the maximum penalty is six months' imprisonment and/or a fine not exceeding the statutory maximum (s. 27(3)). See 4.3.5.

4.2.2.1 '*Publishes*', '*distributes*' 'Publication or distribution' means publication or distribution to the public or a section of the public (s. 19(3)). This definition removes the previous exemption for material circulated to members of an association (Public Order Act 1936, s. 5A(6)) and brings within the ambit of this offence the underground distribution of obnoxious material to members of amorphous organisations in which there is often nothing approaching a private or personal relationship between the members. The argument that the right to freedom of expression requires that organisations not banned by law should enjoy freedom to express their own views within their own groups is countered by the justification of applying the law in circumstances where the very nature of incitement has an impact on persons outside the organisation. Those who already hold racist views may be incited or incited further to racial hatred (see Cmnd 9510, para. 6.7, and also *DPP* v *Whyte* [1972] AC 849 in which the House of Lords held that the Obscene Publications Act 1959 protected not only the wholly innocent from corruption but equally the less innocent from further corruption and the addict from feeding or increasing his addiction).

Equally the decision in *R* v *Britton* [1967] 2 QB 51 must now be considered bad law. The Court of Appeal held that the delivery by a 'wretched little youth' of a pamphlet entitled 'Blacks not wanted here' to Sidney Bidwell, a Member of Parliament, was not publication to the public at large. Lord Parker CJ in a narrow judgment held that an MP and his family were not a section of the public within the meaning of the Race Relations Act 1965.

Some further comparison can be made with the terms of the Obscene Publications Act 1959 which provides that a person publishes an article who 'distributes, circulates, sells, lets on hire, gives, or lends it, or who offers it for sale or for letting on hire'.

4.2.2.2 Other definitions For the meaning of 'written material', 'threatening, abusive or insulting', 'racial hatred', and 'intends to or is likely to', see 4.2.1.2 to 4.2.1.5.

4.2.2.3 Specific defence Where the prosecution have not shown that the defendant intended to stir up racial hatred (and the prosecution therefore rely on the second limb of the offence, namely, that racial hatred is likely to be stirred up), it is a defence for the accused to prove that:

(a)   he was not aware of the content of the written material, and
(b)   he did not suspect and had no reason to suspect that it was threatening, abusive or insulting (s. 19(2)).

The defendant must prove the defence on a balance of probabilities. Note that this defence differs from the wording in s. 18(5). This subsection re-enacts in part the Public Order Act 1936, s. 5A(3).

See also parallel provisions in the Obscene Publications Act 1959, s. 2(5), the Obscene Publications Act 1964, s. 1(3), and the Misuse of Drugs Act 1971, s. 28.

4.2.3   Public performance of a play

The Public Order Act 1986, s. 20, amends s. 5 of the Theatres Act 1968 (the Act which abolished censorship in the theatre) so as to create an offence of stirring up racial hatred by means of a public performance of a play. This offence corresponds with the provisions in the other five offences in Part III of the Public Order Act 1986.

A person is guilty of an offence if:

(a)   he presents or directs the public performance of a play, and
(b)   the performance of the play involves the use of threatening, abusive or insulting words or behaviour, and
(c)   *either* he intends thereby to stir up racial hatred, *or*, having regard to all the circumstances (and, in particular, taking the performance as a whole), racial hatred is likely to be stirred up thereby.

For penalty, see 4.3.5.

Under the Theatres Act 1968, s. 5, the prohibited conduct extended only to words and not behaviour, and the offence required proof of both elements in (c) above, namely, both a specific intent and a likelihood of stirring up racial hatred (thus following the repealed Race Relations Act 1965, s. 6).

A 'play' means (Theatres Act 1968, s. 18(1); Public Order Act 1986, s. 20(5)):

(a)   any dramatic piece, whether involving improvisation or not, which is given wholly or in part by one or more persons actually present and performing and in which the whole or a major proportion of what is done by the person or persons performing, whether by way of speech, singing or action, involves the playing of a role; and
(b)   any ballet given wholly or in part by one or more persons actually present and performing, whether or not it falls within paragraph (a).

A 'public performance' includes (Theatres Act 1968, s. 18(1); Public Order Act 1986, s. 20(5)):

(a)   any performance in a public place within the meaning of the Public Order Act 1936 (see 8.3), and
(b)   any performance which the public or any section thereof are permitted to attend, whether on payment or otherwise.

A director does not escape liability by being absent during the performance (s. 20(4)(c)).

For definitions of 'threatening, abusive or insulting' and 'racial hatred', see 4.2.1.2 and 4.2.1.4.

4.2.3.1   Exceptions   Performances are exempted when given solely or primarily as a rehearsal, or for the purpose of making a recording, broadcast or cable programme, so long as the performance is not attended by persons not connected with the giving of the performance (s. 20(3)). For definitions of 'recording' see 4.2.4, 'broadcast' and 'cable programme service' see 4.2.5.

A performer is not a presenter, unless he steps outside the director's instructions, and a performer does not aid and abet a director by taking part in the performance (s. 20(4)).

4.2.3.2   Specific defence   Where the prosecution have not shown that the defendant intended to stir up racial hatred (and the prosecution therefore rely on the second limb of the offence, namely, that racial hatred is likely to be stirred up), it is a defence (s. 20(2)) for the defendant to prove (on a balance of probabilities) that he did not know and had no reason to suspect that:

(a)   the performance would involve the use of the offending words or behaviour, or
(b)   the offending words or behaviour were threatening, abusive or insulting, or
(c)   the circumstances in which the performance would be given would be such that racial hatred would be likely to be stirred up.

4.2.4 Distributing, showing or playing a recording

Under the Public Order Act 1986, s. 21, a person is guilty of an offence if:

(a)   he distributes, shows or plays a recording of visual images or sounds, and

(b)   the images or sounds are threatening, abusive or insulting, and

(c)   *either* he intends thereby to stir up racial hatred, *or*, having regard to all the circumstances, racial hatred is likely to be stirred up thereby.

For penalty, see 4.3.5.

A 'recording' means any record from which visual images or sounds 'may, by any means, be reproduced (s. 21(2)). This definition is specifically designed to include video recordings.

The distribution etc. does not have to be in public but must be to the public or a section of the public (s. 21(2)). See 4.2.2.1.

For other definitions see above.

The *specific defence* (see 4.2.2.3, 4.2.3.2, 4.2.5.2 and 4.2.6.4) similarly applies to this offence where the defendant proves that he was not aware of the content of the recording and did not suspect, and had no reason to suspect, that it was threatening, abusive or insulting (s. 21(3)).

4.2.5 Broadcasting or including programme in cable programme service

Part III of the Public Order Act 1986 was extended to certain limited aspects of broadcasting at a late stage in the passage of the Bill through Parliament. The official justification for the original exclusion of broadcasting (and the inclusion of cable programmes) was that whereas the means of transmission with cable is owned by individual companies and must therefore be controlled, the means of transmission by broadcasting is owned by broadcasting authorities which are responsible to Parliament. Note, however, the exemptions below.

Under the Public Order Act 1986, s. 22, a person is guilty of an offence if:

(a)   he provides a broadcasting or cable programme service in which threatening, abusive or insulting words or behaviour are broadcast or included in a cable service programme, or

(b)   he produces or directs such a programme, or

(c)   he uses the offending words or behaviour in the programme, and

(d)   *either* he intends thereby to stir up racial hatred, *or*, having regard to all the circumstances, racial hatred is likely to be stirred up thereby.

For penalty, see 4.3.5.

A 'broadcast' means a broadcast by wireless telegraphy (within the meaning of the Wireless Telegraphy Act 1949) for general reception, whether by way of sound broadcasting or television (s. 29). For the meaning of 'cable programme service' see the Cable and Broadcasting Act 1984. A programme means any item which is broadcast or included in a cable programme service (s. 29).

4.2.5.1   Exemptions   Broadcasts of programmes by the British Broadcasting

Corporation and the Independent Broadcasting Authority, and the reception or retransmission of such programmes by cable, are exempted from this section (s. 22(7)).

4.2.5.2 Specific defences   Where the prosecution have not shown that the defendant intended to stir up racial hatred (and the prosecution therefore rely on the second limb of the offence, namely that racial hatred is likely to be stirred up):

(a)   it is a defence for the person providing the service, or the producer or director of the programme, to prove that:

(i)   he did not know and had no reason to suspect that the programme would involve the offending material, and
(ii)   it was not reasonably practicable for him to secure the removal of the material (s. 22(3)); and

(b)   it is a defence for the producer or director of the programme, or the person who used the offending words or behaviour, to prove that he did not know and had no reason to suspect that:

(i)   the programme would be shown, or
(ii)   the circumstances would be such that racial hatred would be likely to be stirred up (s. 22(4) and (5)), and

(c)   it is a defence if a person did not know and had no reason to suspect that the offending material was threatening, abusive or insulting (s. 22(6)).

Under (a) and (b) it is for the defendant to prove the defence on a balance of probabilities. Under (c) it is for the prosecution to disprove the defence beyond reasonable doubt.

4.2.6   Possession of racially inflammatory material

The Public Order Act 1986, s. 23, deals with (a) the possession of written material, and (b) the possession of a recording of visual images or sounds.

(a)   A person is guilty of an offence if:

(i)   he has in his possession written material, and
(ii)   the written material is threatening, abusive or insulting, and
(iii)   he has it with a view to its being displayed, published, distributed, broadcast or included in a cable programme service (whether by himself or another), and
(iv)   *either* he intends racial hatred to be stirred up thereby, *or* having regard to all the circumstances racial hatred is likely to be stirred up thereby.

(b)   A person is guilty of an offence if:

(i)   he has in his possession a recording of visual images or sounds, *and*

(ii)   the images or sounds are threatening, abusive or insulting, *and*

(iii)   he has the recording with a view to its being distributed, shown, played, broadcast or included in a cable programme service (whether by himself or another), *and*

(iv)   *either* he intends racial hatred to be stirred up thereby, *or* having regard to all the circumstances racial hatred is likely to be stirred up thereby.

For penalty, see 4.3.5.

4.2.6.1   Possession   'In the ordinary use of the word "possession", one has in one's possession whatever is, to one's own knowledge, physically in one's custody or under one's physical control' (per Lord Diplock in *DPP* v *Brooks* [1974] 2 All ER 840, 842, a dangerous drugs case).

4.2.6.2   Display   'Display' is not defined in Part III of the Public Order Act 1986. It carries its ordinary meaning of opening up to view, exhibiting, showing. See also public displays of indecent matter in the Indecent Displays (Control) Act 1981.

4.2.6.3   Other definitions   For definitions of 'threatening, abusive or insulting' see 4.2.1.2, 'written material' see 4.2.1.3, 'racial hatred' see 4.2.1.4, 'published' and 'distributed' see 4.2.2.1, 'recording' see 4.2.4, 'broadcast' and 'cable programme service' see 4.2.5.

4.2.6.4   Purpose of this offence   This offence was designed to convict those who manufacture or supply racially inflammatory material in circumstances where it is difficult to prove a specific instance of distribution (Cmnd 9510, para. 6.8). It does seem, however, to go much further than that. In particular, some fears have been voiced that an innocent or curious recipient of material, for example, a leaflet handed over in the street, or a collector of material with the sole purpose of exposing it might be guilty of this offence.

These fears derive from the words 'having regard to all the circumstances, racial hatred is likely to be stirred up'. In the alternative to a specific intention to stir up racial hatred, the offence is made out on the likelihood of racial hatred being stirred up if the material were published, distributed etc. Therefore no actual publication or distribution is required, and any hypothetical publication or distribution could be said to be likely to cause racial hatred to be stirred up. Libraries may therefore be at risk of prosecution for storing racially inflammatory matter. So too may journalists who collect material as background information for future stories.

Two provisions may safeguard the innocent possessor. First, the Public Order Act 1986, s. 23(2), provides that, in considering whether racial hatred is likely to be stirred up, regard must be had to such publication, distribution etc. 'as he has, or it may reasonably be inferred that he has, in view'. This should provide a sufficient defence for the innocent handler of offending material. Secondly, the Attorney-General's consent to prosecution is required (s. 27(1))—see 4.3.2.

4.2.6.5   Specific defence   Where the prosecution have not shown that the

defendant intended to stir up racial hatred (and the prosecution therefore rely
on the second limb of the offence, namely, that racial hatred is likely to be
stirred up), it is a defence for the accused to prove (on a balance of
probabilities) that:

(a)   he was not aware of the content of the written material or recording,
and
(b)   he did not suspect, and had no reason to suspect, that it was
threatening, abusive or insulting (s. 23(3)).

4.3   THE NEW OFFENCES: MISCELLANEOUS

4.3.1   Arrest

A constable (not necessarily in uniform) may arrest without warrant anyone he
reasonably suspects to be committing an offence of stirring up racial hatred by
words or behaviour contrary to the Public Order Act 1986 (s. 18(3)). This is a
new power, but one which accords with the power of arrest under the Public
Order Act 1986, s. 4 (threatening words or behaviour etc.). This power of
arrest is unaffected by the requirement of the Attorney-General's consent to
prosecute (Prosecution of Offenders Act 1985, s. 25).

There is no specific power of arrest for the other offences in Part III of the
Public Order Act 1986. A constable will be able to arrest a person for any of
these offences when the general arrest conditions of the Police and Criminal
Evidence Act 1984, s. 25, apply (see 5.2). Otherwise the summons procedure
can be used to ensure a person's attendance at court.

4.3.2   Attorney-General's consent to prosecution

No proceedings for any offence under Part III of the Public Order Act 1986
may be instituted in England and Wales without the consent of the
Attorney-General (s. 27(1)). This does not prohibit a private prosecution if
consent can be obtained. In practice the role of the Attorney-General has
necessarily restricted the number of prosecutions brought under the previous
incitement to racial hatred provisions. Successive Attorneys-General have
expressed their reluctance to authorise prosecutions which they believe may
fail, giving the reason that unsuccessful prosecutions do more harm than good
to racial equality. The consent requirement may also discourage the police
from bringing cases. Between 1965 and 1973, for example, only seven
prosecutions (against 15 people) were authorised by the Attorney-General.

Other examples of prosecutions requiring the Attorney-General's consent
include the Explosives Act 1883, s. 7, the Prevention of Corruption Act 1906, s.
2, the Official Secrets Act 1911, s. 8, and the Sexual Offences Act 1956, ss. 10,
11 and 37.

If the post of Attorney-General is vacant or if he is absent or ill or if he
delegates the function, the Solicitor-General may act in his place (Law Officers
Act 1944, s. 1).

Where the Attorney-General consents to a prosecution under these
provisions, a further consent is required for the prosecution of an alleged

conspiracy contrary to the Criminal Law Act 1977, s. 1(1) (see *R* v *Pearce* (1981) 72 Cr App R 295).

4.3.3 Fair and accurate reports of parliamentary or judicial proceedings

The offences set out in ss. 18–23 do not apply to:

(a) a fair and accurate report of proceedings in Parliament (s. 26(1));
(b) a fair and accurate report of public court (and tribunal) proceedings, provided the report is published contemporaneously with or as soon as reasonably practicable after the proceedings (s. 26(2)—the proviso, which does not apply to proceedings in Parliament, is designed to prevent words spoken in court proceedings from being taken out of context at a later date).

4.3.4 Offences by corporations

The Public Order Act 1986, s. 28, makes provision for the conviction of directors, managers, secretaries (company secretaries) or other company officers, or others purporting to act in that capacity, if the body corporate is convicted and it is shown that the offence was committed with their consent or connivance. On conviction the officer faces the same penalty as if convicted in a personal capacity.

4.3.5 Penalties

The offences set out in ss. 18–23 carry the same maximum penalties (s. 27(3)):

(a) two years' imprisonment and/or a fine on indictment,
(b) six months' imprisonment and/or a fine (not exceeding the statutory maximum) on summary conviction.

These are the same penalties as on conviction under the repealed Public Order Act 1936, s. 5A. For details of the fine scale, see 1.8.

Sentences of imprisonment are usually imposed for incitement to racial hatred, although sometimes suspended. In *R* v *Malik* [1968] 1 All ER 582 the sentence of 12 months for addressing a Black Power meeting at Reading was upheld—the meeting was lawful but the speech was not. In *R* v *Relf* (1979) 1 Cr App R (S) 111 nine months was imposed for publishing leaflets containing derogatory references to the West Indian community which were displayed in various public places, and in *R* v *Edwards* (1983) 5 Cr App R (S) 145, 12 months was imposed for a comic strip intended for publication in a magazine and designed to prejudice children against Jews. Sentences of 12 months' imprisonment imposed on John Tyndall, chairman of the British National Party, and John Morse, editor of the party newspaper, *British Nationalist*, were reduced on appeal when half of the sentences were suspended (*The Times*, 21 October 1986). Articles in the newspaper had made attacks on Asians, Jews and black people, and had condemned multiracial society.

4.3.6 Entry and search

In relation to s. 23 only (possession of racially inflammatory material), a justice of the peace may issue a warrant to enter and search specified premises, if he is satisfied by information on oath laid by a constable that there are reasonable grounds for suspecting that a person has racially inflammatory material in his possession (s. 24(1)). A similar procedure applies in Scotland (s. 24(2)). 'Premises' is defined in s. 24(4).

A constable entering or searching premises with a warrant may use reasonable force if necessary (s. 24(3)).

4.3.7   Forfeiture

In relation to offences under s. 18 (relating to the display of written material) s. 19 (publishing or distributing written material), s. 21 (distributing, playing or showing a recording) and s. 23 (possessing racially inflammatory matter), a court may on conviction order the forfeiture of any written material or recording produced to the court and shown to relate to the offence (s. 25(1)). Once forfeited the material will be destroyed by the police, but not until the ordinary time for an appeal has expired or an appeal has been finally decided or abandoned (s. 25(2)–(4)).

Similar forfeiture provisions exist in a number of statutes, including the Obscene Publications Act 1959, the Firearms Act 1968, the Misuse of Drugs Act 1971, and the Forgery and Counterfeiting Act 1981.

4.4   FOOTBALL EXCLUSION ORDERS: RACIAL HATRED

The six new offences of incitement to racial hatred in Part III of the Public Order Act 1986 are 'offences connected with football' for the purposes of Part IV of the Public Order Act 1986. This means that a court can make an order excluding an offender from association football matches if he is convicted of an offence of incitement to racial hatred while he is on a journey to or from a football match (Public Order Act 1986, s. 31(3)(c)) or while he is at a football match or was entering or leaving or trying to enter or leave the football ground (s. 31(2)). For further details see 11.2.

5

Police Powers

5.1 PREVENTIVE POWERS: BREACH OF THE PEACE, BINDING OVER

Neither the Public Order Act 1986 nor the Police and Criminal Evidence Act 1984 affects the common law power of police constables (and ordinary citizens) to prevent a breach of the peace. In this context police officers may arrest, disperse or detain and if necessary take before a magistrates' court to be bound over those committing or about to commit or renew a breach of the peace. No other form of preventive detention by the police is lawful.

5.1.1 Meaning of breach of the peace

Although the concept of a breach of the peace is as old as the common law itself its definition has emerged somewhat uncertainly despite frequent use in public order law (particularly under the offences in the Public Order Act 1936, s. 5, and unlawful assembly—both now repealed—and in by-laws). The Law Commission Working Paper on offences against public order (No. 82, 1982, p. 144) preferred to avoid precise definition because it could 'indirectly affect the scope of the common law powers'. Nevertheless, the most authoritative definition of a breach of the peace appears in *R* v *Howell* [1982] QB 416, 427:

> We are emboldened to say that there is a breach of the peace whenever harm is actually done or is likely to be done to a person or in his presence to his property or a person is in fear of being so harmed through an assault, an affray, a riot, unlawful assembly or other disturbance. It is for this breach of the peace when done in his presence or the reasonable apprehension of it taking place that a constable, or anyone else, may arrest an offender without warrant.

In *R* v *Chief Constable of Devon & Cornwall (ex parte Central Electricity Generating Board)* [1982] QB 458 Lord Denning MR, on the particular facts of the case, in which local farmers and residents were protesting at the possible siting of a nuclear power station at Luxulyan in Cornwall by the unlawful (contrary to The Town and Country Planning Act 1971, s. 281(2)) obstruction of the Board's right to enter and survey land, took (at p. 471) a much broader view of breach of the peace:

> I think that the conduct of these people, their criminal obstruction, is itself a breach of the peace. There is a breach of the peace whenever a person who is

lawfully carrying out his work is unlawfully and physically prevented by
another from doing it. He is entitled by law peacefully to go on with his work
on his lawful occasions. If anyone unlawfully and physically obstructs the
worker—by lying down or chaining himself to a rig or the like—he is guilty of
a breach of the peace. Even if this were not enough, I think that their
unlawful conduct gives rise to a reasonable apprehension of a breach of the
peace.

This approach seems to weaken the element of violence and in *R* v *Howell* the
Court of Appeal (at p. 427) criticised the definition in *Halsbury's Laws of
England* (4th ed. vol. 11, para. 108) for failing to relate different kinds of
behaviour to violence and stated that the word 'disturbance' when used in
isolation could not describe a breach of the peace. Similarly, shouting and
swearing do not of themselves amount to a breach of the peace unless giving
rise to a reasonable apprehension of violence (*R* v *Brown*, CA, 24 October
1985, ref. No. 1738 B89, a domestic dispute, following *R* v *Howell*; and see
Ritchie v *M'Phee* (1882) 10 R (J) 9). See also *Wooding* v *Oxley* (1839) 9 C&P 1,
disturbance by noise not amounting to a breach of the peace at a meeting (see
10.3). But in *G* v *Chief Superintendent of Police, Stroud, The Times*, 29
November 1986, it was held that a mere disturbance could amount to a
likelihood of a breach of the peace (see 5.12.1.4).

It is submitted that *R* v *Howell*, in which the authorities were considered at
great length and which was not considered in the Luxulyan case, is to be
preferred as the authoritative statement on breach of the peace.

5.1.2 Exercise of preventive powers

There is a power of arrest without warrant for breach of the peace where (a) a
breach of the peace is committed in the presence of the person making the
arrest, or (b) the arrestor reasonably believes that a breach of the peace will be
committed in the immediate future by the person arrested although he has not
yet committed any breach, or (c) where a breach of the peace has been
committed and it is reasonably believed that a renewal of it is threatened (*R* v
Howell [1982] QB 416, 426). Apart from breach of the peace powers the police
have no preventive detention powers.

Circumstance (b) is the most contentious. The anticipated breach of the
peace must be 'a real possibility' before action can be taken (*Piddington* v *Bates*
[1961] 1 WLR 162). There must be 'a real and imminent risk' of a breach of the
peace (*R* v *Chief Constable of Devon & Cornwall (ex parte Central Electricity
Generating Board)* [1982] QB 458, 476). But this element was greatly
developed by the use of police road blocks in the miners' strike, most notably in
the Dartford Tunnel incident in which police powers to prevent an anticipated
breach of the peace were invoked to stop striking miners leaving Kent and
travelling over 100 miles north (see 6.7). Although in *Moss* v *McLachlan, The
Times*, 29 November 1984, another case involving the movement of striking
miners (the facts of the case are set out at 6.7.3), the Divisional Court said that
the police could only act if 'they honestly and reasonably formed the opinion
that there is a real risk of a breach of the peace in the sense that it is in close

proximity both in place and time'. For a full discussion of these cases and the question of 'imminence', see (1985) 149 JPN 403 and 423.

The arrest can be made by a police officer or an ordinary citizen (*R* v *Howell* [1982] QB 416, 426). The police have a general duty at common law to enforce the law (*R* v *Commissioner of Police of the Metropolis (ex parte Blackburn)* [1968] 2 QB 118). It is also the duty of every citizen to take reasonable steps to make a person who is breaking or threatening to break the peace refrain from doing so, including in appropriate cases detaining that person against his will, but in the case of a citizen who is not a constable 'it is a duty of imperfect obligation' (*Albert* v *Lavin* [1982] AC 546, 565). Where any arrest is made by a private citizen he should take the arrested person before a justice of the peace or a police officer as soon as reasonably possible (see 5.6).

The power can be exercised by:

(a)   preventing the person from going in a particular direction (refusal to comply would amount to obstructing a police officer in the execution of his duty: Police Act 1964, s. 51(3), see 5.12) or dispersing a crowd of persons or splitting them up; or

(b)   detaining the person, if necessary at a police station, for so long as is necessary in the circumstances (unreasonably lengthy detention would amount to false imprisonment and be actionable in the civil courts for damages), for example, to allow for cooling down or to prevent two sides fighting each other, or to take the arrested person before the magistrates' court with a view to being bound over (see 5.1.4).

Where there is a clear breach of the peace a police officer is entitled to use reasonable force to prevent it continuing, particularly if he anticipates that there will be a further breach of the peace unless he intervenes (*Joyce* v *Hertfordshire Constabulary* (1985) 80 Cr App R 298, fighting amongst spectators at a football match). Indeed it is his duty to do so (*Albert* v *Lavin*, in which a constable forcibly prevented a person from boarding a bus after the person had physically queue-barged at the bus stop to the resentment of others in the queue). No criminal charge need be brought for the exercise of the power to be lawful, although if criminal offences have been committed the police will have additional and alternative powers.

5.1.3   Not a criminal offence

Breach of the peace is not, except in Scotland, a criminal offence in itself. It may be a constituent part of a criminal offence, as in the repealed offence of threatening behaviour etc. contrary to the Public Order Act 1936, s. 5. Otherwise it can lead to binding over (see 5.1.4) but not to a penalty since there can be no conviction. An information charging that a person was guilty of conduct in the vicinity of the Taff Merthyr colliery which might lead to breaches of the peace contrary to the common law could not lead to a conviction for which a penalty could be imposed. It could only lead, where the facts were proved, to the defendant being bound over to keep the peace, with or without sureties (*Davies* v *Griffiths* [1937] 2 All ER 671). An arrest for a breach of the peace may, of course, lead to a charge where an offence has been committed, for example, assault, criminal damage or affray.

5.1.4 Binding over

If a police officer (or other citizen) exercises the common law power of arrest for a breach of the peace, the person arrested, in the discretion of the arrestor, can be released without charge or can be taken to a magistrates' court to show cause why he should not be bound over under the Justices of the Peace Act 1361 to keep the peace and/or to be of good behaviour. This does not amount to a conviction nor is it a penalty. It is an undertaking as to future conduct with or without (often without) any admissions about past behaviour. As Blackstone put it (B1 Com, bk 4, ch. 18):

> This preventive justice consists in obliging those persons, whom there is probable ground to suspect of future misbehaviour, to stipulate with and to give full assurance to the public, that such offence as is apprehended shall not happen; by finding pledges or securities for keeping the peace, or for their good behaviour.

The Justices of the Peace Act 1361 gives justices the power:

> to take of all them that be [not] of good fame, where they shall be found, sufficient surety and mainprise of their good behaviour towards the King and his people . . . to the intent that . . . the peace [be not] blemished.

The court must allow the person, if he wishes, to say why he should not be bound over (*Sheldon* v *Bromfield Justices* [1964] 2 QB 573; *R* v *Keighley Justices (ex parte Stoyles)* [1976] Crim LR 573)). No order should be made unless there may be a breach of the peace in the future (*R* v *Aubrey-Fletcher (ex parte Thompson)* [1969] 2 All ER 846). Orders have been made where public meetings have been held persistently in circumstances likely to cause disorder (*Wise* v *Dunning* [1902] 1 KB 167; *Duncan* v *Jones* [1936] 1 KB 218; *Davies* v *Griffiths* [1937] 2 All ER 671), where an intention to lead an unlawful procession has been evinced (*R* v *Little and Dunning (ex parte Wise)* (1910) 74 JP 7; cf. *Beatty* v *Gillbanks* (1882) 9 QB 308), after the use of abusive words and conduct (*Wilson* v *Skeock* (1949) 113 JP 294; *Ward* v *Holman* [1964] 2 QB 580) and on dismissing an information under the Public Order Act 1936 (*R* v *Woking Justices (ex parte Gossage)* [1973] 1 QB 448). A magistrate was wrong to refuse to bind over defendants charged with causing or attempting to cause criminal damage to the perimeter fence of an RAF base where the defendants indicated that they intended to continue acts of criminal damage until the government revised its policy on the use of nuclear weapons. But the same magistrate was not wrong to refuse to imprison the defendants—against whom no evidence had been offered—for failing to consent to a binding-over order under the Magistrates' Courts Act 1980, s. 115(3), where there would otherwise have been 'a quite glaring inequality of treatment' because other defendants who were convicted of the offence charged were merely fined (*Lanham* v *Bernard; Lanham* v *Toye, The Times*, 23 June 1986).

A binding-over order can only be made on admissible evidence, not on the word of a prosecuting advocate or a police officer who has no personal knowledge of the facts (*Brooks and Breen* v *Nottinghamshire Police* [1984] Crim LR 677), unless the person agrees to be bound over. Otherwise the facts which justify a court making a binding-over order must be strictly proved (*Shaw* v *Hamilton* (1982) 75 Cr App R 288, 290). Binding over a witness (see below) is 'a serious step and should only be taken where facts are proved by evidence before the court which indicates the likelihood that the peace will not be kept' (*R* v *Swindon Crown Court (ex parte Pawittar Singh)* (1984) 79 Cr App R 137; see also *R* v *Kingston Crown Court (ex parte Guarino)* [1986] Crim LR 325).

A binding-over order may only be made on the person consenting and acknowledging his 'indebtedness'. The essence of a binding-over order is that a person acknowledges that he is indebted to the Queen, that by that acknowledgement he becomes bound to pay the sum fixed by the court if he fails to keep the peace, and, therefore, the justices cannot bind over a person unless he acknowledges the debt, and, if he refuses to do so, their only sanction is to commit him to prison (*Veater* v *G* [1981] 1 WLR 567). If the person refuses he may be committed to prison for a period not exceeding six months or until he sooner complies (Magistrates' Courts Act 1980, s. 115(3); *R* v *Trueman* (1913) 77 JP 428). This provision has caused much controversy in recent years, for example, when hunt saboteurs have refused to be bound over to keep the peace and have been sent to prison despite the fact that they have committed no criminal offence.

Offenders aged *over 17 and under 21* may be committed on refusing to be bound over; their refusal constitutes 'a kindred offence' to contempt of court (Contempt of Court Act 1981, s. 12(1)) and is punishable by detention in accordance with the Magistrates' Courts Act 1980, s. 115(3), and the Criminal Justice Act 1982, s. 9(1) (*Howley* v *Oxford* (1985) 81 Cr App R 246, followed in *Chief Constable of the Surrey Constabulary* v *Ridley and Steel* [1985] Crim LR 725). There is power to bind over a juvenile if he consents, but no power to detain him if he refuses (*Conlan* v *Oxford* (1984) 79 Cr App R 157).

The person must be bound over for a *stipulated sum* with or without sureties and for a *stipulated time* (*R* v *Edgar* (1913) 77 JP 356). There is no limit on these provisions although they must be reasonable in all the circumstances. Usually the period will be 12 months. It is a denial of justice, unless the recognisance is trivial, not to inquire into the person's means before setting the level of the recognisance (*R* v *Central Criminal Court (ex parte Boulding)* (1984) 79 Cr App R 100).

There is a right of appeal to the Crown Court against a binding-over order (Magistrates' Courts (Appeals from Binding Over Orders) Act 1956, s. 1), where the appeal is by way of rehearing (*Shaw* v *Hamilton* (1982) 75 Cr App R 288).

A breach of the recognisance must be properly proved (*R* v *Pine* (1934) 24 Cr App R 10; Archbold, para. 5-117) and, probably, beyond reasonable doubt. It used to be thought that these were civil proceedings so that the civil standard of proof applied (see *R* v *Southampton Justices (ex parte Green)* [1975] 2 All ER 1073), but doubt has been cast on this belief by *R* v *Bolton Justices (ex parte Graeme), The Times*, 14 March 1986). If the breach is proved the only power in the court is to forfeit all or part of the recognisance(s).

Apart from the above powers the power of the court to make a binding-over order may arise in the following ways:

(a)   In a criminal case a witness or a defendant (even if acquitted) may be bound over (Justices of the Peace Act 1968, s. 1(7), and see generally Archbold, para. 5-116 et seq.).

(b)   On complaint under the Magistrates' Courts Act 1980, ss. 115 and 116, a magistrates' court may require any person to enter into a recognisance, with or without sureties, to keep the peace or be of good behaviour towards the complainant, and may commit him, if he fails to comply with the order, to custody for a period not exceeding six months or until he sooner complies with the order.

(c)   A defendant may in limited circumstances be bound over to come up for judgment (Powers of Criminal Courts Act 1973, s. 1(1); Supreme Court Act 1981, s. 79(2)(b); and see Archbold, para. 5-114).

(d)   The Court of Appeal may exceptionally quash a conviction and bind over a defendant to keep the peace or be of good behaviour (*R* v *Sharp and Johnson* [1957] 1 QB 552, an affray case).

There have been several unsuccessful attempts to abolish or amend the law on binding-over orders, including the attempt of Sydney Silverman MP in 1962 to repeal the 1361 statute and any similar form of preventive justice.

5.2   POWERS OF ARREST UNDER THE POLICE AND CRIMINAL EVIDENCE ACT 1984

Apart from the common law power of arrest for a breach of the peace, all powers of arrest without warrant are now governed by the Police and Criminal Evidence Act 1984 (except those which are specifically created by statute after the passing of the Police and Criminal Evidence Act 1984 on 31 October 1984, for example under the Public Order Act 1986, see below). The power of arrest without warrant is dealt with in ss. 24 to 26 and sch. 2 of the Police and Criminal Evidence Act 1984, which are set out in full in appendix 3. The following paragraphs summarise these provisions.

5.2.1   Arrest for an arrestable offence

Summary arrest (arrest without warrant) can be made for an arrestable offence, which now means any offence for which the sentence is fixed by law (murder and treason), any offence carrying a maximum penalty of five years' imprisonment or more (for example riot and violent disorder, but not affray and offences contrary to ss. 4 and 5 of the Public Order Act 1986) and certain specified statutory offences including certain lesser offences under the Official Secrets Acts 1911 and 1920, taking a motor vehicle without authority (Theft Act 1968, s. 12), going equipped for burglary etc. (Theft Act 1968, s. 25) and certain offences connected with customs, prostitution and corruption (Police and Criminal Evidence Act 1984, s. 24).

These powers of arrest can be exercised even when it would be practicable or appropriate to proceed by way of summons. Under the Police and Criminal Evidence Act 1984, s. 24, a police officer has wider powers than other persons and may arrest a person who is, or whom he reasonably suspects to be, committing *or about to commit* any of the above arrestable offences, and any person who has, or whom he reasonably suspects of having, committed any such offence.

5.2.2   Arrest for a non-arrestable offence subject to conditions

Where a constable has reasonable grounds for suspecting that any offence which is not an arrestable offence (however trivial, for example dropping litter) has been committed or attempted or is being committed or attempted, he must proceed by way of summons unless it is 'impracticable or inappropriate' to do so, in which case he may arrest the person (Police and Criminal Evidence Act 1984, s. 25).

A summons is 'impracticable or inappropriate' if any one of five 'general arrest conditions' is satisfied (s. 25(3)):

(a)   the name of the person is unknown,
(b)   the name is doubted,
(c)   the address has not been given or is unsatisfactory,
(d)   to prevent injury to the person or loss of or damage to property, to prevent an offence against public decency, or to prevent an unlawful obstruction of the highway, or
(e)   to protect a child or other vulnerable person.

For the precise wording of the arrest conditions, see Appendix 3.

5.2.3   Other statutory powers of arrest

All prior statutory powers of arrest without warrant are repealed by the Police and Criminal Evidence Act 1984, s. 26, except those listed in sch. 2. The provisions preserved by sch. 2 include the Public Order Act 1936, s. 7(3) (which covers the offences contrary to s. 1, which prohibits the wearing of uniforms), the Street Offences Act 1959, s. 1(3) (loitering or soliciting in a street or public place for the purpose of prostitution), the Criminal Law Act 1977, ss. 6(6), 7(11), 8(4), 9(7) and 10(5) (offences relating to entering and remaining on property) and the Prevention of Terrorism (Temporary Provisions) Act 1984, ss. 12 and 13 (various offences connected with terrorism).

5.2.4   Arrest for fingerprinting

The Police and Criminal Evidence Act 1984, s. 61, deals with the taking of fingerprints of persons detained at police stations. Section 27 deals with the taking of fingerprints of those persons who have been convicted of a criminal offence but have not been in police detention for the offence, for example, if they were summonsed by post and have not had their fingerprints taken in the course of the investigation of the offence by the police or since their conviction. Section 27(3) provides a power of arrest for failure to comply with s. 27, for example by failing to attend at a police station to be fingerprinted.

5.3   POWERS OF ARREST UNDER THE PUBLIC ORDER ACT 1986

5.3.1   Arrestable offences

The offences of riot (Public Order Act 1986, s. 1), violent disorder (s. 2), and contaminating or interfering with goods (s. 38) are arrestable offences within the meaning of the Police and Criminal Evidence Act 1984, s. 24 (see 5.2.1) because they each carry a maximum penalty of five or more years' imprisonment.

5.3.2   Non-arrestable offences with specific power of arrest

The Public Order Act 1986 creates specific powers of arrest without warrant for the following offences: affray (s. 3(6)), threatening behaviour etc. (s. 4(3)), disorderly conduct (s. 5(4)), breach of conditions on public processions (s. 12(7)), breach of an order prohibiting processions (s. 13(10)), breach of conditions on public assemblies (s. 14(7)), incitement to racial hatred by words or gestures (s. 18(3)) intimidation including watching and besetting contrary to the Conspiracy and Protection of Property Act 1875, s. 7 (Public Order Act 1986, sch. 2, para. 1), entering premises in breach of a football exclusion order (s. 32(4)) and breach of direction to trespassers to leave land (s. 39(3)).

5.3.3   No power of arrest

The following offences are neither arrestable offences nor are they provided with a specific power of arrest, although a power of arrest is available to a police constable if it appears to him that service of a summons is impracticable or inappropriate because any of the five general arrest conditions is satisfied under the Police and Criminal Evidence Act 1984, s. 25 (see 5.2.2): the offence of organising a public procession in breach of the advance notice requirements (s. 11), stirring up racial hatred by publishing or distributing written material (s. 19), by the public performance of a play (s. 20), by distributing, showing or playing a recording (s. 21), by broadcasting (s. 22) and by possessing racially inflammatory material (s. 23).

5.4   INFORMATION TO BE GIVEN ON ARREST

An arrest is unlawful unless at the time of the arrest or as soon as is practicable after the arrest the arrested person is informed that he is under arrest and of the ground for the arrest (Police and Criminal Evidence Act 1984, s. 28; *Christie* v *Leachinsky* [1947] AC 573; *R* v *Inwood* [1973] 2 All ER 645). There is no need for the reason to be given where it is obvious (*R* v *Hamilton* [1986] Crim LR 187), although the words 'That's enough, you're locked up' are insufficient where there are several possible offences (*R* v *Lowe* [1986] Crim LR 49). Notification must also be given of the reason for a personal search, which constitutes an affront to personal dignity (*Brazil* v *Chief Constable of Surrey* [1983] Crim LR 483).

If the arrest (or search) is unlawful, for any reason, an action for false imprisonment or assault may lie. But note that in *Connolly* v *Metropolitan Police Commissioner* (*The Guardian*, 1 May 1980) a jury awarded only £1 damages for failure to give adequate notification on arrest.

5.5   ARREST WITH WARRANT

An arrest may be effected under the authority of a warrant issued pursuant to some statutory provision, usually the Magistrates' Courts Act 1980, s. 1. A police officer or any other person lays before a justice of the peace an information in writing and substantiated on oath that a person has, or is suspected of having, committed an offence. The application is made *ex parte* and the justice's decision is not reviewable by a higher court unless made in bad faith. A warrant can only be issued for an indictable offence or for an offence punishable with imprisonment or if the address of an accused is too uncertain for service of a summons. It may or may not be backed for bail. See generally *Stone's Justices' Manual*.

5.6   ARREST BY PRIVATE PERSON

Where a private person (who is not a constable) makes a lawful arrest either at common law or under statute he should take the arrested person before a justice of the peace or a police officer, not necessarily forthwith, but as soon as reasonably possible. In *John Lewis & Co. Ltd* v *Tims* [1952] AC 676, the owners of a shop were not liable in damages for false imprisonment where two store detectives had taken a woman suspected of theft back into the shop for the manager to consider the case, decide that he should prosecute and call the police. The result would have been different if there had been no reasonable suspicion of theft or the delay in calling the police had been unreasonable.

5.7   POLICE ROAD-BLOCKS

For the police power to impose road-blocks to prevent freedom of movement see 6.7.

5.8   NO POWER TO 'READ THE RIOT ACT'

The offence of failing to disperse within one hour of a riot after a request by a justice of the peace contrary to the Riot Act 1714 was abolished in 1967 (see 2.2.12). In the White Paper (Cmnd 9510, para. 6.14) the government rejected proposals for a statutory power to disperse an assembly with a related criminal offence of failure to comply with police directions. In doing so they accepted Lord Scarman's view in his report on the Brixton disorders (Cmnd 8427) that the police had adequate powers at common law to disperse an assembly in order to prevent or deal with a breach of the peace.

5.9   POWER TO IMPOSE CONDITIONS ON PROCESSIONS AND ASSEMBLIES AND TO PROHIBIT PROCESSIONS

For a detailed consideration of the new powers to control processions and assemblies under Part II of the Public Order Act 1986, see chapters 8 and 9.

5.10   BAIL CONDITIONS

Some concern has been voiced over the imposition of bail conditions in public order cases in recent years. The police have often requested stringent bail conditions, particularly in picketing cases, preventing persons from going within a certain distance of the object of the picketing. In some courts in Nottinghamshire during the miners' dispute a standard form was in use for the vast majority of cases, with the standard conditions already typed on the bail form. These types of conditions are often widely drawn and can only be challenged in individual cases by application to a judge in chambers (Criminal Justice Act 1967, s. 22 as amended; RSC, Ord. 79, r. 9), for which legal aid is not available. Appeals to the Crown Court, for which legal aid is available, can only be made when bail is refused (Supreme Court Act 1981, s. 81, and Bail Act 1976, s. 5—both amended by the Criminal Justice Act 1982, s. 60).

In *R* v *Mansfield Justices (ex parte Sharkey and others), The Times*, 13 October 1984, the Divisional Court criticised the practice of the clerk to the justices in affixing standard conditions to bail forms even while applications were being made for unconditional bail (and also the practice of putting together in the dock defendants who had been arrested at different places or on different occasions). Nevertheless the court held that the fact that the outcome of the application was correctly anticipated did not vitiate the decision. A condition of bail that a striking miner, charged with an offence under the Public Order Act 1936, s. 5, should 'not visit any premises or place for the purpose of picketing or demonstrating in connection with the current trade dispute between the National Union of Mineworkers and National Coal Board other than peacefully to picket or demonstrate at his usual place of employment' was properly imposed.

Over 200 travellers arrested during the police operation to prevent the 'peace convoy' from reaching Stonehenge were granted bail by Salisbury magistrates on condition that they left the County of Wiltshire by midnight (*The Times*, 23 June 1986). In other cases courts have imposed conditions that defendants could not go within 25 miles of Stonehenge (see NCCL, *Stonehenge*).

5.11   METROPOLITAN POLICE ACT 1839 AND TOWN POLICE CLAUSES ACT 1847

In the metropolitan police district the Commissioner of Police can control the streets of London under powers which are wider than the Public Order Act 1936 powers were before their repeal. It remains to be seen whether they will be replaced in practice by the new Public Order Act 1986 powers to control processions and assemblies (see chapters 8 and 9). The Public Order Act 1986 certainly does not repeal either the Metropolitan Police Act 1839 or the Town Police Clauses Act 1847 (which contains similar powers for all districts outside London).

The Metropolitan Police Act 1839, s. 52, allows the Metropolitan Police Commissioner:

(a) *to make regulations* (i) for the route to be observed by all carts, carriages, horses and persons, and (ii) for preventing obstruction of the streets and thoroughfares in all times of public processions, public rejoicings or illuminations, and

(b) *to give directions* to the constables for keeping order and to constables and traffic wardens for preventing any obstruction of the thoroughfares in the immediate neighbourhood of Her Majesty's palaces and the public offices, the High Court of Parliament, the courts of law and equity, the police courts, the theatres and other places of public resort, and in any case when the streets or thoroughfares may be thronged or may be liable to be obstructed.

The penalty for wilful non-compliance 'after being made acquainted with the regulations or directions' is a fine not to exceed level 2 (Metropolitan Police Act 1839, s. 54 as amended).

Before the passing of the Public Order Act 1986 the use of the Metropolitan Police Act 1839, s. 52, was preferred to the limited powers granted to the Commissioner on reasonable apprehension of serious public disorder under the Public Order Act 1936, s. 3 (see chapter 8). For example, during the dispute between the print unions and Mr Rupert Murdoch's News International, the Metropolitan Police Act 1839, s. 52, was invoked to control the vicinity of the News International plant at Wapping (see letter to the *Guardian*, 11 April 1986, from Deputy Assistant Commissioner Wyn Jones, although earlier reports suggested that the police might have been relying on their breach of the peace powers). The use of these powers at Wapping covered a wide geographical area with serious effects upon the daily life and movement of the residents who were not given notice of the 'regulations' or 'directions' either in detail or in general terms. For an account of the effect of the policing of the Wapping dispute see NCCL, *No Way in Wapping*, in which the conclusion was drawn that the use of either powers under the Metropolitan Police Act 1839, s. 52, or breach of the peace preventive powers was probably unlawful in the particular circumstances.

Regulations or directions under the Metropolitan Police Act 1839, s. 52, may be challenged by way of judicial review (see 8.7) or, on conviction for a breach, by way of case stated to show that they are unreasonable on *Wednesbury* principles (see 8.7) or that they are *ultra vires* s. 52 of the Act (*Papworth* v *Coventry* [1967] 2 All ER 41).

Outside London the local authority can make similar orders and give similar directions under the Town Police Clauses Act 1847, s. 21. An order was made by Salisbury District Council in June 1986 after an application had been made by the Chief Constable of Wiltshire. The order banned 'hippies' from the city centre for two specified days and restricted them to a route along Salisbury's ring road, so as to prevent them from making a nude protest in Salisbury at the ban on their annual pilgrimage to Stonehenge (*The Times* and *The Guardian*, 14 June 1986).

5.12   OBSTRUCTING THE POLICE IN THE EXECUTION OF THEIR DUTY

It is a criminal offence to (resist or) wilfully obstruct a police constable in the execution of his duty (or a person assisting a constable in the execution of his duty), punishable on summary conviction with a maximum penalty of one month's imprisonment and/or a fine not to exceed level 3 (Police Act 1964, s. 51(3)).

This offence is used frequently in public order situations. It is a most powerful weapon in the hands of the police. It is used against those who refuse to move on or to stand back, against those who refuse to obey instructions, for example, at the picket line or on a demonstration, against those who interfere with police work, by trying to prevent or by objecting to an arrest or a search. Often an arrest for this offence is preceded by a warning that continued conduct or a failure to comply will lead to arrest. But the law does not require a police officer to give any warning before making an arrest. The scope of the offence has been much extended by judicial decision and it is therefore difficult to defend successfully.

5.12.1   Ingredients of the offence

5.12.1.1   Wilfully   '"Wilfully" means that the act is done deliberately and intentionally, not by accident or inadvertence, but so that the mind of the person who does the act goes with it' (Lord Russell of Killowen CJ in *R* v *Senior* [1899] 1 QB 283, 290–1; see also *R* v *Walker* (1934) 24 Cr App R 117; *Eaton* v *Cobb* [1950] 1 All ER 1016; *Arrowsmith* v *Jenkins* [1963] 2 QB 561). The obstruction must be deliberate and intentional and something done without lawful excuse (*Rice* v *Connolly* [1966] 2 QB 414). There must be some form of hostility to the police (*Willmott* v *Atack* [1977] QB 498; applied in *Wershof* v *Metropolitan Police Commissioner* [1978] 3 All ER 540 but distinguished in *Green* v *Moore* (1982) 74 Cr App R 250 where it was said that in *Willmott* v *Atack* the police officers were obstructed but the purpose was to assist the police by persuading the man to go quietly, whereas in *Green* v *Moore* Green's intention was to assist the landlord, whose public house was being investigated for after-hours drinking, and not the police). A genuine motive of preventing a perceived unjustified arrest is immaterial (*Hills* v *Ellis* [1983] 1 All ER 667). 'Wilfully' implies an element of *mens rea*, for the act not only has to be done deliberately, but also with the knowledge and intention that it will obstruct (*Lewis* v *Cox* (1985) 80 Cr App R 1, persistent inquiry of the police as to where a friend was being taken).

5.12.1.2   Obstruct   When this offence first appeared in the 19th century the obstruction had to be physical obstruction. The offence of wilful obstruction was part of the special offence of assaulting a constable (see Police Act 1964, s. 51(1)). Today, however, to obstruct is to do any act which makes it more difficult for the police to carry out their duty (*Rice* v *Connolly* [1966] 2 QB 414). But intention by itself to make the task of the police more difficult cannot amount to obstruction; there must be an act making that task more difficult (*Bennett* v *Bale* [1986] Crim LR 404).

There is a moral or social duty to assist the police but not a legal duty; a refusal to give information or to answer questions is not wilful obstruction although providing false or misleading information would be (*Rice* v *Connolly*; *Ricketts* v *Cox* (1982) 74 Cr App R 298). Warning speeding motorists or unlawful drinkers after hours that the police are at hand is obstruction (*Hinchcliffe* v *Sheldon* [1955] 1 WLR 1207; *Betts* v *Stevens* [1910] 1 KB 1; *Green* v *Moore* (1982) 74 Cr App R 250). The consumption of alcohol after a road traffic accident with the purpose of frustrating the breathalyser procedure is obstruction (*Dibble* v *Ingleton* [1972] 1 QB 480). It is an obstruction to disobey a police officer's instruction to reverse the wrong way down a one-way street when life and property are at risk (*Johnson* v *Phillips* (1975) 3 All ER 682). A police constable, having stopped a motor vehicle under the Road Traffic Act 1972, s.159, after suspecting it of being stolen by the driver, was entitled in the execution of his duty to detain and seize the vehicle and to arrest the driver (*Lodwick* v *Sanders* (1985) 80 Cr App R 304). Passengers in vehicles belonging to the 'peace convoy' aid and abet the drivers to obstruct the police where their presence amounts to encouragement, even though no words of encouragement have been given (*Smith* v *Reynolds and Others* [1986] Crim LR 559). See also the picketing cases discussed in 6.8.

5.12.1.3   A constable   Every police officer in England and Wales holds the office of constable (*Lewis* v *Cattle* [1938] 2 KB 454). The constable does not have to be in uniform. Nor is it a defence that the defendant did not know that the person was a constable (*R* v *Maxwell and Clanchy* (1909) 2 Cr App R 26), although a genuine mistake of fact, for example, that he was a thug and not a constable, would be material on the issue of reasonableness of the resistance offered and on the issue of self-defence (*Kenlin* v *Gardiner* [1967] 2 QB 510; *R* v *Mark and Mark* [1961] Crim LR 173).

5.12.1.4   In the execution of his duty   If the police officer is acting outside the execution of his duty he is exceeding his authority, and as a consequence any arrest (see below) is unlawful and any resistance by way of reasonable force is lawful and cannot amount to an assault (see *R* v *Marsden* (1868) LR 1 CCR 131; *Kenlin* v *Gardiner* [1967] 2 QB 510; *R* v *Fennell* [1971] 1 QB 428). Any detention following an unlawful arrest will amount to false imprisonment. A constable will be acting outside the scope of his duty when, for example, he exceeds his powers of arrest either at common law or under the Police and Criminal Evidence Act 1984 (see 5.1.2 and 5.2).

This aspect of the offence has caused the courts some difficulty. Most of the cases concern alleged assaults (it is an offence under the Police Act 1964, s. 51(1), to assault a constable in the execution of his duty) committed as a reaction to police interference with the liberty of the subject (see, for example, *Kenlin* v *Gardiner*; *Donnelly* v *Jackman* [1970] 1 WLR 562; *Daniel* v *Morrison* (1980) 70 Cr App R 142; *Bentley* v *Brudzinski* (1982) 75 Cr App R 217; *Ludlow* v *Burgess* (1982) 75 Cr App R 227; *Collins* v *Wilcock* [1984] 3 All ER 374). A police officer was outside the scope of his duty in attempting to prevent a breach of the peace by trying to restrain a person who was using force to prevent an unlawful search by another police officer (*McBean* v *Parker* [1983] Crim LR 399), but within the scope of his duty in going to the assistance of a police sergeant who was being attacked while lawfully leaving private premises and in endeavouring to prevent a breach of the peace (*Robson* v *Hallett* [1967] 2 QB 939; and see *Kay* v *Hibbert* [1977] Crim LR 226). The courts should be reluctant to conclude from words used and demeanour exhibited by a police officer, which falls short of physical force, that there has been a detention so as to take the officer outside the execution of his duty (*Weight* v *Long* [1986] Crim LR 746). If there is no legal justification for police officers forcibly entering private premises they will not be in the execution of their duty (*R* v *Richards and Leeming* (1985) 81 Cr App R 125, in which the police received a telephone call alleging a domestic fight and wrongly indicated that they would enter the premises, without permission if none was forthcoming, in order to assure themselves that no one had been injured; and see 10.2). The search of a defendant in an unlicensed night café was lawful and therefore the constable was within the execution of his duty where the entry had been lawful under the Greater London Council (General Powers) Act 1968 and the Gaming Act 1845, despite the fact that the sole purpose of the visit was to detect drug offences and no warrant had been issued under the Misuse of Drugs Act 1971, s. 23(3) (*Foster* v *Attard* [1986] Crim LR 627). Failure to explain the reason for a search takes a police officer outside the execution of his duty (*McBean* v *Parker* [1983] Crim LR 399, and see 5.4).

The police were entitled to remove a car to the police station after the driver had given a positive breath test, and were accordingly within the execution of their duty, except where there was somebody who could demonstrate the right and the capacity to look after the car (*Liepins* v *Spearman* [1986] RTR 24; see also *Stunt* v *Boston* [1972] RTR 435 and 6.6). A constable was within the execution of his duty when he guided a girl inmate of a probation hostel by the elbow away from a possible further disturbance (*King* v *Hodges* [1974] Crim LR 424). In *G* v *Chief Superintendent of Police, Stroud, The Times,* 29 November 1986, it was held that the reasonableness of the constable's belief that a breach of the peace was likely to occur could only be reviewed by making allowance for the circumstances in which a constable had to make a spur-of-the-moment decision in an emergency.

5.12.2   Power of arrest

The Police Act 1964, s. 51, provides no power of arrest without warrant. Before the Police and Criminal Evidence Act 1984 an arrest under this section could only be effected where the arresting officer honestly and reasonably believed that the obstruction actually caused or was likely to cause a breach of the peace or was calculated to prevent the lawful arrest or detention of another (*Wershof* v *Metropolitan Police Commissioner* [1978] 3 All ER 540). Now, however, either the common law breach of the peace arrest power or the Police and Criminal Evidence Act, s. 25, arrest power will apply (see 5.1.2 and 5.2).

5.12.3   Obstruction under the Misuse of Drugs Act 1971

It is an offence contrary to the Misuse of Drugs Act 1971, s. 23(4)(a), intentionally to obstruct a constable in the exercise of his powers under s. 23 of the Act to search and obtain evidence. It is an offence if the defendant does any act (such as swallowing or disposing of any item connected with the use of drugs) which obstructs a constable who is lawfully detaining him or wishes to detain him for the purpose of searching him for illicit drugs, provided that (a) the defendant knows that the constable is detaining or wishes to detain him for a search, and (b) the obstruction is intentional, that is, the act viewed objectively through the eyes of a bystander does obstruct the constable's detention or search and viewed subjectively through the eyes of the defendant is intended so to obstruct (*R* v *Forde (James)* (1985) 81 Cr App R 19).

6

Use of the Highway

6.1 DEFINITION OF 'HIGHWAY'

The importance of defining the scope of the term 'highway' lies in the use which may be made of the highway, the restrictions which may be placed upon its use and the offences which relate to its use.

There is no statutory definition of a highway. The Highways Act 1980, s. 328, defines a highway as meaning the whole or part of a highway other than a ferry or waterway. The Highways Act 1835, s. 5, states that a highway shall be understood to mean all roads, bridges (not being county bridges), carriageways, cart-ways, horse-ways, bridle-ways, footways, causeways, church-ways and pavements. The Road Traffic Act 1972, s. 196(1), defines a road as any highway and any other road to which the public have access; this does not exclude footpaths and bridle-ways (*Lang* v *Hindhaugh, The Times*, 25 March 1986).

At common law a highway is a way over which there exists a public right of passage, that is to say, a right for all of Her Majesty's subjects at all seasons of the year freely and at their will to pass and repass without let or hindrance (*Ex parte Lewis* (1888) 21 QBD 191, 197; and see *Halsbury's Laws of England*, 4th ed., vol. 21, para. 1 et seq.). The right to close off a piece of land may prevent it from becoming a highway in this sense (see (1976) 126 NLJ 50, the subways of Piccadilly Circus underground station are not part of the highway). In *R* v *Dubbins, The Times*, 22 and 29 May 1986, an attempt to persuade a stipendiary magistrate that The Highway, a road in Wapping, was not a highway as a result of police restrictions imposed under the Metropolitan Police Act 1839, s. 52, during the printers' dispute was unsuccessful, the magistrate finding that the road had not ceased to be a highway with any degree of finality, as, for example, under a court order. The defendant, who was alleged to have sat down in the road outside the Wapping plant, was later acquitted on other grounds, the magistrate indicating that he was not satisfied that in the confusion a warning to move had been given or that any warning would have been heard (*The Guardian*, 29 June 1986).

6.2 RIGHT OF PASSAGE

The law relating to the use of the highway plays a prominent part in public order law. There is no specific common law or statutory right of assembly, although the courts often acknowledge the existence of general rights of assembly and free speech (see 8.2). The Public Order Act 1986 makes no provision for positive rights (the only reference to rights appears in the restrictions on processions and assemblies in ss. 12 and 14). From time to time judges refer to general concepts, for example: 'The right to demonstrate and protest are, like the right of free speech, rights which it is in the public interest that individuals should possess and exercise without impediment, so long as no wrongful act is done' (Lord Denning MR in *Hubbard* v *Pitt* [1976] QB 142, 178). But these concepts or principles are not specifically recognised by the law, either in statute law or in the development of the common law by judicial decision.

The only right which is clearly recognised is *the right to pass and repass along the highway*, the right to make ordinary and reasonable use of the highway as a highway (*Harrison* v *Duke of Rutland* [1893] 1 QB 142; *Hickman* v *Maisey* [1900] 1 QB 752). This is a public right (*Boyce* v *Paddington Borough Council* [1903] 1 Ch 109, 114). In *Iveagh* v *Martin* [1961] 1 QB 232, 273, Paull J said:

> On a highway I may stand still for a reasonably short time, but I must not put my bed upon the highway and permanently occupy a portion of it. I may stoop to tie up my shoelace, but I may not occupy a pitch and invite people to come upon it and have their hair cut. I may let my van stand still long enough to deliver and load goods, but I must not turn my van into a permanent stall.

Any *obstruction of the highway* is a criminal offence (see below). It is therefore arguable that meetings or processions on the highway are prima facie unlawful (see Goodhart (1937) 6 CLJ 161; cf. *Brownlie's Law of Public Order and National Security*, 2nd ed., pp. 42 et seq.); and that they are at the very least a temporary obstruction of the highway and that their existence, in these days of busy streets and pavements (part of the highway), may only be legitimised by the exercise of police discretion to refrain from prosecution.

But there are also powerful arguments in favour of a more flexible approach to the use of the highway. It can be said that Part II of the Public Order Act 1986 recognises the existence of processions and assemblies—and therefore their right to use the highway and if necessary to obstruct the highway—because it expressly or by necessary implication permits them where the specified conditions, such as advance notice of processions (see 8.4 below), are fulfilled. In *R* v *Clark (No. 2)* [1964] 2 QB 315 Lord Parker CJ, referring (at p. 320) to the judgment of Lord O'Brien CJ in the Irish case of *Loudens* v *Keaveney* [1903] 2 IR 82 said:

> He pointed out that many processions are perfectly lawful, and that no public nuisance is created by obstruction thereby unless the user of the highway in all the circumstances is unreasonable. He pointed out that there may be considerable, even complete, obstruction and yet the use of the street may be quite reasonable.

Lord Scarman too has argued (*The Red Lion Square Disorders*, Cmnd 5919, para. 122) that a procession which allows room for others to go on their way is lawful, although he believed it was open to question whether a public meeting (or assembly) held on the highway could ever be lawful, for it would not in any way be incidental to the exercise of the right of passage.

These uncertainties could be cured by the creation of a positive right of assembly including a right to picket peacefully (see 8.2 and Thornton, *We Protest*). In the absence of such a right it must be assumed that custom and practice will tolerate an extensive use of the highway for the use of public protest.

6.3   RESTRICTIONS ON THE RIGHT TO USE THE HIGHWAY

6.3.1   Public Order Act 1986

Part II of the Public Order Act 1986 provides police controls over public processions and assemblies (for full details see chapters 8 and 9).

6.3.2   Criminal offences

It is an offence if a person, without lawful authority or excuse, in any way wilfully obstructs the free passage of the highway (Highways Act 1980, s. 137; see 6.5). Many other offences connected with violence and disorder can be committed in public places (see chapters 2 and 3).

6.3.3   Road Traffic Act 1972

The police have certain powers to stop motorists and pedestrians on the highway (see 6.7.2).

6.3.4   Road Traffic Regulation Act 1984

The highway authority can close or restrict a road for roadworks or by reason of the likelihood of danger to the public or of serious damage to the highway (s. 14, and see 7.4.3).

6.3.5   Local Acts

In London the Metropolitan Police Act 1839 permits the police to make regulations or to give directions for preventing obstruction of the streets (see 5.11). Outside London the Town Police Clauses Act 1847 gives district councils similar powers. Other local Acts of Parliament give local authorities wide powers to make by-laws to cover public meetings in their area, often laying down special conditions for the use of parks and other public places (see 6.4).

6.3.6   Access to Parliament

Parliament can regulate access to the Houses of Parliament by sessional orders (see Erskine May, *Parliamentary Practice*, 20th ed., pp. 223–4) and in practice the Metropolitan Police Commissioner gives directions during the sitting of Parliament under the Metropolitan Police Act 1839, s. 52, in furtherance of sessional orders to constables 'to disperse all assemblies or processions of persons likely to cause obstruction or disorder' within a specified area (see *Papworth* v *Coventry* [1967] 2 All ER 41; *Pankhurst* v *Jarvis* (1910) 101 LT 946; *Despard* v *Wilcox* (1910) 102 LT 103).

6.3.7   Restrictions on picketing
See 6.8.

6.3.8   Street collections, leafleting etc.
See 6.11.

6.3.9   Nuisance
See 6.12.

6.4   BY-LAWS

Many activities on the highway and in other public places such as parks and gardens are restricted by local by-laws. A copy of the by-laws should be on sale at the local town hall and also available for inspection.

By-laws are the laws and regulations of local authorities. They are authorised by various enabling statutes and must be confirmed by the relevant Secretary of State. The Local Government Act 1972, s. 235, for example, enables district councils and London boroughs to make by-laws for good rule and government and for the suppression of nuisances. This general power covers topics such as music near houses, churches and hospitals; noisy hawking; indecent language; violent behaviour on school premises; fighting; indecent bathing; indecent shows; nuisances contrary to public decency; wilful jostling; flags; defacing pavements; advertising bills and advertising vehicles; dangerous games; spitting; noisy animals; and many other topics.

A number of statutes authorise the making of by-laws on a number of specific topics, for example, charitable collections (see 6.11), priority and queues in relation to persons waiting to enter public vehicles (Highways Act 1980, s. 35(6)), preservation of order and prevention of damage in national parks and country parks (National Parks and Access to the Countryside Act 1949, s. 90, and Countryside Act 1968, s. 41), prevention of nuisance and preservation of order on commons (Commons Act 1899, ss. 1 and 10), access to and preservation and protection of ancient monuments (Ancient Monuments and Archaeological Areas Act 1979, s. 19) and regulation of pleasure fairs and roller-skating rinks (Public Health Act 1961, s. 75).

By-laws cover, therefore, nearly every activity in public places. The wording of each by-law may differ from one locality to another, but many by-laws are repeated in different parts of the country. Many by-laws prohibit indecent language or behaviour, or behaving in a disorderly or offensive manner with intent to provoke a breach of the peace or whereby a breach of the peace may be occasioned. Others punish riotous, violent or indecent behaviour.

Typical by-laws governing the use of pleasure grounds, gardens and open spaces vested in or maintained by a local authority will, among other things:

(a)   prohibit holding or taking part in public discussion or any public meeting, and giving or reading any public speech, lecture, sermon or address;

(b)   prohibit bill-posting or the erection of placards or notices;

(c)   prohibit wilful obstruction or annoyance of any other person or officer of the council;

(d)   prohibit the erection of a stall or booth or other structure;

(e)   prohibit the playing of a radio, loudspeaker or musical instrument so as to cause a nuisance or annoyance;

(f)   prohibit the sale or distribution of books, pamphlets, leaflets or advertisements; and

(g)   provide for a person's removal by an officer of the council or a constable for infringement of any by-law.

6.4.1   Criminal proceedings

The penalty for infringing a by-law is a fine at the level set out in the by-law or, where not expressed, a fine not exceeding level 2 (Local Government Act 1972, s. 237).

Any person may institute criminal proceedings for breach of a by-law unless the statute under which the by-law is made restricts the right to prosecute (*R v Stewart* [1896] 1 QB 300).

When a charge is brought the defendant may challenge the validity of the by-law (even though confirmed by the Secretary of State) on the grounds that it is *ultra vires* the enabling statute or obviously unreasonable or inconsistent with or repugnant to the general law. The magistrates are bound to decide on any objection to the validity of a by-law and an appeal against their decision lies to the Divisional Court by way of case stated.

Ministry of Defence by-laws aimed at preventing trespass on the United States Air Force base at Mildenhall, Suffolk, (and also prohibiting leafleting, displaying posters and banners, and interfering with fences) were held by local magistrates to be unlawful. John Bugg, a former policeman who had been charged under a by-law with entering the base though not an authorised person after he had gone into the base through a hole cut by members of the Campaign for Nuclear Disarmament, had argued that the by-laws dealt with matters that were already covered by provisions in existing statutes and that they were not in keeping with the intention of the original by-laws which was to protect people from straying on to land when guns were being fired (*The Guardian*, 23 July 1986). On appeal the High Court overruled the decision of the magistrates. The correct approach was for by-laws to be presumed valid until a descendant showed that they were not, rather than the prosecution having to prove beyond reasonable doubt as the magistrates held, that the by-laws were valid (*The Times*, 20 December 1986). Meanwhile a number of further prosecutions have been discontinued.

6.4.2   Civil proceedings

Under the civil law a breach of a by-law may also in some cases be sufficient to sustain an action in damages (see *Newman* v *Francis* (1953) 51 LGR 168), and the threatened breach of a by-law may be restrained by an injunction (*Burnley Borough Council* v *England* (1977) 76 LGR 393). See generally *Encyclopedia of Local Government Law*, vol. 1, ch. 6.

6.4.3   Licensing

Other local controls are imposed by systems of licensing by the local authority, for example, street and house-to-house collections (see 6.11), street trading (Local Government (Miscellaneous Provisions) Act 1982, s. 3 and sch. 4), sale of food by hawkers (Food Act 1984, s. 66), public entertainments (Local

Government (Miscellaneous Provisions) Act 1982, s. 1) and caravan sites (Caravan Sites and Control of Development Act 1960 and Caravan Sites Act 1968). Pedlars' licences (Pedlars Act 1871, s. 5) are issued by the police.

6.5 OBSTRUCTION OF THE HIGHWAY

It is an offence if a person, without lawful authority or excuse, in any way wilfully obstructs the free passage of the highway (Highways Act 1980, s. 137). The offence is punishable on summary conviction with a maximum fine not to exceed level 3 (Highways Act 1980, s. 310). For fine scales see 1.8.

The specific power of arrest set out in the Highways Act 1980, s. 137(2), is repealed by the Police and Criminal Evidence Act 1984, s. 26, so that the power of arrest is now governed by the Police and Criminal Evidence Act 1984, s. 25 (arrest for non-arrestable offences subject to general arrest conditions, see 5.2). This means that a constable can arrest without warrant where it appears to him that service of a summons is impracticable or inappropriate because he has 'reasonable grounds for believing that arrest is necessary to prevent the relevant person . . . (v) causing an unlawful obstruction of the highway' (Police and Criminal Evidence Act 1984, s. 25(3)(d)).

This offence is a serious restriction on any form of public protest. It is one of the most commonly used charges in public order law and the breadth of the offence is often seen as a *de facto* licensing power over public gatherings (see De Smith, *Constitutional and Administrative Law*, 5th ed., p. 509). The police use it to remove sit-down demonstrators, to prevent demonstrators outside South Africa House from straying outside the barrier positions agreed with the police, to keep marchers from leaving the agreed police route, to control pickets, and in every conceivable public order context on the highway.

There is no requirement of violence or threat of violence, and when cases reach court prosecutors commonly agree to offer no evidence if the defendant agrees to be bound over (see 5.1), a concession not usually made in more serious cases. Often the police will give a warning to move before making an arrest, although there is no legal requirement to do so and the failure to give a warning will not invalidate the arrest and the charge. Nevertheless a failure to give a warning may be relevant to the reasonableness or otherwise of the use of the highway (*R v Dubbins*, see 6.1). In addition the police will sometimes use the charge of obstructing a police officer (see 5.12) where a person is obstructing the highway—whether by sitting down, speaking, listening, leafleting or collecting—and refuses to move on after a police request to do so. This has been a widespread practice in the environs of Stonehenge where members of the 'peace convoy' have refused to comply with police instructions to move (see *Smith v Reynolds and others* [1986] Crim LR 559).

6.5.1 Elements of the offence

6.5.1.1 Without lawful authority or excuse These words rarely provide a defence for an accused. A police officer would have lawful authority to create road blocks or barriers in certain limited circumstances (see 6.7) or to control traffic, particularly where life or property were at risk (*Johnson v Phillips* [1975] 3 All ER 682, and see 5.12). Any other citizen may have difficulty in establishing a defence under these words once an obstruction has been proved (*Nagy* v *Weston* [1966] 2 QB 561). Peaceful picketing does not provide a defence of lawful authority or excuse (*Broome* v *DPP* [1974] AC 587).

6.5.1.2 Wilfully 'Wilfully' means intentionally as opposed to accidentally, that is, by an exercise of his or her free will (*Arrowsmith* v *Jenkins* [1963] 2 QB 561, in which a conviction was upheld despite the fact that the area was frequently used for meetings, the police had advance notice and the defendant believed her meeting was lawful). There is no wilful obstruction where there is neither intention, nor recklessness, nor even ordinary negligence (*Eaton* v *Cobb* [1950] 1 All ER 1016, the driver of a stationary motor car had not wilfully obstructed the free passage of the highway by accidentally striking a passing cyclist). It is no defence that the local authority has acquiesced in the obstruction for a long time before deciding to prosecute (*Redbridge London Borough Council* v *Jacques* [1970] 1 WLR 1604; *Cambridgeshire & Isle of Ely County Council* v *Rust* [1972] 3 All ER 232, 237), but reasonable excuse may sometimes apply to a temporary obstruction, if not a permanent one (*Dixon* v *Attfield* [1975] 1 WLR 1171).

For the meaning of 'wilfully' in the offence of obstructing a police officer, see 5.12.

6.5.1.3 Obstructs Whether a particular use of the highway amounts to an obstruction is whether the use is *unreasonable* having regard to all the circumstances including its duration, position and purpose, and whether it causes an actual, as opposed to a potential, obstruction (*Nagy* v *Weston* [1966] 2 QB 561 cited by Lord Denning MR in *Hubbard* v *Pitt* [1976] QB 142, 174).

A procession is a reasonable and therefore lawful use of the highway unless it amounts to a public nuisance (*R* v *Clark (No. 2)* [1964] 2 QB 315, see 6.2).

In *Cooper* v *Metropolitan Police Commissioner* (1986) 82 Cr App R 238 a club tout was convicted of the offence. He had been seen on four separate occasions during a 13-minute period to approach small groups of pedestrians on a footway four feet wide and engage them in conversation 'for a minute or so', to persuade them to enter the club. On each occasion the free passage of the footway was blocked to other pedestrians using it with the result that some members of the public passing along had to step out on to the roadway in order to pass by. The court held that on a charge of obstruction of the highway magistrates, as a matter of common sense, must decide, first whether there was an obstruction at all. In doing so they should consider whether or not the user amounting to an obstruction is or is not a reasonable use of the highway, which is a question of fact, depending on all the circumstances, including the length of time the obstruction continues, the place where it occurs, the purpose for which it is done and whether it does in fact cause an actual obstruction as opposed to a potential obstruction. Secondly, if they are of the view that there was a prima facie obstruction, they should go on to consider whether the defendant was, in fact, exercising no more than his ordinary right of passing or repassing.

In *Waite* v *Taylor* (1985) 149 JP 551 a busker was convicted of the offence for juggling with lit fire sticks in Union Street, Bath (presumably this would not have been an offence in Covent Garden). May LJ found that the underlying principle of the law of obstruction was as follows:

In so far as a highway is concerned members of the public have the right to pass and repass along it. That does not, however, mean that one must keep moving all the time. However, if one does stop on a highway then prima facie an obstruction occurs, because by stopping you are on a piece of the very highway that somebody else may wish to pass and repass along. Where, however, your stopping is really part and parcel of passing and repassing along the highway and is ancillary to it (such as a milkman stopping to leave a milk bottle on a doorstep) then this is not an obstruction within the meaning of the subsection with which we are concerned.

On the other hand, where stopping on the highway cannot properly be said to be ancillary to or part and parcel of the exercise of one's right to pass and repass along that highway, then the obstruction becomes unreasonable and there is an obstruction contrary to the provisions of the subsection.

The obstruction must, therefore, at least be an actual obstruction, although restricting access to any part of the highway may be an obstruction in the absence of any person being inconvenienced (*Wolverton Urban District Council* v *Willis* [1962] 1 All ER 243). This element is usually proved by the evidence of the arresting officer.

But in *Hirst and Another* v *Chief Constable of West Yorkshire, The Times*, 19 November 1986, it was held that *Waite* v *Taylor* applied too rigid a test. Members of a group of animal rights supporters had exhibited banners bearing slogans and had offered leaflets to passers-by in a spacious pedestrian precinct outside a shop which sold furs. The Divisional Court, in quashing the conviction, followed the approach in *Cooper* v *Metropolitan Police Commissioner* and emphasised the test of reasonableness laid down in *Nagy* v *Weston*. Glidewell LJ said that the correct approach was first to consider whether there was an actual obstruction. Unless it was *de minimis* any stopping on the highway would be prima facie an obstruction. The second question was whether the obstruction was wilful or deliberate. Finally, had the prosecution proved that the obstruction was without lawful authority or excuse? Lawful authority included permits and licences for market and street traders and collectors for charity. Lawful excuse embraced activities lawful in themselves which were reasonable.

It will be a good defence if there was no obstruction in fact or the obstruction was trivial, for example, because it was so short in duration. In *Hubbard* v *Pitt* [1976] QB 142 Lord Denning MR considered (at pp. 174–5) that the presence of half a dozen people on Saturday morning for three hours on the pavement outside an estate agent's premises without interfering with the free passage of people to and fro was not an obstruction. A partial obstruction of the highway created by addressing a crowd is an offence even though there is enough room for persons and vehicles to pass (*Homer* v *Cadman* (1886) 55 LJ MC 110). A queue outside a shop is an obstruction if the shopkeeper is carrying out his business in an unusual way (*Fabbri* v *Morris* [1947] 1 All ER 315), but not otherwise (*Dwyer* v *Mansfield* [1946] 2 All ER 247). Selling hot dogs from a van in a busy street (*Pitcher* v *Lockett* [1966] Crim LR 283) or selling refreshments from a mobile snack-bar on the highway (*Waltham Forest London Borough Council* v *Mills* [1980] Crim LR 243) is an obstruction. Exclusive use of the highway for seven hours by a parked truck for the purpose of vacuum-cleaning a house was not an obstruction in fact (*Dunn* v *Holt* (1904) 73 LJ KB 341).

It is an offence to incite others to cause a public nuisance by obstructing the highway (*R* v *Moule* [1964] Crim LR 303 and *R* v *Adler* [1964] Crim LR 304, both cases of leaders instructing the crowd to sit down in the road; and see 6.12.2).

It is also an offence contrary to the Town Police Clauses Act 1847, s. 28, punishable on summary conviction with a maximum penalty of 14 days' imprisonment or a fine not exceeding level 3, for any person to commit any one of a multitude of activities in a street to the obstruction, annoyance or danger of the residents or passengers. By-laws also provide similar offences of obstruction in public places.

6.6   REMOVAL OF VEHICLES FROM THE HIGHWAY

There are statutory and common law powers for the removal of motor vehicles from the highway.

Vehicles can be removed:

(a)   If abandoned, by the local authority. On conviction for the unauthorised dumping of vehicles the maximum penalty on summary conviction is three months' imprisonment and/or a fine not exceeding level 4 (Refuse Disposal (Amenity) Act 1978, ss. 2–4).

(b)   If illegally, obstructively or dangerously parked, or abandoned or broken down, by the police (Road Traffic Regulation Act 1984, ss. 99–104).

(c)   If causing an obstruction on the highway or likely to cause injury (*Stunt* v *Boston* [1972] RTR 435), or where the driver has given a positive breath test and there is nobody who can demonstrate the right and the capacity to look after the car (*Liepins* v *Spearman* [1986] RTR 24), at common law.

The confiscation by the police of vehicles belonging to members of the 'peace convoy' may not easily come within any of these categories (see 7.4).

6.7   POLICE ROAD-BLOCKS

There is no general power vested in the police, either at common law or by statute, to create road-blocks. Specific powers are considered in the following paragraphs.

6.7.1   Under the Police and Criminal Evidence Act 1984

The Police and Criminal Evidence Act 1984, s. 4, permits the police, on written authorisation by an officer not below the rank of superintendent, to conduct 'road checks' to see if vehicles are carrying (a) persons who have committed or are intending to commit or have witnessed a 'serious arrestable offence' (Police and Criminal Evidence Act 1984, s. 116) or (b) escaped prisoners. Road checks are limited to a particular 'locality' for up to seven days (although renewable) and must be based on reasonable suspicion that the person is in the locality.

The Police and Criminal Evidence Act 1984, s. 1, also provides that a constable, whether in uniform or not, may stop and search any person or vehicle, and may detain the person or vehicle for the search, on reasonable suspicion that he will find stolen or prohibited articles (including offensive weapons, see 3.1).

6.7.2   Under the Road Traffic Act 1972

A police constable in uniform may stop a motorist (or a pedestrian) on a road (Road Traffic Act 1972, s. 159) and request drivers to supply their name and address as well as the name and address of the owner of the vehicle, but not to require them to change their route. The purpose of these powers is to enable the officer to check the status of the vehicle, and if necessary its roadworthiness, and to delay pedestrians for the purposes of traffic control. Failure to comply with these requirements is a criminal offence. The constable is entitled to detain the vehicle for a reasonable time so as to enable him, if he suspects the vehicle to be stolen, to effect an arrest and explain to the driver the reason for the arrest (*Lodwick* v *Sanders* (1985) 80 Cr App R 304).

6.7.3   At common law

A constable has the right at common law to control traffic on public roads (see *Gelberg* v *Miller* [1961] 1 All ER 291; *Daniel* v *Morrison* (1980) 70 Cr App R 142), and to cause others to disobey traffic regulations but only when life and property are at risk (*Johnson* v *Phillips* [1975] 3 All ER 682).

A police constable has the power to stop and turn back motor vehicles if he has reasonable grounds for apprehending that a breach of the peace is imminent (*Moss* v *McLachlan, The Times*, 29 November 1984). For a full discussion of breach of the peace see 5.1. In *Moss* v *McLachlan*, a case generally considered to turn on its particular facts, striking miners were turned back some two miles from one colliery, where there had earlier been disorder, and some five miles from another. The Divisional Court emphasised that the possibility of a breach of the peace must be real, imminent and immediate, in the sense that it was in close proximity both in place and time, to justify any preventive action. Accordingly the police were on the facts within the execution of their duty and convictions for obstructing the police by refusing to turn back were upheld.

This action, sometimes known as the 'intercept policy', was widely used by the police in Nottinghamshire and elsewhere during the miners' dispute. Those who disobeyed or queried the instructions were arrested for obstructing the police (see 5.12). It is a policy which is considered by some to be stretching police powers at common law to the limit, if not beyond. In *Foy* v *Chief Constable of Kent* (20 March 1984, unreported), a more extreme example, the same policy was applied to stop Kent miners at the Dartford Tunnel some 200 miles from their destination. An application for an interim injunction to restrain the Chief Constable of Kent from acting unlawfully in obstructing the miners from using the highway and in falsely imprisoning them in the county of Kent was refused (see *The Guardian*, 21 March 1984) and the action was not pursued.

Similar action was taken by West Country police forces in the summer of 1986 to stop and redirect the 'peace convoy'. Road-blocks were also used to support High Court injunctions obtained by landowners to prevent the holding of a pop concert at Stonehenge and the congregation of persons for that purpose (see *R* v *Salisbury Magistrates' Court (ex parte Mastin)* [1986] Crim LR 545 and 3.3) although there is arguably no legal justification for such action. The police have often been uncertain which, if any, powers they were using. The threat of a breach of the peace was in many instances absent.

The element of imminence, confirmed in *R* v *Howell* [1982] QB 416 (see 5.1) appears to have replaced the notion that an apprehended breach of the peace must be expected to take place in the presence of the apprehending constable. And now even the concept of imminence is interpreted widely. During the miners' strike Sir Michael Havers, the Attorney-General, supported police interference with miners' freedom of movement, but his assessment of the law omitted the requirement of imminence:

> If a constable reasonably comes to the conclusion that persons are travelling for the purpose of taking part in a picket in circumstances where there is likely to be a breach of the peace, he has the power at common law to call upon them not to continue their journey and to call upon their driver to take them no further. (HC Deb. vol.56, Written Answers, col.279.)

If the driver refuses to comply he commits the offence of obstructing the police (see 5.12) and may be arrested without warrant. The arrested driver would then have to try to argue in court that the element of imminence was lacking and that the constable was therefore acting outside the execution of his duty—a difficult task in view of the decision in *Moss* v *McLachlan*.

6.7.4   Under the Metropolitan Police Act 1839, s. 52

In the metropolitan police district the Commissioner of Police has power to make regulations and to give directions for keeping order and preventing obstruction of the highway (see 5.11). District councils have similar powers outside London under the Town Police Clauses Act 1847. The validity of these powers for the creation of road-blocks is uncertain and untested in the courts. It has been suggested that the police action under s. 52 in relation to the print dispute in Wapping was probably unlawful as being unreasonable and unnecessary and exercised unjustly and unfairly over residents and visitors (NCCL, *No Way in Wapping*).

6.8   PICKETING

6.8.1   Industrial picketing

There is no special law of picketing, nor is there a comprehensive right to picket enshrined in statute or carefully developed by the courts at common law. Nor is picketing defined in the law. In *News Group Newspapers Ltd* v *Society of Graphical & Allied Trades 1982, The Times*, 1 August 1986, Stuart-Smith J adopted (at pp. 44–5 of the transcript) the argument that a definition of 'picket' extracted from the Trade Union and Labour Relations Act 1974, s. 15(1)(see below), would have as its essentials a person who, in contemplation or furtherance of a trade dispute attends at or near a place of work for the purpose of obtaining or communicating information or persuading any person to work or abstain from working. His lordship also, however, adopted the *Oxford English Dictionary* (1906) definition of 'men acting in a body or singly who are stationed by a trades-union or the like to watch men going to work during a strike or at a non-union workshop, and to endeavour to dissuade or deter them'.

But, despite the unpopularity of pickets with the law, occasional judicial pronouncements have recognised the practice of picketing, notably Lord Denning MR in *Hubbard* v *Pitt* [1976] QB 142, 177:

> Picketing is lawful so long as it is done merely to obtain or communicate information, or peacefully to persuade; and is not such as to submit any other person to any kind of constraint or restriction of his personal freedom: see *Hunt* v *Broome* [1974] AC 587, 597 by Lord Reid.

Pickets have the right to use the highway like anybody else, but their use of the highway for picketing (or the use of the highway by those who demonstrate in support of a picket) is strictly limited to that which is reasonable in the circumstances. It is the police on the spot who will decide in the first instance what is reasonable; if charges are brought then the magistrates will decide.

If pickets resist police instructions, for example, not to picket in a particular place or to move to a different gate of the factory or to stop talking to a lorry driver seeking to enter the premises, they can be arrested for *obstruction of the highway* (see 6.5) or, more commonly, for *obstructing a police officer* in the execution of his duty (see 5.12 and note in particular the limitations on the power of arrest). If the action of the pickets is reasonable and the police arrest is unreasonable the magistrates' court will acquit the picket. But more often, particularly in serious disputes during which local magistrates' courts are swamped with public order cases, the picket's conduct will be found to be unlawful and pending his trial his activities may be seriously curtailed by the imposition of heavy bail conditions (see 5.10).

Pickets also have a limited immunity under the law. Immunity from civil (but not criminal) proceedings is provided for a person who, in contemplation or furtherance of a trade dispute, attends at or near his own place of work for the purpose only of 'peacefully obtaining or communicating information, or peacefully persuading any person to work or abstain from working' (Trade Union and Labour Relations Act 1974, s. 15 as amended by the Employment Acts 1980 and 1982).

Legal restrictions on pickets are as follows:

(a) Peaceful picketing should be *at or near the picket's workplace*; if not there is no immunity from civil proceedings (Trade Union and Labour Relations Act 1974, s. 15) although secondary picketing is not in itself a crime. An exception is created for a trade union official who attends to picket at the place of work of a member of his union whom he is accompanying and whom he represents (Trade Union and Labour Relations Act 1974, s. 15(1)(b)).

(b) Section E of the Code of Practice (Employment Code of Practice (Picketing) Order 1980, SI 1980 No.1757) is headed 'Limiting numbers of pickets'. It suggests that pickets and their organisers should ensure that in general the *number of pickets* does not exceed six at any entrance to a workplace (para.31). The Code does not make it a criminal offence or tortious to have more than six persons on a picket line, but by the Employment Act 1980, s. 3(8), a court may consider the provisions of the Code where relevant in any proceedings (as Scott J did in *Thomas* v *National Union of Mineworkers (South Wales Area)* [1985] 2 WLR 1081, by granting an injunction against the South Wales Area of the union, restraining them from organising picketing or demonstrations at colliery gates by more than six persons; see also *News Group Newspapers Ltd* v *Society of Graphical & Allied Trades 1982, The Times*, 1 August 1986).

(c)   The attendance of some 50 to 70 striking miners on a daily basis at colliery gates shouting abuse at vehicles carrying working miners may amount to *unreasonable interference* with the working miners' right to use the highway without unreasonable harassment and therefore be actionable in tort (*Thomas* v *National Union of Mineworkers (South Wales Area)*). However, doubt was cast on the existence of this newly created tort in *News Group Newspapers Ltd* v *Society of Graphical & Allied Trades 1982, The Times*, 1 August 1986 (transcript, p.32).

(d)   *Breach of the peace powers* (see 5.1) are often invoked by the police to curb the numbers of pickets (see *Piddington* v *Bates* [1961] 1 WLR 162, in which the decision of police officers to restrict pickets to two in number on the back gate of a factory was upheld) or to require would-be pickets to desist (*Kavanagh* v *Hiscock* [1974] QB 600, a picket who broke through a police cordon to speak to a coach driver and his passengers).

(e)   Forty pickets on the move circling around the main entrance of a factory is an unreasonable use of the highway and therefore an obstruction of the highway (*Tynan* v *Balmer* [1967] 1 QB 91).

(f)   A picket is entitled to invite a driver to stop and listen to him provided this is done in a reasonable way, but he cannot compel him because there is no statutory duty on the driver to stop or remain for longer than he chooses to stay (*Broome* v *DPP* [1974] AC 587). If a picket does seek to compel a driver, the picket will be guilty of the offence of obstructing the highway (see 6.5).

(g)   The Public Order Act 1986, s. 14, empowers the police to impose conditions on public assemblies (meaning an assembly of 20 or more in a public place which is wholly or partly open to the air: Public Order Act 1986, s. 16). Despite the White Paper's pronouncement (para. 5.14) that the right of peaceful picketing will not in any way be infringed, these new powers are intended to apply to picketing (see chapter 9) and where applicable will enable the police to restrict a picket by location, duration and numbers (although, presumably, if the numbers fall below 20 the picket is no longer an assembly).

6.8.2   Consumer picketing

Although consumer picketing is widespread in the United States and developing in this country and although the Royal Commission on Trade Unions and Employers' Associations (Cmnd 3623) recommended that statutory protection be extended to this area of peaceful assembly, the law provides no special protection to consumer picketing. The immunity of the Trade Union and Labour Relations Act 1974, s. 15, is restricted to trade disputes and does not therefore apply to disputes between seller and buyer, between producer and consumer.

Consumer picketing is therefore lawful only in so far as it does not infringe any other law, such as the law of libel and slander and notably, once again, the law of the highway. There have been few cases in this area to provide guidance, but in *Hubbard* v *Pitt* [1976] QB 142 an injunction was granted against a group of persons who regularly picketed outside a local estate agent's office complaining publicly and with the use of placards about the estate agent's policy on tenanted property (for the full terms of the injunction see 7.2.2.3). Nevertheless, although the injunction restraining the defendants from picketing was upheld, the trial judge's ruling that the right to picketing was limited to trade disputes was not allowed to stand. Lord Denning MR, in particular, relied on the principle of lawful picketing. He concluded that the pickets were not unlawful: they behaved in an orderly and peaceful manner throughout; they were arranged with the full knowledge and agreement of the police; the presence of half a dozen people on Saturday morning for three hours was not an unreasonable use of the highway and did not interfere with the free passage of people to and fro; there was nothing in the nature of a public nuisance, no crowds collected, no queues were formed, no obstruction caused, no breaches of the peace; nor was it a nuisance for a group of people to attend at or near the plaintiffs' premises in order to obtain or to communicate information or in order peacefully to persuade, unless associated with obstruction, violence, intimidation, molestation or threats.

See also *Hirst* v *Chief Constable of West Yorkshire, The Times*, 19 November 1986, in which convictions for obstructing the highway were quashed because the court below had failed to consider the reasonableness of the pickets' use of the highway (see 6.5.1.3).

6.9   STREET OFFENCES

6.9.1   Prostitution

It is an offence:

(a)   for a common prostitute,
(b)   to loiter or solicit,
(c)   in a street or public place,
(d)   for the purpose of prostitution (Street Offences Act 1959, s. 1).

This offence is punishable on summary conviction with a fine not exceeding level 2 for a first offence or not exceeding level 3 for a second or subsequent offence. The power of a constable to arrest anyone he reasonably suspects to be committing an offence is specifically preserved by Police and Criminal Evidence Act 1984, s. 26 and sch.2 (see 5.2 and appendix 3).

Proof that a woman is a common prostitute may be given by showing that she has persisted in conduct after being cautioned. The system of formal cautioning prevents a woman from being charged for this offence until she has received two formal and recorded cautions for offences which she admits (see Home Office Circular No. 109/1959). She can challenge a caution by applying to the magistrates' court within 14 days and is entitled to a hearing in camera (Street Offences Act 1959, s. 2).

The word 'common' is not mere surplusage; it applies to a woman who offers herself commonly, who is prepared for reward to engage in acts of lewdness with all and sundry, as opposed to a single act of lewdness for reward (*R* v *Morris-Lowe* [1985] 1 All ER 400). 'Public place' is not defined in this Act; for a discussion of definitions of 'public place' see 8.3. Solicitation by men is dealt with in 6.9.2.

Since the abolition of imprisonment for this offence many prostitutes have to work to pay their fines, a practice which is openly accepted by many urban magistrates' courts, although some courts have sought to imprison prostitutes by means of heavy fines with imprisonment in default.

Prostitution in private is not an offence, but an offence is committed if the person solicited is in a street or public place and the prostitute is on a balcony or at a window (*Smith* v *Hughes* [1960] 2 All ER 859) although not if she offers her services by displaying a notice on a board and is not present (*Weiss* v *Monahan* [1962] 1 All ER 664; *Burge* v *DPP* [1962] 1 All ER 666, *Behrendt* v *Burridge* [1976] 3 All ER 285; cf. *Shaw* v *DPP* [1962] AC 220, the *Ladies Directory* case in which a conspiracy to corrupt public morals was charged—this offence is unlikely to be charged in ordinary cases of prostitution today).

Under the Vagrancy Act 1824, s. 3, every common prostitute wandering in the public streets or public highways, or in any place of public resort, and behaving in a riotous or indecent manner is guilty of a summary offence punishable with a maximum penalty of one month's imprisonment and/or a fine not to exceed level 3.

6.9.2 Solicitation by men

It is an offence for a man:

(a)   persistently to solicit or importune,
(b)   in a public place,
(c)   for immoral purposes (Sexual Offences Act 1956, s. 32).

This offence is punishable on conviction on indictment with a maximum penalty of two years' imprisonment and/or a fine and on summary conviction with six months' imprisonment and/or a fine not exceeding the statutory maximum. Anyone may arrest without warrant a person committing this offence (Sexual Offences Act 1956, s. 41) but a constable may only do so under the 'general arrest conditions' of the Police and Criminal Evidence Act 1984, s. 25 (see 5.2).

There is probably little or no difference between soliciting and importuning (see *Field* v *Chapman, The Times*, 9 October 1953), but it must be persistent, that is at least more than one act. Two acts are sufficient (*Dale* v *Smith* [1967] 1 WLR 700, 'Hello' said more than once in a public lavatory was held to be importuning). The immoral purpose need not be a criminal offence in itself, for example, persistent suggestions that acts should take place between consenting adult males in private, which is not a criminal offence by virtue of the Sexual Offences Act 1967, s. 1, may amount to an immoral purpose (*R* v *Ford* [1978] 1

All ER 1129). Whether the activity amounts to an immoral purpose is a matter for the jury (*R* v *Grey* (1982) 74 Cr App R 324). It can therefore be argued on behalf of defendants that if the importuning is proved the jury could still find that there was no immoral purpose because of the change of attitudes in recent years. See also *Hampshire* v *Mace* [1986] Crim LR 752.

6.9.3   Indecency between men

It is an offence for a man:

(a)   to commit an act of gross indecency with another man,
(b)   in public or in private (except if they are consenting adults—over 21—in private) (Sexual Offences Act 1956, s. 13).

This offence is punishable on indictment with a maximum penalty of two years' imprisonment or five years' imprisonment if by a man over 21 with a man under 21 and/or a fine, or on summary conviction with six months' imprisonment and/or the statutory maximum fine. Prosecutions must be brought within 12 months of the alleged offence (Sexual Offences Act 1967, s. 7).

'With another man' cannot be construed as meaning 'against' or 'directed towards'; both men must participate in the indecency (*R* v *Preece and Howells* (1976) 63 Cr App R 28).

6.9.4   Kerb-crawling

The Sexual Offences Act 1985 (in force from 16 September 1985) creates two separate offences.

6.9.4.1.   Sexual Offences Act 1985, s. 1   A man commits the offence of kerb-crawling if:

(a)   he solicits a woman (or different women) for the purpose of prostitution, and
(b)   he does so either from a motor vehicle while it is in a street or public place, or in a street or public place while in the immediate vicinity of a motor vehicle that he has just got out of or off, and
(c)   he does so persistently or in such a manner or in such circumstances as to be likely to cause annoyance to the woman (or any of the women) solicited or to cause nuisance to other persons in the neighbourhood.

The offence is triable summarily only, with a maximum penalty of a fine not exceeding level 3. This is an arrestable offence where the 'general arrest conditions' of the Police and Criminal Act 1984, s. 25, apply (see 5.2).

Soliciting is not defined (see 6.9.2). The purpose of prostitution is not limited to sexual intercourse; it includes all the services of a prostitute (Sexual Offences Act 1985, s. 4(1)).

6.9.4.2   Sexual Offences Act 1985, s. 2   A man commits an offence if:

(a)   he solicits a woman (or different women) for the purpose of prostitution, and

(b)   he does so persistently, and
(c)   he does so in a street or public place.

The offence is triable summarily only, with a maximum penalty of a fine not exceeding level 3. It is an arrestable offence if the general arrest conditions of the Police and Criminal Evidence Act 1984 apply, s. 25 (see 5.2).

6.10 LITTER

There are a number of criminal offences connected with litter.
    It is the offence of leaving litter, if any person:

(a)   throws down, drops or deposits, *and* leaves,
(b)   any thing whatsoever in such circumstances as to cause, or contribute to, or tend to lead to, the defacement by litter of any place in the open air,
(c)   unless authorised by law or with the consent of the owner, occupier or other relevant person having control of the place (Litter Act 1983, s. 1).

The deposit etc. of litter must be in, into or from any place in the open air to which the public are entitled or permitted to have access without payment, which includes any covered place open to the air on at least one side (for other definitions of 'public place' see 7.3). 'Leaves' does not mean 'abandons'; the accused is guilty if the article has been left for only a short time (*Witney* v *Cattanach* [1979] Crim LR 461).
    Prosecution may be brought by the police or by any private person whether aggrieved or not (see *Snodgrass* v *Topping* (1952) 116 JP 332) or by a member or officer of a local authority (Local Government Act 1972, s. 222).
    The penalty on summary conviction is a fine not exceeding level 3. In passing sentence the court shall take into account the purpose of the section, the nature of the litter, and any risk of injury to persons or animals or of damage to property (Litter Act 1983, s. 1(4)).
    It is an offence punishable on summary conviction with a fine not exceeding level 1 wilfully to remove or otherwise interfere with any litter bin (Litter Act 1983, s. 5(9)). The offender may be ordered to pay compensation up to £20 to the litter authority (Litter Act 1983, s. 5(10)).
    It is an offence punishable on summary conviction with imprisonment for up to 14 days or a fine not exceeding level 1 for any person to throw rubbish into a town garden, or trespass in it, or steal or damage the flowers or plants, or commit any nuisance in it (Town Gardens Protection Act 1863, s. 5). A town garden is any enclosed garden or ornamental ground set apart in any city or borough for the use and enjoyment of the inhabitants (s. 1), but not Crown property (s. 7). It is an offence punishable on summary conviction with a fine not exceeding level 1 to damage any allotment not exceeding 40 poles (about 1,000 square metres) in extent or any crops or fences or buildings on an allotment (Allotments Act 1922, s. 19). See also 3.3.
    It is an offence punishable on summary conviction with a fine not exceeding level 1 for any person (other than an authorised council employee) to sort over or disturb the contents of dustbins in the street or on a forecourt or to sort over

or disturb refuse material on a council dump (Public Health Act 1936, s. 76, as amended).

It is an offence punishable on summary conviction with a fine not exceeding level 3 for a householder to fail to comply with a notice from the council requiring him to place refuse in receptacles which are of a kind or a number reasonably specified in the notice (Control of Pollution Act 1974, s. 13(1A)).

It is an offence punishable on summary conviction with 14 days' imprisonment or a fine not exceeding level 3:

(a)   to throw or lay down any stones, coal, slate, shells, lime, bricks, timber, iron or other materials, or

(b)   to throw from the roof or any part of any house or other building any slate, brick, wood, rubbish or other thing (except snow), or

(c)   to throw or lay down any dirt, litter or ashes, or night soil, or any carrion, fish, offal or rubbish, on any street, or

(d)   to cause any offensive matter to run from any manufactory, brewery, slaughterhouse, butcher's shop, or dunghill into any street to the obstruction, annoyance or danger of the residents or passengers (Town Police Clauses Act 1847, s. 28 as amended; note that this section contains a large number of other offences with a public nuisance element).

6.11   STREET COLLECTIONS, LEAFLETING ETC.

The law relating to street collecting, leafleting and selling papers is confused, both in the multiplicity of laws and regulations and in the application of the law. There are statutes and regulations governing street collections and charitable collections from house to house. Some police forces use the laws against begging and peddling under the Vagrancy Act 1824 against collectors and sellers. Local authorities also have a multitude of powers in by-laws to restrict this kind of activity in specified streets, parks and open places. Some by-laws give council officials or the police the power to remove persons infringing the requirements of local laws (see 6.4).

But practice and police interpretation of the law are erratic. In some areas the police restrict activity by strict enforcement of the law of the highway, and the use of the offence of obstruction of a police officer in the execution of his duty (see 5.12), usually for failing to comply with a police instruction to desist or to move on. Sometimes the police take the view that selling magazines is lawful but that collecting money is not. The sale of *The Miner*, a broadsheet supporting the miners' strike, was usually considered to be illegal because the police felt it was less a newspaper and more a device to get round the collection regulations, although frequently collecting food or collecting money at street meetings would be permitted. Also during the miners' strike a number of police commanders in London came to working agreements with miners' support groups to decide what would be permitted.

The prudent course is to consult the police and the local authority before embarking upon collecting or selling.

The main areas of activity and their legal implications can be summarised as follows.

6.11.1   Street collections

Money may be collected *for charitable purposes* at open-air meetings in public places and at private meetings with the permission of the organisers without infringing the law, as long as it is not collected in such a way that it creates an obstruction of the highway (see 6.4), for example, by causing a crowd to gather on the pavement outside a hall, or the collector commits an offence under s. 4 or s. 5 of the Public Order Act 1986 (see 2.5 and 2.6). But otherwise the collection of money in a street, including alongside a procession, requires a licence under the Police, Factories, etc. (Miscellaneous Provisions) Act 1916, s. 5. Such a licence is obtained from the local district council outside London or from the police in London or from the Common Council in the City of London. Making a street collection without a licence is a criminal offence. For full details of these provisions see below. Collecting money for non-charitable purposes constitutes begging and is an offence contrary to the Vagrancy Act 1824 (see 6.11.6.5). Collecting for workers on strike and their families does not constitute begging (see 6.11.6.5).

Similar considerations apply to the *sale of articles for charitable purposes*. A licence is required for the sale of, for example, jumble or charity mugs or T-shirts in the street under the Police, Factories, etc. (Miscellaneous Provisions) Act 1916, s. 5. The sale of articles for charitable purposes without a licence is a criminal offence under the Act (see 6.11.6.1). The sale of articles for non-charitable purposes would also require a licence under the street-trading provisions (see 6.11.6.4). In practice it is best to obtain a market stall or use council premises with permission in order to avoid a conviction for street trading.

Food and household items may be collected for charitable purposes as long as the collection does not create an obstruction of the highway, for example, by setting up a table on the pavement and causing pedestrians to walk in the road to get round it.

6.11.2   Door-to-door collections

It is illegal under the House to House Collections Act 1939 to go from door to door asking for donations of money or goods without a licence. For full details of the statutory provisions see 6.11.6.2. 'Goods' includes jumble although the collection of jumble for an obvious cause like the local church or boy scouts is unlikely to lead to prosecution. Door-to-door collection should be distinguished from door-to-door sales (see 6.11.6.3). A licence for door-to-door collections can be obtained from the district council or in London from the police or in the City of London from the Common Council. If a licence is refused an appeal lies to the Home Secretary (House Collections Act 1939, s. 2(4)). Sometimes a licence can take a long time to obtain. For example, in the miners' dispute the Dover District Council took over three months to decide to refuse to grant a licence to a local miners' support group.

6.11.3   Leaflets and petitions

There is no requirement to obtain a licence or certificate for handing out leaflets or collecting signatures for a petition. A leaflet must have on it the name and the address of the printer.

Some by-laws, however, contain restrictions on the places where leafleting may take place. Leafleting may be restricted if the police consider it to be causing an obstruction of the highway because of the position of the leafleter(s) on the road or pavement (for the offence of obstruction of the highway see 6.5). If the police tell a leafleter to move on, even for no good reason, the leafleter may be at risk of possible arrest and prosecution for obstructing the police in the execution of their duty (see 5.12). It would also be an offence to hand out leaflets which are threatening, abusive or insulting so as to infringe s. 4 or s. 5 of the Public Order Act 1986 or which are intended or likely to stir up racial hatred under the provisions of ss. 17–19 of the Public Order Act 1986. In one case during the Vietnam War convictions for insulting behaviour were obtained where leaflets opposing the war and inviting servicemen to desert were handed out to persons entering a club for United States servicemen.

By contrast in Holland the courts have held that art. 7 of the Constitution which guarantees freedom of expression renders unlawful regulations to prohibit the use of the highway for displaying 'advertising or publicity material' without prior permission from the local authority (see Sieghart, *The International Law of Human Rights*, p. 331, n. 13). In California the Court of Appeal has upheld First Amendment rights protecting free speech for school employees in an industrial dispute to leaflet at the private business offices of two school board members (see Thornton, *We Protest*, p. 16).

6.11.4 Selling newspapers

It is not illegal for persons over 18 years of age to sell newspapers in the street or from door to door, as long as the sale is for campaigning purposes. If the sale is for profit it becomes street trading (see 6.11.6.4) or, if door to door, peddling (see 6.11.6.3), both of which are illegal without a licence. In *West Yorkshire Metropolitan Police* v *Teal and Bolloten* (Leeds Crown Court, 20 November 1981, unreported) convictions for selling newspapers, *Brixton News Sheet*, from door to door and asking for donations from householders without a pedlar's licence under the Vagrancy Act 1824, s. 3, were quashed on appeal.

Difficulties sometimes arise, however, because the police consider some magazines or newspapers to be less of a campaigning document and more of a device to get round the charitable collection regulations, as was sometimes the case with *The Miner*, a broadsheet supporting the miners' strike.

Newspaper sellers may also fall foul of the law if they are considered to be an obstruction of the highway. There is no police policy on obstruction; it is up to the individual constable on the spot to decide whether a seller is causing an obstruction. But senior police officers have indicated that the decision will usually depend upon the number of sellers, where they are positioned and the time of day, for example, the rush hour.

A by-law against selling any paper devoted wholly or mainly to giving information as to the probable result of races, steeplechases, or other competitions was held invalid for being uncertain and unreasonable (*Scott* v *Pilliner* [1904] 2 KB 855).

6.11.5   Placards, banners etc.

As with leafleting (see 6.11.3), there is no requirement under the general law
for permission from the police or the local authority for the carrying of placards
or banners, although some local by-laws impose a measure of control on their
use (see 6.4). In general terms they must not obstruct the highway (see 6.4),
they must not carry messages which could be considered threatening, abusive
or insulting within the meaning of ss. 4 and 5 of the Public Order Act 1986 (see
2.5 and 2.6) or which are intended or likely to stir up racial hatred within the
meaning of ss. 17–19 of the Public Order Act 1986 (see chapter 4) and they must
not be dangerous or likely to cause injury (see 3.1).

6.11.6   Summary of main points of law

6.11.6.1   Street collections   Each district council, the police authority for the
Metropolitan Police District (the Home Secretary), and the Common Council
of the City of London may make regulations to provide in which streets or
public places and under what conditions a person may be permitted to collect
money or sell articles for the benefit of charitable or other purposes (Police,
Factories, etc. (Miscellaneous Provisions) Act 1916, s. 5 as amended).

'Street' includes any highway and any public bridge, road, lane, footway,
square, court, alley or passage, whether a thoroughfare or not (s. 5(4)), but
'public place' is not defined (for a discussion of the various meanings of 'public
place' see generally 8.3).

It is an offence punishable on summary conviction with a fine not exceeding
level 1 to contravene any such regulation.

In London, for example, detailed regulations (Street Collections
(Metropolitan Police District) Regulations 1979 SI No. 1230) provide that a
permit must be obtained from the Commissioner before a collection can be
made. Applications for a permit must be in writing on a special form (a copy of
the form is set out at the end of this section). The regulations provide that no
collection shall be made in such a manner as to cause danger, obstruction,
inconvenience or annoyance to any person, nor shall any collector importune
any person to the annoyance of that person. While collecting collectors must
remain stationary and two collectors shall not be nearer than 25 metres.
Collections must be in a collecting box. Within three months of the collection a
statement of account must be given to the Police Commissioner (a standard
form is set out in 6.11.7).

Most police permits (in London) are granted for annual events like Poppy
Day. A licence is more difficult to obtain if the organiser is not a national
charity. The Commissioner will require assurances of compliance with the
regulations, and he is assisted by an advisory committee made up of
representatives of the London Boroughs Association and others before making
a decision.

In *Meaden* v *Wood* [1985] Crim LR 678 the defendant had been collecting for
the striking miners in a paved pedestrian precinct without a permit. The
stipendiary magistrate held that the 1979 regulations were *ultra vires* the 1916
Act in that the Act did not authorise the Home Secretary to delegate his powers

to regulate street collections to the Commissioner and dismissed the information. The Divisional Court allowed the prosecutor's appeal on the basis that the Act provided the Home Secretary with an administrative power which permitted delegation to the police for the purposes of deciding whom to permit to collect money in the street within the system which the Home Secretary had set up.

6.11.6.2   Charitable collections from house to house   These are controlled by a system of licensing under the House to House Collections Act 1939 which distinguishes between promoters—meaning persons who cause others to act, whether for remuneration or not, as collectors—and collectors. This system should be distinguished from the system of trading from house to house which is governed by the Pedlars Act 1871 (6.11.6.3).

Every collection from house to house (including public houses) for charitable purposes, meaning any charitable, benevolent or philanthropic purpose (House to House Collections Act 1939, s. 11(1)), must be:

(a)   the subject of a licence granted by the district council or, in London, by the Commissioner of Police in the Metropolitan Police District or by the Common Council in the City of London, or

(b)   the subject of a certificate granted by the police if the collection is local in character and likely to be completed in a short period of time, or

(c)   the subject of an exemption granted by the Home Secretary where he is satisfied that a person is promoting a charitable purpose throughout the whole or a substantial part of England, and

(d)   made by a collector with a prescribed badge or certificate of authority identifying the collector and the charitable purpose.

The sale of toiletries with part of the proceeds going to the Children's Research Fund was a 'collection' within the meaning of the House to House Collections Act 1939, s. 11(1), which provides that a 'collection' means 'an appeal to the public, made by means of visits from house to house, to give, whether for consideration or not, money or other property' (*Carasu Ltd* v *Smith* [1968] 2 QB 383). However, in *Murphy* v *Duke* [1985] QB 905 the sale of goods was held not to be a collection, the only differences being that the toiletries were actually made by beneficiaries of the charitable funds and the sales agents were supplementing their income (see the Trading Representations (Disabled Persons) Amendment Act 1972). Accordingly, the sales agents were entitled to a pedlar's certificate from the chief constable under the Pedlars Act 1871.

Offences.   It is an offence:

(a)   To collect without a licence—the maximum penalty on summary conviction is three months' imprisonment and/or a fine not exceeding level 2 (a collection for a charitable purpose includes the exchange of goods for money: *Cooper* v *Coles, The Times*, 10 July 1986).

(b)   To promote (to cause others to collect) a collection without a

licence—the maximum penalty on summary conviction is six months'
imprisonment and/or a fine not exceeding level 3.

(c) To contravene the regulations, for example, as to the wearing of badges
of identity—the penalty on summary conviction is a fine not exceeding level 1.

(d) To use the wrong identity badge or to use a badge etc. calculated to
deceive—the maximum penalty on summary conviction is six months'
imprisonment and/or a fine not exceeding level 3.

(e) To fail as a collector to give the police his name and address—penalty
on summary conviction a fine not exceeding level 1.

(f) Knowingly or recklessly to make a false statement in furnishing
information for the purposes of this Act—the maximum penalty on summary
conviction is six months' imprisonment and/or a fine not exceeding level 3.

6.11.6.3 Door-to-door selling Door-to-door salesmen for non-charitable
purposes, itinerant salesmen travelling on foot, hawkers and pedlars etc. must
obtain a pedlar's certificate from the local police under the Pedlars Act 1871,
and any person who acts as a pedlar without a certificate commits a summary
offence punishable with a fine not exceeding level 1. The following categories
are excluded: commercial travellers, persons seeking orders for goods or acting
through dealers, persons selling or seeking orders for books, vegetables, fish,
fruit or victuals, persons selling goods in a legal public market, and persons
standing in the streets and selling goods. Door-to-door sales of newspapers of a
campaigning nature are generally considered not to be in breach of the 1871
Act where neither the sellers nor their organisation are making any profit (see
West Yorkshire Metropolitan Police v *Teal and Bolloten*, discussed in 6.11.4).

6.11.6.4 Street trading The law on street trading is contained in the Local
Government (Miscellaneous Provisions) Act 1982, s. 3 and sch. 4. This Act
provides a detailed system of street trading licences and consents with criminal
offences for non-compliance. In particular a council may designate any street in
their district into one of three categories: a 'prohibited street' in which street
trading is prohibited entirely, a 'licence street' where trading may only take
place under a licence granted by the council, and a 'consent street' where
trading may only take place under a consent granted by the council (sch. 4).
The difference between a licence and a consent seems to be that the former
relates to persons trading from stalls in fixed and regular positions on a
permanent basis, whereas the latter is intended to cover itinerant or
intermittent traders perhaps operating from small movable stalls or vehicles.
These matters were considered in *R* v *Penwith District Council (ex parte May)*
(22 November 1985, unreported, ref. No. CO/109/85), in which a decision of
the Penwith District Council refusing a trading consent to the Penzance and
District Campaign for Nuclear Disarmament to sell and distribute literature,
badges and similar material in a pedestrian precinct was quashed for being
made without good reason. See generally *Stone's Justices' Manual 1986*, para.
4-5911 et seq.

6.11.6.5 Begging It is an offence contrary to the Vagrancy Act 1824, ss. 3
and 4, to beg in a public place, street, highway, court or passage, or to gather
alms or to procure charitable contributions of any kind under false pretences.

This offence is punishable on summary conviction with a fine not exceeding level 3. During the miners' strike some collectors were charged with begging, although there is authority that workmen on strike seeking assistance are not begging. In *Pointon* v *Hill* (1884) 12 QBD 306 it was held that colliers on strike going from house to house begging for assistance in money or kind for the wives and children of colliers were not within the meaning of the Act because it was not their habit and mode of life to wander abroad and beg. In *Mathers* v *Penfold* [1915] 1 KB 514) an authorised union member who sought contributions during a building dispute for strikers and their families was not guilty under the Act because the Act was aimed not at persons collecting for an object of a charitable nature but at persons who had 'given up work and adopted begging as a habit or mode of life'.

6.11.6.6   Obstruction of the highway   Those who collect or leaflet or seek signatures for petitions or sell newspapers may in certain circumstances be guilty of obstructing the highway contrary to the Highways Act 1980, s. 137 (see 6.4). No offence will be committed if the use of the highway is reasonable (see *Hirst and Another* v *Chief Constable of West Yorkshire, The Times,* 19 November 1986; 6.5.1.3).

6.11.7   Street Collections (Metropolitan Police District) Regulations 1979

6.11.7.1   Form of Application for Permit
To the Commissioner of Police of the Metropolis
   We, the undersigned, hereby, on behalf of the society, committee or other body named in paragraph 1 below, make application for a permit for a street collection.
   We apply for the collection to be authorised to be held in connection with a procession and for one or more of the special permissions referred to in the provisos to regulations 9, 12 and 13, as follows:
   [Either delete or complete as appropriate.]

   1.   Name of society, committee or body of persons applying for permit for the collection (chief promoter).
   2.   Address of chief promoter.
   3.   Names and addresses of the individuals through whom this application is made who will be jointly responsible for the collection.
   4.   Name of charity or fund which is to benefit.
   5.   Address of the principal office of the charity or fund and name of the secretary or other chief executive officer.
   6.   Objects of the charity or fund.
   7.   Date upon which it is proposed to make the collection.
   8.   Locality within which it is proposed to make the collection.
   9.   Method proposed to be adopted in making the collection.
   10.   Payments (if any) proposed to be made to persons connected with the promotion or conduct of the collection, including the name and address of each recipient and the amount to be paid in each case.
   11.   Disposal of the proceeds (including any deduction proposed to be made from proceeds before distribution to the charity or fund, for expenses or

any other purposes; the purpose and estimated amount of any such deduction; and the distribution of proceeds between the charities or funds, if more than one is to benefit).

Signed ....
         ....
         ....
         ....
         ....
Date   ....

6.12   PUBLIC NUISANCE

It is an offence at common law to commit a public nuisance. The offence is triable either way. It is punishable on indictment with an unlimited term of imprisonment and/or a fine and summarily with a maximum of six months' imprisonment and/or a fine not exceeding the statutory maximum.

6.12.1   Meaning of public nuisance

The common law offence of public nuisance is not often used, and it is arguably too wide and vague a concept to form part of the criminal law. A public nuisance is one which inflicts damage, injury or inconvenience on all the Queen's subjects or on all members of a class who come within the sphere or neighbourhood of its operation (see *Halsbury's Laws of England*, 4th ed., vol. 34, para. 305). Archbold (42nd ed., para. 27–45) classifies public nuisances into four categories: (a) interference with comfort, enjoyment or health; (b) acts dangerous to public safety; (c) acts injurious to public morals, decency or order; and (d) unlawful treatment of dead bodies. 'Nuisance may be defined, with reference to highways, as any wrongful act or omission upon or near a highway, whereby the public are prevented from freely, safely, and conveniently passing along the highway' (Lord Simonds in *Jacobs* v *London County Council* [1950] AC 361, 375).

6.12.2   Examples

The offence is more easily explained by example than by definition. For present purposes illustrations will only be taken from a public order context. It is a nuisance at common law to obstruct the highway without authority or to render it dangerous for an appreciable period of time (see *R* v *Train* (1862) 2 B & S 640), for example, by selling goods or entertaining the public so as to cause crowds to gather (see *R* v *Lewis* (1881) 72 LT Jo 117, collecting crowds by exhibiting attractive objects in a shop). Unauthorised encampments may amount to a public nuisance (*Attorney-General* v *Stone* (1895) 60 JP 168).

Many of the old examples of public nuisance are now covered by local by-laws (for example, controlling fairs and circuses) or by statute (for example, under the Obscene Publications Act 1959 and the Control of Pollution Act 1974). In the 1960s a number of nuclear disarmament protesters were convicted of incitement to commit a public nuisance by obstructing the highway (see *R* v *Moule* [1964] Crim LR 303, leading demonstrators round Trafalgar Square and

6.11.7.2 Form of statement

Name and address of society, committee or body to whom the permit for the collection was granted (chief promoter): ....

Name of charity or fund to benefit ....

Date of collection ....

Show NIL entries

Proceeds of collection	Amount	Total	Expenses and application of proceeds	Amount	Total
From collecting boxes			Printing and stationery		
			Postage		
			Advertising		
			Collecting boxes		
			Badges or other emblems		
			Other items (specify items separately)		
Interest on proceeds			Payments referred to in reg. 18(2)		
			Disposal of balance (insert particulars)		
Other items (specify items separately)					
Total	£	£	Total	£	£

(If the expenses of the collection were defrayed otherwise than from the proceeds of the collection—either wholly or in part—the particulars of the amount should be inserted on both sides of the account, i.e., in the 'proceeds' column and as an item of 'expenses').

Certificate of two of the persons who applied for the permit

We certify that to the best of our knowledge and belief the above is a true account of the proceeds, expenses and application of the proceeds of the collection.

Date: .... 19 .... Signed ....

Certificate of accountant (or other responsible person referred to in regulation 19(1)(a))

I certify that I have obtained all the information and explanations required by me and that the above is in my opinion a true account of the proceeds, expenses and application of the proceeds of the collection.

Date .... 19 .... Signed .... Qualifications ....

(Name in block capitals) ....

Address ....

down Whitehall and instructing them to sit down in the road; *R* v *Adler* [1964] Crim LR 304, instructing a crowd to sit down in the road; although in *R* v *Clark (No. 2)* [1964] 2 QB 315, following *Loudens* v *Keaveney* [1903] 2 IR 82, the conviction was quashed where the defendant had simply led and directed a CND demonstration along a route chosen in an attempt to circumvent a police cordon). Conspiracy to commit a nuisance remains an offence (Criminal Law Act 1977, s. 1(1)).

In recent times the existence of the offence has been confirmed in a bomb-hoax case (*R* v *Madden* (1975) 61 Cr App R 254; bomb hoaxes are now governed by the Criminal Law Act 1977, s. 51, see 3.8). It has been used to prosecute pop festivals on health grounds, the repetition over a long period of obscene telephone calls (*R* v *Norbury* [1978] Crim LR 435), bringing dangerous animals on to or near the highway (*R* v *Wheeler, The Times*, 17 December 1971, pumas and leopards), and glue sniffing on a school playground after school hours where there was undue interference with the comfortable and convenient enjoyment of land (*Sykes* v *Holmes and Maw* [1985] Crim LR 791). Note that glue sniffing is not included in drunk and disorderly behaviour contrary to the Licensing Act 1872, s. 12 (*Neale* v *R.M.J.E.* (1985) 80 Cr App R 20), although driving whilst unfit through drink or drugs contrary to the Road Traffic Act 1972, s. 5(2), does cover glue sniffing.

In *News Group Newspapers Ltd* v *Society of Graphical & Allied Trades 1982, The Times*, 1 August 1986, a civil case, it was held that when marches or demonstrations are peaceful and orderly no nuisance is created. However, when marchers or demonstrators get out of control, attack the police and the employees of the plaintiffs and obstruct the highway by masses of people, that is not a reasonable use of the highway and amounts to a nuisance.

7

Law of Trespass

This chapter deals with trespass to land. It looks at the discussion and development of the law of trespass arising out of the activities of the 'peace convoy'. It assesses the scope of the civil law of trespass, particularly the summary procedure for the recovery of land and the use of injunctions; it explains the new criminal trespass law (Public Order Act 1986, s. 39); and it describes the other criminal offences relating to the law of trespass. It concludes with a section on the law relating to the peace convoy and the public order law issues involved.

7.1 INTRODUCTION

In the summer of 1986 the government decided to reconsider the law of trespass, particularly whether the limited law of criminal trespass should be extended. This arose out of the temporary occupation of land by members of the peace convoy and other travellers in their attempts to hold a festival at Stonehenge to celebrate the summer solstice.

No previous government had considered legislating for a full law of criminal trespass. In 1974 the Law Commission (Working Paper No. 54) proposed two criminal offences of entering and remaining on property despite the fact that the then government had decided 'not to create at that stage an offence of criminal trespass'. This proposal, arising out of complaints about squatters, was enacted in a modified form in the Criminal Law Act 1977 (see 7.3.7.2). But these offences dealt principally with residential premises; they did not cover the adverse occupation of open land.

Otherwise unwanted occupiers of fields would normally be ejected by the civil law procedures (see 7.2.2) or by the police arresting those who had committed criminal offences such as damage to crops or by self-help by the owner sometimes with the help of the police where a breach of the peace was anticipated (see 5.1).

In early June 1986 a Minister of State at the Home Office was still maintaining the position that there was no need for a law of criminal trespass, that a criminal trespass offence would create more problems than it would solve, particularly for innocent ramblers or visitors to property, that the Public Order Bill gave the police sufficient powers to act to remove wrongdoers, and that the Public Order Bill was not the right place for a new law of criminal trespass anyway. But in late June 1986 (*The Times*, 24 June 1986) the Attorney-General informed the House of Commons that (a) the Home

Secretary was considering strengthening police powers under the Public Order Bill or creating a limited form of criminal trespass 'to make trespass on private land by hippie convoys a criminal offence' (the Home Secretary quoted in the *Sunday Times*, 29 June 1986), and (b) the Lord Chancellor was considering improvements to the civil procedure for the summary repossession of land. The Attorney-General made it clear that the government retained reservations about a criminal trespass offence and the sort of cases which, in his view, should never be made criminal offences.

The result of the fresh consideration of the law of trespass was (a) the insertion of a new clause entitled 'Power to direct trespassers to leave land' in the Public Order Bill in the House of Lords on 6 October 1986—this clause became s. 39 of the Public Order Act 1986, and (b) the publication by the Lord Chancellor of a consultation paper on summary proceedings for possession of land, which has led to changes in civil procedure.

7.2   CIVIL LAW

7.2.1   Meaning of trespass

A person commits trespass to land if he intentionally, negligently or recklessly enters or remains on land in the possession of another. A trespass is a tort (civil wrong) actionable in the civil courts. See generally Street, *The Law of Torts*, 7th ed., ch. 5, and *Winfield and Jolowicz on Tort*, 12th ed., ch. 13.

It is trespass to go on to land or to put or leave anything (including vehicles) on to land or even to fire a gun on to land. In law a squatter is a trespasser. He has no interest in the house or land he occupies which would enable him to defend possession proceedings brought against him by the owner or a person (such as a tenant) entitled to occupation. If the owner or occupier wishes to eject trespassers he should issue civil proceedings. Alternatively, he may invoke the new criminal trespass law (see 7.3.2 to 7.3.6).

Not all forms of entry on to private land amount to trespass. A lawful visitor such as the postman or a person delivering a leaflet has implied permission to walk up to the front door of a private house (*Robson* v *Hallett* [1967] 2 QB 939), unless that permission is withdrawn by a clear notice or by telling the visitor to go away. A police constable who has entered private premises without permission or other lawful authority becomes a trespasser at the very latest on being told to leave and refusing to do so (*Davis* v *Lisle* [1936] 2 KB 434, and see 10.1.2). Even the entry by a constable on to unattended private premises to secure a bicycle which might otherwise be stolen does not prevent the constable from being a trespasser (*R* v *Prebble* (1858) 1 F & F 325, where the constable could not sue for injury sustained on the premises).

There can also, although it is less common, be trespass to the highway if the highway is used for purposes other than those 'reasonably incident to its user' as a highway (*Liddle* v *Yorkshire (North Riding) County Council* [1934] 2 KB 101, 127; and see chapter 6), for example, using the highway to make notes of the performances of racehorses in neighbouring fields (*Hickman* v *Maisey* [1900] 1 QB 752). Picketing or holding meetings on the highway may amount to trespass, although actions are rare (cf. *Hubbard* v *Pitt* [1976] QB 142). Leaving a car in a narrow lane for the purposes of trespassing in a neighbouring field does not make the car either 'the symbol of a trespass or the instrument of a nuisance' (*Randall* v *Tarrant* [1955] 1 WLR 255; for the law of public nuisance see 6.12). Trespassing in pursuit of a fox is not a claim of title so as to oust the jurisdiction of justices; nor will it justify an assault upon a person rightfully obstructing the hunt (*Paul* v *Summerhayes* (1878) 4 QBD 9). But it is a good defence to a charge of obtaining game by unlawfully going on land in search or pursuit of game to prove that the defendant had a bona fide belief that he had permission to go on the land and reasonable grounds for that belief (*Dickinson* v *Ead* (1914) 78 JP 326).

7.2.2 Owners' and occupiers' remedies under the civil law

7.2.2.1 Possession order The possessor of land (usually the owner or tenant) can sue a trespasser for *the return of the possession of the land* (within 12 years). This is the most effective way of removing trespassers from open land. Once an order for possession has been granted and a writ of possession has issued from the court and been served on the trespassers either:

(a)   the trespassers can be forcibly ejected by the sheriff in High Court proceedings or by the bailiffs in county court proceedings (the sheriff or bailiff may evict anyone he finds on the premises, even though that person was not a party to the proceedings: *R* v *Wandsworth County Court (ex parte London Borough of Wandsworth)* [1975] 1 WLR 1314)—the police are empowered to assist the sheriff (Sheriffs Act 1887, s. 8(2)) but not a bailiff unless a breach of the peace is imminent (see 5.1)—or

(b)   the possessor can take contempt proceedings against the trespassers which could lead ultimately to imprisonment.

Summary procedure for possession of land.   Following the Department of the Environment's *Consultation Paper on Squatting* (August 1975), rules of court (RSC, Ord. 113, in the High Court, CCR, Ord. 24, in the County Court) were drafted to provide a special procedure for speedy and effective action to reclaim land and eject trespassers. In the High Court, which has some advantages for the owner over the county court procedure, application is made by originating summons supported by affidavit. Service of the summons and affidavit can be made either on named defendants to the proceedings or, where it is not reasonably practicable to identify the trespassers, on unnamed persons by affixing copies of the documents to the main door or 'other conspicuous part of the premises'. This summary procedure is designed to operate without a trial with witnesses, although defendants with a genuine claim will be entitled to a full trial of the action. The strict procedure must normally be complied with (*Re 9 Orpen Road, Stoke Newington* [1971] 1 WLR 166, 168), but the judge has a discretion to waive any irregularity if no injustice would be caused (*Burston Finance Ltd* v *Wilkins and persons unknown, The Times*, 17 July 1975). This procedure is limited to the recovery of land (RSC, Ord. 113, r. 1). An order for possession will not normally be made for five days (five clear days in the High Court, i.e., excluding Saturdays, Sundays and public holidays; five days in a county court), but the period may be shorter in case of urgency. From 12 January 1987 the period of five days will be reduced to two days for non-residential premises (*TheTimes*, 23 December 1986). The abridgement of the period may be obtained administratively (*Westminster City Council* v *Monahan*

[1981] 1 WLR 698, 702). There is no power to suspend the order for possession unless the owner consents (*McPhail* v *Persons Unknown* [1973] Ch 447; *Swordheath Properties Ltd* v *Floydd* [1978] 1 WLR 550). Nor is there a power to grant an injunction under this summary procedure. But in the case of re-entry after enforcement of an order, an order of restitution is available on *ex parte* application (RSC, Ord. 46, r. 3; CCR, Ord. 24, r. 6(1) and Ord. 26, r. 17(4) and (5)). An order of restitution can be enforced against unnamed persons, whether they were originally in occupation or not, provided there is a connection between them and those who were in occupation (*Wiltshire County Council* v *Frazer* [1986] 1 WLR 109).

It is a criminal offence to resist or intentionally obstruct an officer of the court (including a sheriff and bailiff) engaged in executing any process issued by the civil court in possession proceedings (Criminal Law Act 1977, s. 10). This is an arrestable offence punishable on summary conviction with a maximum penalty of six months' imprisonment and/or a fine not exceeding level 5. It is a defence to prove on a balance of probabilities that the defendant believed that the person was not an officer of the court (Criminal Law Act 1977, s. 10(3)).

Misuse of summary procedure.   Although this procedure was designed for the eviction of unwanted squatters, since the decision in *Greater London Council* v *Jenkins* [1975] 1 WLR 155 it has become a common method of gaining possession against licensees after determination of the licence. Orders in the county court for the recovery of land occupied by trespassers rose by 26% to 8,547 in the year cited in the Judicial Statistics 1985 (Cmnd 9464). The broad category of licensees includes 'short-life' licensees occupying local authority or housing association or other property under a temporary arrangement, such as some hostels and women's refuges, those housed by local authorities under Part III of the Housing Act 1985 during the first 12 months of their occupancy, residents of hostels, lodging houses and bed and breakfast hotels, most service occupiers, and many flat-sharing and family arrangements.

Lord Chancellor's proposals.   In a consultation paper, *Summary Proceedings for Possession of Land* (15 September 1986), the Lord Chancellor has proposed:

(a)   that the period of five days should be reduced to two or three days, with the present power to shorten the period in urgent cases remaining,

(b)   that the form of service on unnamed defendants, such as placing in the ground at conspicuous points a number of stakes with sealed transparent envelopes containing the documents, should be provided for specifically in the rules without the need for specific directions, and

(c)   that cases should be heard by a master in the High Court or a registrar in a county court with the power to transfer appropriate cases to a judge. These proposals all become law on 12 January 1987. The five-day-period is reduced to two days and remains five days in the case of residential premises (*The Times*, 23 December 1986).

7.2.2.2 Damages   The possessor of land can sue a trespasser for damages (compensation) if any loss or damage has been caused (and the trespasser can be identified and is likely to have money to pay the compensation).

Use of the Highway

7.2.2.3 Injunction The possessor of land can sue a trespasser or potential trespasser for an injunction restraining the trespasser from committing, continuing or repeating the trespass.

Injunctions in public order cases are rare, except in relation to land. An unusual interlocutory injunction was obtained in *Hubbard* v *Pitt* [1976] QB 142 restraining peaceful protestors who had been picketing outside an estate agent's office from:

> besetting the plaintiffs' premises . . . or otherwise molesting the plaintiffs, their servants, agents or clients, or their tenants or any other person transacting or seeking to transact business with the plaintiffs or committing any nuisance against the plaintiffs in respect of their premises, and/or from doing any act calculated to damage the plaintiffs in their business and/or from interfering with the plaintiffs' contractual relations with their clients and any other persons, and/or from publishing or causing to be published certain words printed on placards and/or contained in a leaflet, and/or from conspiring to do such or similar acts.

The Court of Appeal upheld the injunction, applying *American Cyanamid Co.* v *Ethicon Ltd* [1975] AC 396 (see RSC, Ord. 29, r. 1) because there was a serious issue to be tried, namely, whether the defendants were committing the tort of private nuisance, and it could not be said that the plaintiffs could not succeed at the trial on their claim for a permanent injunction.

Interlocutory injunctions will be granted in clear cases even though to do so would be to give the plaintiff substantially if not all the remedy he claims, for example, to prevent the wrongful exclusion of members from meetings of an association (*Woodford* v *Smith* [1970] 1 All ER 1091, a local ratepayers' and residents' association) or to restrain trespassers from entering or remaining on land (*Manchester Corporation* v *Connolly* [1970] Ch 420, [1970] 1 All ER 961, caravans on an illegal site).

In the print dispute at Wapping Mr Rupert Murdoch's News International issued writs against the print unions seeking injunctions to restrict the picketing outside the Wapping plant (*The Guardian*, 14 June 1986). The High Court granted an injunction against some but not all defendants (*News Group Newspapers Ltd* v *Society of Graphical & Allied Trades 1982, The Times*, 1 August 1986). The principal terms of the injunction were as follows, that named defendants:

> and each of them be restrained forthwith whether by themselves, their servants, officers, agents or otherwise howsoever from inciting, inducing, procuring, persuading, assisting, encouraging, financing and/or in other ways organising:

> (a)   at or near the premises of News International at Pennington Street, London E1, demonstrations and/or marches and/or picketing which involves the commission of any tortious act or acts, in particular but without prejudice to the generality of the foregoing, nuisance and/or obstruction of the highway, interference with the commercial contracts of the plaintiffs,

intimidation and/or assault of the plaintiff's employees or visitors, save and except that the named defendants may organise:

  (i) pickets, provided they do not exceed six in number at the entrance to the main gate for the purpose of peacefully obtaining or communicating information;
  (ii) peaceful, disciplined and orderly marches along the highway into Wellclose Square save and except as the police otherwise direct;

  (b) at or near the premises of News Group Newspapers Ltd at Bouverie Street, London EC4, demonstrations and/or marches and/or picketing which involve the commission of any tortious act or acts and in particular but without prejudice to the generality of the foregoing intimidation and/or assault of the employees of News Group Newspapers, Times Newspapers Ltd and London Post (Printers) Ltd or visitors of News Group Newspapers save and except that the defendants may organise pickets, provided they do not exceed six in number at any entrance to the premises for the purpose of peacefully obtaining and communicating information and provided always that they are ex-employees of News Group Newspapers (or in the case of a trade union official if he is accompanying and representing such ex-employee) for the purpose of peacefully persuading persons not to work;
  (c) at or near the premises of Times Newspapers Ltd at 200 Grays Inn Road, demonstrations and/or marches and/or picketing which involve the commission of any tortious act or acts and in particular but without prejudice to the generality of the foregoing intimidation and/or assault of the employees of News Group Newspapers, Times Newspapers or London Post (Printers) or visitors of Times Newspapers save and except that the defendants may organise pickets, provided they do not exceed six in number, at the entrance to the premises for the purpose of peacefully obtaining or communicating information and provided always that they are ex-employees of Times Newspapers (or in the case of a trade union official if he is accompanying and representing such ex-employee) for the purpose of peacefully persuading persons not to work.

In a separate case the High Court granted injunctions against print workers restraining them from assaulting employees or property of TNT Roadfreight (UK) Ltd, the newspaper distribution firm owned by News International Ltd (*The Guardian*, 19 August 1986).

In *Thomas* v *National Union of Mineworkers (South Wales Area)* [1985] 2 WLR 1081 (see 6.6) an interlocutory injunction was granted to working miners restraining the South Wales branch of the NUM from organising picketing at or near the specified colliery entrances otherwise than for the purpose of peacefully obtaining or communicating information or peacefully persuading miners not to work and otherwise than in numbers not exceeding six.

Landowners in the vicinity of Stonehenge obtain High Court injunctions annually to prevent the holding of a pop concert and the congregation of persons there for that and other purposes. In 1985 and 1986 landowners local to

Stonehenge, including the National Trust and the Ministry of Defence, obtained injunctions preventing approximately 50 named persons from entering their land, thereby setting up, with the assistance of the Wiltshire police's 'Stonehenge Intelligence Unit', what became known as the 'exclusion zone' around Stonehenge. The injunctions restrained the defendants, their servants or agents from entering or remaining on land which was delineated on a plan annexed to the writ of summons until the trial of the action or further order.

7.2.2.4 *Right of re-entry*   The possessor can exercise his common law right of re-entry and use reasonable force to eject the trespasser (*McPhail* v *Persons Unknown* [1973] Ch 447; *Hemmings* v *Stoke Poges Golf Club* [1920] 1 KB 720), although this course is not advisable in view of the risks of injury or damage to property in the process and in view of the offence of violence for securing entry to premises contrary to the Criminal Law Act 1977, s. 6 (see 7.3.7.1). A trespasser who has entered land without force should be requested to leave first before there is any attempt to eject him. In the 'Advice for farmers and landowners', issued by the Ministry of Agriculture, Fisheries and Food (19 August 1986), guidance on the civil law is given to those faced with mass trespass on their land. The use of force is not advised.

7.3   CRIMINAL LAW

There is no comprehensive criminal law of trespass. But the Public Order Act 1986, s. 39, provides a new law of criminal trespass, entitled 'Power to direct trespassers to leave land'. This makes it an offence in certain specified circumstances to enter land as a trespasser and to fail to leave it after a request by the occupier and a direction by the police to do so. This means that the familiar notice 'Trespassers will be prosecuted' is not quite the empty threat it used to be. But it is still not a crime to walk across someone else's land without permission or to refuse to leave when told to do so.

7.3.1   Conspiracy to trespass

For a brief period it was a crime to conspire to trespass even though a trespass by one person in similar circumstances was not criminal (*Kamara* v *DPP* [1974] AC 104, in which students from Sierra Leone occupied their High Commission in London with the aid of an imitation firearm—they were also convicted of unlawful assembly). But the Criminal Law Act 1977, s. 1 (following the Law Commission's proposals: Working Paper No. 54), abolished the offence of conspiracy to trespass by limiting indictable conspiracies to agreements to pursue a course of conduct which, if carried out, would necessarily amount to or involve the commission of a criminal offence (and not a tort). This Act also abolished a number of obsolete offences of entering or remaining on property contrary to the Statutes of Forcible Entry 1381 to 1623 and the common law offences of forcible entry and detainer. The Law Commission, looking towards the protection of property rights and the preservation of public order (Working Paper No. 54, para. 33), proposed two new offences—of entering property by force adversely to any person in physical occupation or entitled to occupy it, and of being unlawfully on property and failing to leave as soon as reasonably practicable after being ordered to leave by a person entitled to occupation. The former became law (see the Criminal Law Act 1977, s. 6, see 7.3.7.1) but the latter, amounting to an offence of criminal trespass, was rejected at the time on the ground that it is undesirable to allow the criminal law to be employed where a civil remedy may be sufficient. It now resurfaces in an amended form in the new criminal trespass offence in the Public Order Act 1986, s. 39.

7.3.2   Power to direct trespassers to leave land

The Public Order Act 1986, s. 39, creates a new two-stage criminal trespass law, described in the marginal note as 'Power to direct trespassers to leave land'. The first stage of the section permits the police in certain specified circumstances to direct trespassers to leave land which they have entered as trespassers. The second stage provides that trespassers who fail to comply with the direction or who trespass again on the same land within three months commit a criminal offence punishable on summary conviction with up to three months' imprisonment.

7.3.3   The new two-stage criminal trespass law: stage one: the direction to leave

Under the Public Order Act 1986, s. 34(1), the 'senior police officer' may direct persons to leave land if he reasonably believes that all four of the following preconditions apply:

(a)   two or more persons have entered the land as trespassers, and
(b)   they are present with the common purpose of residing there for any period, and
(c)   reasonable steps have been taken by or on behalf of the occupier to ask them to leave, and
(d)   (i) any of them caused damage to property on the land, or
            (ii) any of them used threatening, abusive or insulting words or behaviour towards the occupier, his family or an employee or agent of his, or
            (iii) they have between them brought 12 or more vehicles on to the land.

7.3.3.1   Senior police officer   The 'senior police officer' who gives the direction to leave does not have to be high-ranking. The phrase means the most senior in rank of the police officers present at the scene (s. 39(5)). It could therefore be a police constable. The phrase is also used with the same meaning in the control of public processions and assemblies by the imposition of conditions (see Public Order Act 1986, ss. 12(2) and 14(2)).

7.3.3.2   The direction   There is no requirement for the direction to be in writing. It may therefore be given either in writing or orally. But in the absence of provision to the contrary the direction must be given directly to the person who is required to leave and not to a third party to be passed on. Presumably it will be a sufficient direction to shout over the fence, 'All of you must leave', at least where the persons on the land are obviously together in one place. It must also be presumed that a direction to adults must include a direction to children.

7.3.3.3 'Reasonably believes'   The most striking feature of s. 39(1) is that the preconditions for giving the direction need not in fact have taken place. The police officer need only reasonably believe that they have taken place. If, for example, the persons on the land are not trespassers because they have been given permission by the owner or occupier of the land to be there, they may nevertheless be directed to leave the land if the owner or occupier has wrongly told the police that they are trespassers. They will, however, have a specific defence (s. 39(4), see 7.3.5) if they refuse to go and are charged, but the burden will rest upon them to prove that their original entry on the land was not as trespassers.

If the police officer's belief is unreasonable, for example, if there is good reason to believe that the persons on the land are not trespassers or if they are ramblers and clearly not intending to stay, the direction will be invalid and any subsequent prosecution should fail. The direction to leave could also be challenged by way of judicial review (see 8.7).

7.3.3.4 The four preconditions   'Two or more persons have entered land as trespassers'.   Section 39 does not apply to entry on to land by one person alone, although if two or more persons enter as trespassers the direction to leave may be given by the police to 'those persons, or any of them' (s. 39(1)).

A trespasser is defined as meaning a person who is a trespasser as against the occupier of the land (s. 39(5)). There is further discussion of the meaning of trespass in 7.1.

Although under the civil law a person may commit trespass by mistake, for example, by going to the wrong house at night, the criminal law does not recognise the concept of innocent trespass. It is not an offence for the purposes of burglary under the Theft Act 1968, s. 9 (see 7.3.7.5) to 'enter as a trespasser' without knowing that fact, or at the very least being reckless as to that fact (*R* v *Collins* [1972] 2 All ER 1105; *R* v *Jones, R* v *Smith* [1976] 1 WLR 672). Nevertheless, under the Public Order Act 1986, s. 39(1), innocent trespass will not prevent the police giving a direction to leave. It is, however, at least arguable that where a criminal charge is brought the specific defence that the original entry was not as a trespasser (see below) will apply where the defendant can prove that he had no knowledge that he was a trespasser at the material time, and was not reckless as to that fact.

For the purposes of s. 39 'land' does not include buildings (for the offences of criminal trespass which relate to buildings and land adjacent to buildings, see the Criminal Law Act 1977 offences discussed in 7.3.7.1 to 7.3.7.4) other than agricultural buildings within the meaning of the General Rate Act 1967, s. 26(4) (including buildings forming part of a market garden and buildings used solely for agricultural operations), or scheduled monuments within the meaning of the Ancient Monuments and Archaeological Areas Act 1979 (Public Order Act 1986, s. 39(5)). Nor does 'land' include land forming part of a highway (Public Order Act 1986, s. 39(5)).

'Present with the common purpose of residing there for any period'. The words 'residing there' are not defined in the section. 'Reside' has different meanings depending on the context. In this context it connotes the idea of a home or a habitation, although s. 39(5) makes it clear that a person may be

regarded as having the purpose of residing in a place notwithstanding that he
has a home elsewhere. It need not necessarily be permanent or exclusive, but it
suggests something lasting. It 'denotes the place where an individual eats,
drinks and sleeps' (*R* v *North Curry (Inhabitants)* (1825) 4 B & C 953, 959).
'Residing' is certainly more than 'remaining', for example, for the purpose of
demonstrating by exhibiting placards or for a sit-in.

The length of 'any period' is not specified. These words appear to add little to
the section. Any person who has with others the common purpose of residing
on land will inevitably intend to remain on the land for a period of time.

This precondition applies only to those who have a common purpose of
residing. It does not apply to those who have no such common purpose, for
example, where one person sets up residence but the others intend to move on.

'Reasonable steps have been taken by or on behalf of the occupier to ask them
to leave'. The words 'reasonable steps' are not further defined. They must be
steps which viewed objectively are reasonable in all the circumstances. It would
not be enough to shout out from the window of a house if the trespassers were
half a mile away or they could not hear because of heavy rain. But, as with the
direction given by the police, the request does not have to be in writing or
expressed in any particular form of words, polite or otherwise.

The occupier is defined as the person entitled to possession of the land by
virtue of an estate or interest held by him (s. 39(5)).

Caused damage to property, used threatening, abusive or insulting words or
behaviour, or brought 12 or more vehicles on to the land   For the meaning of
'damage' in the context of the offence of criminal damage contrary to the
Criminal Damage Act 1971 see 3.3. The Public Order Act 1986, s. 39(5),
defines 'property' as meaning property within the meaning of the Criminal
Damage Act 1971, s. 10(1), namely, property of a tangible nature, whether real
or personal, including money, and (a) including wild creatures which have been
tamed or are ordinarily kept in captivity, and any other wild creatures or their
carcasses, but (b) not including mushrooms growing wild on any land or
flowers, fruit or foliage of a plant growing wild on any land. 'Mushrooms'
includes any fungus and 'plant' includes any shrub or tree.

For the meaning of 'threatening, abusive or insulting words or behaviour' see
the discussion of the offences contrary to ss. 4 and 5 of the Public Order Act
1986 in 2.5 and 2.6.

'Vehicle' is defined in the Public Order Act 1986, s. 39(5), as including a
caravan as defined in the Caravan Sites and Control of Development Act 1960,
s. 29(1), namely, any structure designed or adapted for human habitation
which is capable of being moved from one place to another (whether by being
towed, or by being transported on a motor vehicle or trailer) and any motor
vehicle so designed or adapted, but it does not include (a) any railway
rolling-stock which is for the time being on rails forming part of a railway
system, or (b) any tent. A structure 'involves the notion of something which is
put together . . . constructed so as to make one whole, which is then called a
structure' (*Hobday* v *Nicol* [1944] 1 All ER 302, 303).

7.3.4 Stage two: the criminal offence

A person is guilty of an offence of criminal trespass contrary to s. 39(2) of the Public Order Act 1986 if:

(a)   the senior police officer has given to that person a direction to leave the land, and
(b)   that person knows that the direction has been given and that it applies to him, and
(c)   he fails to leave the land as soon as reasonably practicable, or
(d)   having left the land he subsequently re-enters the land as a trespasser within three months.

The offence is triable summarily only, with a maximum penalty on conviction of three months' imprisonment and/or a fine not exceeding level 4 (for fine scale see 1.8).

Apart from the specific defences provided by the Public Order Act 1986, s. 39(4) (see 7.3.5), a person will not be guilty of the offence of criminal trespass if the senior police officer's belief was not reasonable in all the circumstances in relation to one or more of the four preconditions (this is a question of fact), or if he was unaware that a direction had been given or knew that a direction had been given but did not know that it applied to him, or that he intended to leave the land but it had not been reasonably practicable to do so (for example, if he was waiting for children to come back from shopping with their mother; see also specific defences, 7.3.5), or that when he re-entered the land within three months (the period runs from the day on which the direction to leave was given) he did not do so as a trespasser (for example, he had implied permission to go on the land or believed that he had permission—see the discussion of innocent trespass, 7.3.3.4). In each case the burden lies upon the prosecution to disprove beyond reasonable doubt any of the above matters.

7.3.5 Specific defences

The Public Order Act 1986, s. 39(4), provides two specific defences to a charge of criminal trespass. In both defences the burden rests on the defendant to prove the defence on a balance of probabilities. These two defences are in addition to the other defences set out above and defences of general application.

The two specific defences are:

(a)   It is a defence for the defendant to show that his original entry on the land was not as a trespasser (s. 39(4)(a)).

He will not be a trespasser if he had a right, whether express or implied, to be there. It is submitted that this defence also applies if in fact he was a trespasser but believed that he was not a trespasser. The Law Commission (Working Paper No. 54, para. 49) suggested that an offence of criminal trespass should have as one of its essentials the defence that the person 'genuinely believed that he was entitled to be on the property'. See also the discussion of innocent trespass, 7.3.3.4. The wording of this defence also suggests that no offence will be committed if the original entry was not a trespass but the person subsequently became a trespasser, for example, if the original permission to enter had been subsequently revoked. The doctrine of trespass *ab initio* would therefore not apply.

(b)   It is a defence for the defendant to show that he had a reasonable excuse for failing to leave the land as soon as reasonably practicable, or for again entering the land as a trespasser (s. 39(4)(b)).

The first part of this defence appears to be unnecessary. Under the offence in the Public Order Act 1986, s. 39(2)(a) the prosecution must prove beyond reasonable doubt that the defendant failed to leave the land as soon as reasonably practicable. Once the defendant raises, for example, the issue that it was not reasonably practicable to leave because he was waiting for a mechanic to repair his vehicle, the prosecution must negative the issue by proof beyond reasonable doubt (as with self-defence, see 2.2.4.4). Whether he has a reasonable excuse is therefore not a separate issue of which he is required to satisfy the court.

It might be a reasonable excuse for re-entry on to the land as a trespasser if the person had left something behind.

7.3.6   Power of arrest

The Public Order Act 1986, s. 39(3), provides a specific power of arrest without warrant for a constable who reasonably suspects that a person is committing an offence of criminal trespass under section 39. The constable must be in uniform. For further discussion of arrest powers see chapter 5.

7.3.7   Other criminal offences

There are, in addition to the new offence defined in the Public Order Act 1986, s. 39, a number of limited offences of criminal trespass in the Criminal Law Act 1977. They are intended principally to protect premises from squatters, although in the main they are cumbersome charges and the police prefer to use either the offences contrary to ss. 1 and 3 of the Criminal Damage Act 1971 of criminal damage (see 3.3) or the offences of possessing anything with the intent to damage property (see *R* v *Buckingham* (1975) 63 Cr App R 159, a jemmy in a haversack) or of being found on enclosed premises.

The additional offences of criminal trespass are described in the following paragraphs.

7.3.7.1   Violence for securing entry (Criminal Law Act 1977, s. 6)   It is an offence if any person without lawful authority or lawful excuse uses or threatens violence (against persons or property) for the purpose of securing entry into any premises (meaning a building or land ancillary to a building: s. 12(1)(a)) for himself or any other person, provided that the defendant knows that there is someone present on the premises who is opposed to the entry. The mere fact of having an interest in or right to possession or occupation of the premises does not constitute lawful authority, but it is a defence for the accused to prove (on a balance of probabilities) that he was acting as or on behalf of 'a displaced residential occupier' of the premises in question or part of them. This is an arrestable offence, triable summarily only, with a maximum penalty of six months' imprisonment and/or a fine not exceeding level 5.

7.3.7.2   Adverse occupation of residential premises (Criminal Law Act 1977, s. 7)
It is an offence if:

(a)   any person is on residential premises ('premises' means a building or land ancillary to a building, which includes the garden of a private house: s. 12(1)(a)) as a trespasser, and
(b)   a displaced residential occupier or 'a protected intending occupier' (defined as a person with a freehold or leasehold interest or an authority to occupy the premises, who requires the premises for his own occupation as a residence but who has been excluded from occupation by a trespasser, and who carries and produces a signed and witnessed notice to that effect) requires the trespasser to leave, and
(c)   the trespasser fails to leave.

It is a defence for the accused to prove (on a balance of probabilities) that he believed that the person requiring him to leave was not a person within (b), or that the premises were used mainly for non-residential purposes, or that the notice under (b) was either defective or not produced.
    This is an arrestable offence, triable summarily only, with a maximum penalty of six months' imprisonment and/or a fine not exceeding level 5.

7.3.7.3   Trespassing with a weapon of offence (Criminal Law Act 1977, s. 8)   It is an offence for any person on premises (meaning a building or land ancillary to a building: s. 12(1)(a)) as a trespasser to have with him without lawful authority or excuse a weapon of offence, namely, any article made or adapted for use for causing injury to or incapacitating a person, or intended by the person having it with him for such use. For a discussion of similar provisions relating to offensive weapons under the Prevention of Crime Act 1953 see 3.1. This is an arrestable offence, triable summarily only (unlike the offence contrary to the Prevention of Crime Act 1953) with a maximum penalty of three months' imprisonment and/or a fine not exceeding level 5.
    It is an offence contrary to the Firearms Act 1968, s. 20, to trespass with a firearm without reasonable excuse.

7.3.7.4   Trespassing on premises of foreign missions etc. (Criminal Law Act 1977, s. 9)   It is an offence to enter or be on the premises of a diplomatic mission, or consular premises, or any other premises entitled to similar inviolability, or the residence of diplomats or other similarly accredited persons, as a trespasser. This is an arrestable offence, triable summarily only, with a maximum penalty of six months' imprisonment and/or a fine not exceeding level 5. Proceedings may only be instituted by or with the consent of the Attorney-General.

7.3.7.5   Burglary (Theft Act 1968, s. 9)   It is an offence if a person:

(a)   enters any building as a trespasser and with intent to steal, commit damage, inflict grievous bodily harm or commit rape, or
(b)   having entered as a trespasser steals, or attempts to steal, or inflicts or attempts to inflict grievous bodily harm.

The offence is triable either way with a maximum penalty on indictment of 14 years' imprisonment.

Michael Fagan was acquitted by a jury of burglary, it having been alleged that he entered Buckingham Palace (including the Queen's bedroom) as a trespasser and stole, by drinking, some wine.

Special provisions are made in the Explosives Act 1875, s. 77, for trespassers on premises where explosives are made or stored.

7.3.7.6 Being found on enclosed premises (Vagrancy Act 1824, s. 4) It is an offence if a person is found in or upon any dwelling-house, warehouse, coach-house, stable or outhouse, or in any enclosed yard, garden or area, for any unlawful purpose.

This commonly used charge is a summary offence punishable on conviction with a maximum penalty of three months' imprisonment and/or a fine not exceeding level 3.

The unlawful purpose must be the commission of some offence which would subject the party to criminal proceedings (*Hayes* v *Stevenson* (1860) 25 JP 39), but the unlawful purpose need not be to commit a crime at the time or place where the defendant is found (*Re Joy* (1853) 22 LT Jo 80).

7.3.7.7 By-laws There are many by-laws which create criminal trespass offences. See, for example, the challenge by John Bugg to Ministry of Defence by-laws at Mildenhall in Suffolk (see 6.4.1).

7.3.8 Action by the police

The police are empowered to act against trespassers:

(a) to arrest without warrant a person reasonably suspected of committing the new criminal trespass offence (Public Order Act 1986, s. 39(3));

(b) to arrest anyone committing any of the new criminal offences in Part I of the Public Order Act 1986, namely, riot, violent disorder, affray, threatening behaviour etc. or disorderly conduct, although in the last two offences no offence will have been committed if the conduct complained of was done inside a dwelling and it only took effect inside the same or another dwelling (see chapter 2);

(c) to arrest for one of the offences under the Criminal Law Act 1977, ss. 6–9, see 7.3.7.1 to 7.3.7.4 and the offence of resisting or intentionally obstructing an officer of the court (s. 10, see 7.2.2.1)—the powers of arrest in the Criminal Law Act 1977 were preserved by the Police and Criminal Evidence Act 1984, sch. 2—or to arrest for burglary (see 7.3.7.5);

(d) to arrest for any other offence committed on the land or premises, for example, criminal damage or assault (including attempts or threats to commit damage or to assault);

(e) to detain or disperse under police preventive powers where a breach of the peace is being committed (for example, by trespassers resisting a farmer's attempts to remove them from his land), or where it is reasonably believed that a breach of the peace is imminent, or where a breach of the peace has been committed and it is reasonably believed that a renewal of it is threatened, and, if necessary, to take that person before the magistrates' court to be bound over (see 5.1).

7.4   THE 'PEACE CONVOY'

The movement of travellers towards Stonehenge at the time of the summer solstice has become an annual feature of West Country life. While politicians have described the members of the 'peace convoy' as 'medieval brigands'—'I want to make life as difficult as possible for them' (Mrs Thatcher, June 1986)—and senior police officers have developed strategies to 'neutralise this invasion', describing them as 'pollution', others have marvelled at the level of intolerance which has been shown to a small group of people who have adopted an alternative life-style and which is exemplified by police tactics such as dawn raids and mass blockades of the highway. Some observers have pointed out that the Nazis came for the gypsies before they came for the Jews. See generally *Stonehenge* (NCCL, July 1986) for a history of the conflict over the convoy and a discussion of the issues involved.

In any event a number of public order law issues have been raised.

7.4.1   The case of farmer Attwell and the law of trespass

In May 1986 approximately 300 'itinerant hippies' (see *The Times*, 31 May 1986) occupied land belonging to a Somerset farmer. At the end of a week the trespassers were evicted by sheriff's officers under the summary procedure for possession (see 7.2.2.1). Some MPs claimed that the case demonstrated a need for a law of criminal trespass, to make it a criminal offence to enter land (open land or buildings) as a trespasser or to remain on land as a trespasser after being required to leave (as the Law Commission recommended in 1974, see 7.3.1). The police, it was said, had been powerless to act.

But the delay in evicting the trespassers may not have been the fault of the law:

(a)   The summary procedure in the High Court (and to a lesser extent in county courts) is normally speedy and effective once put into motion, and possession orders can be obtained from the duty judge at weekends or out of court hours. In cases of urgency—and Mr Attwell's case was urgent because he claimed that damage was being caused to his property—the normal five-day period can be waived. It seems that Mr Attwell had two problems. First he lacked funds to bring proceedings. The financial limits may have prevented his obtaining legal aid (eventually the newspaper *Today* paid for his legal fees). Secondly there may have been some delay in the proceedings at his local court.

(b)   In any event the police were not powerless to act. If criminal offences had been committed, such as criminal damage, the police were entitled, in fact had a duty, to enter the land and arrest those responsible or at least attempt to find out who was responsible. If it was impossible to identify the culprits the police were entitled to use their preventive powers (see chapter 5) to prevent a breach of the peace, which was certainly imminent in view of the behaviour of local residents who were threatening to use shotguns. By this means the police could have moved the trespassers on and, if they had refused to comply with police instructions to move on, arrested them (if the general arrest conditions of the Police and Criminal Evidence Act 1984, s. 25, applied) for obstructing the police in the execution of their duty (see 5.12) or for any other criminal offence committed (for example, assault or threatening, abusive or insulting words or behaviour under the Public Order Act 1936, s. 5). Why the police did not act is uncertain. Some have suggested that they still had many cases outstanding from the year before. Proceedings against 119 people were discontinued at Salisbury Magistrates' Court because, said the prosecutor, the charges were 'so cold and old' (*The Guardian*, 2 December 1986). But it is more likely that the police were displaying their usual reluctance to become involved in anything to do with the civil law (a common complaint of those involved in domestic disputes, particularly of women in domestic violence cases).

7.4.2   Sites for the travellers

The provision of adequate sites for travellers to stay on has been at the heart of the peace convoy problem. It is clear that there has been a failure to provide adequate sites for travellers in general. The Department of the Environment has estimated that some 40% of travellers camp on illegal sites. One solution lies in the Caravan Sites Act 1968. The Act provides that it is the duty of every local authority (council of a county, metropolitan district or London borough) to provide sites with adequate accommodation for 'gypsies', defined in the Caravan Sites Act 1968 as persons of nomadic habit of life, whatever their race or origin. This would appear to include the members of the peace convoy. The only exceptions specified in the Caravan Sites Act 1968 are members of an organised group of travelling showmen or persons engaged in travelling circuses. But many local authorities, usually in response to local resentment, have failed to provide sites, even emergency sites, and have passed the problem back to the police. Some authorities have invoked planning laws to prevent sympathetic landowners from permitting travellers to stay on their land. If local authorities do avoid their responsibilities the Caravan Sites Act 1968 provides a procedure to force them by way of mandamus in the High Court to comply.

7.4.3   Freedom of movement

As chapters 8 and 9 show, there is no clearly defined right of assembly in law, only the right to pass and repass along the highway without let or hindrance. Restrictions have been placed on the travellers' freedom of movement in four particular ways. First, the police have used road-blocks to divert the convoy. The legality of this tactic has been questioned since the only justification could be to prevent a breach of the peace (see 5.1) and the somewhat bedraggled travellers have, in the main, been extremely peaceful. Questions of privacy have been raised by the gathering of information by police at these road-blocks, by asking for names and addresses, date and place of birth, occupation, colour of eyes, height and vehicle registration number. Secondly, a general order was made under the Town Police Clauses Act 1847, s. 21, by Salisbury District Council in June 1986 (see 5.11) banning 'hippies' from the city centre for two specified days to prevent a protest march taking place. Thirdly, wide-ranging bail conditions were imposed by Salisbury and Wiltshire magistrates on over 200 travellers requiring them to leave the county of

Wiltshire by midnight (*The Times*, 23 June 1986; see 5.10). Fourthly, Wiltshire Council made a road closure order in relation to a road leading to Stonehenge. The police had asked for the order primarily on the basis that closure would assist their operations, even though the Road Traffic Regulation Act 1984, s. 14, requires that there should be a likelihood of danger to the public or of serious damage to the highway before an order is made.

7.4.4   Confiscation of vehicles

Many vehicles have been confiscated by the police and put up for auction if not claimed (*The Guardian*, 25 June 1986). The authority for the confiscation seems to be uncertain. At first the police claimed that they were exercising powers under the Road Traffic Act 1972, although no power of confiscation (as, for example, in the case of items seized in drugs cases) exists under that Act.

The police are entitled to remove a vehicle from the highway if it is abandoned or an obstruction or is likely to cause injury or is illegally parked or where the driver has given a positive breath test and there is nobody who can demonstrate the right and the capacity to look after the car (*Stunt* v *Boston* [1972] RTR 435; *Liepins* v *Spearman* [1986] RTR 24). But the confiscation by the police of convoy vehicles may not easily come within any of these categories. At Southampton County Court a dozen travellers obtained an injunction restraining the Chief Constable of Hampshire from disposing of their vehicles. The vehicles had been kept in a police pound after the police had mounted an operation, at a cost of nearly £500,000, to evict the travellers from Stoney Cross in the New Forest (*Daily Telegraph*, 1 August 1986). See generally 6.6.

8

New Controls over Processions and Marches

This chapter explains the new police powers to control public processions, and in particular the requirement for advance notice of processions (Public Order Act 1986, s. 11), the new tests for imposing conditions on processions (s. 12), the power to ban processions (s. 13), new criminal offences for breaching the controls (ss. 11–13), and judicial review to challenge the controls. This chapter also considers the extent of the right of assembly and the meaning of procession and public place. Public assemblies are considered separately in chapter 9.

8.1 INTRODUCTION

Part II of the Public Order Act 1986 creates new police controls over public processions and assemblies (the controls over public assemblies are considered separately in chapter 9). In relation to processions the 1986 Act requires advance written notice of processions, imposes new conditions on processions, and provides for the banning of processions in limited circumstances.

8.1.1 Public Order Act 1936, s. 3

Previous controls were governed by the Public Order Act 1936, s. 3 (set out in appendix 2), which provided that where the Chief Officer of Police had reasonable ground for apprehending that a public procession might occasion *serious public disorder* he could either impose conditions on the procession (usually rerouting) or apply to the local authority for a banning order which the Home Secretary had to approve. In London the Metropolitan Police Commissioner or, where applicable, the City of London Police Commissioner could apply directly to the Home Secretary for a ban. In all cases bans were limited to three months in duration. Criminal sanctions were provided for organisers and participants who knowingly failed to comply with these provisions.

In practice the vast majority of processions and marches passed off peacefully (see White Paper, Cmnd 9510, para. 4.1), with full cooperation with the police including adequate advance notice. Much rerouting was ordered and complied with, often by agreement in advance, and usually where there was no threat or likelihood of public disorder, let alone serious public disorder. The police frequently acted without relying on particular statutory or common law provisions and, on the whole, some sort of balance was created between the interests of marchers and protesters on the one hand and the flow of traffic and pedestrians on the other. In other words life went on in the streets (particularly in London) on a fairly normal basis, with the bigger marches being held at weekends. Even Oxford Street in London has been used for big demonstrations, as well as Piccadilly and Trafalgar Square, without undue inconvenience.

Only rarely did trouble flare up during the course of a march and the police found they had ample powers to prevent a breach of the peace or to make arrests—for obstructing the highway, obstructing a police officer, for possession of offensive weapons, for threatening behaviour etc., or for assault or criminal damage. Some marches posed obvious problems in advance, such as National Front marches intending to pass through racially sensitive areas, and although the problem was not a new one it led to the growing use of the power to ban marches in recent decades (see 8.6).

8.1.2 The new powers

The Public Order Act 1986 extends considerably the previous controls over processions in the Public Order Act 1936. It provides for the first time a national requirement that organisers must give advance notice of processions (including all marches and moving demonstrations). It provides new tests for imposing controls by the police on processions. Under the 1936 Act the police could only impose conditions such as rerouting where they had reasonable grounds for apprehending serious public disorder. Under the new Act the police can impose conditions if either they anticipate serious public disorder or if they anticipate serious damage to property or serious disruption to the life of the community or if the purpose of the organisers is the intimidation of others. The 1986 Act also provides a new range of offences for organisers and participants of processions who breach the controls.

The government introduced the Public Order Act 1986 evincing a determination to uphold the right of peaceful protest without causing undue inconvenience to the rights of others (Cmnd 9510, para. 4.1). It remains to be seen whether the impact of the Act's provisions will maintain that balance for the future.

8.2 A RIGHT OF ASSEMBLY?

There is no statutory right of assembly either in the Public Order Act 1986 or elsewhere. Nor does the common law specifically recognise the right of assembly (or of free speech). But from time to time judges either as legal arbiters or as prominent figures (such as Lord Scarman in the Red Lion Square report, Cmnd 5919) have referred publicly to the existence of fundamental rights in general and to the rights of peaceful assembly and public protest in particular.

In his dissenting judgment in *Hubbard* v *Pitt* [1976] QB 142 Lord Denning MR said (at p.178):

The right to demonstrate and the right to protest on matters of public concern . . . are rights which it is in the public interest that individuals should possess; and, indeed, that they should exercise without impediment so long as no wrongful act is done.

Lord Denning repeated these sentiments in a later case concerned with the banning of processions, adding that the right to meet together, to go in procession, to demonstrate and to protest on matters of public concern was an undoubted right of Englishmen (*Kent* v *Metropolitan Police Commissioner, The Times*, 15 May 1981, see 8.7).

It should also be noted that although Part II of the Public Order Act 1986 (processions and assemblies) makes no provision for positive rights, the imposition of controls and conditions on processions and assemblies does acknowledge that there is, in general terms, a right to process and assemble. It can be said that the law expressly or by implication permits the acts if the specified conditions are fulfilled.

But if rights do exist under the common law they do so purely in the negative sense. Processions, marches and demonstrations are not lawful because the law recognises the right of assembly; they are lawful only when and if they infringe no other law. 'They are, so long as they are peaceful and orderly, not actionable, even though they may cause some inconvenience to others (Stuart-Smith J in *News Group Newspapers Ltd* v *Society of Graphical & Allied Trades 1982, The Times*, 1 August 1986, at p. 24 of the transcript). The common law only permits that which is not forbidden. And the positive value, if any, of any rights under the common law is substantially undermined by the prominence which the law gives to the right to pass and repass along the highway (*Harrison* v *Duke of Rutland* [1893] 1 QB 142; *Hickman* v *Maisey* [1900] 1 QB 752, and see chapter 6). The use of the highway for peaceful protest is not lawful because the right of peaceful protest is protected but because, negatively, there has been no obstruction of the highway in the particular case.

There is a further irony in this, namely, that every procession or demonstration on the highway is inevitably a temporary obstruction of the highway. Any demonstration, whether static or moving, which obstructs passage along the highway is prima facie unlawful (see chapter 6). Nevertheless the Court of Appeal has held that a procession is lawful unless it amounts to a public nuisance, quashing the conviction of the field secretary of the Campaign for Nuclear Disarmament on a charge of inciting persons to commit a public nuisance by obstructing the highway, it being alleged that he had told the crowd which route to follow (*R* v *Clark (No. 2)* [1964] 2 QB 315, see 6.2).

Certainly Lord Scarman has argued (*The Red Lion Square Disorders*, Cmnd 5919, para. 122) that a procession which allows room for others to go on their way is lawful. But he drew a distinction between the moving procession and the static assembly, suggesting that it was open to question whether a public meeting (or assembly) held on the highway could ever be lawful, for it would not in any way be incidental to the exercise of the right of passage. A similar view on the right of public meeting was expressed in the opening words of Lord Hewart CJ's judgment in *Duncan* v *Jones* [1936] 1 KB 218, 221, a case concerning the right to speak at a public meeting in a street:

> There have been moments during the argument in this case when it appeared to be suggested that the court had to do with a grave case involving what is called the right of public meeting. I say 'called', because English law does

not recognise any special right of public meeting for political or other purposes. The right of assembly, as Professor Dicey puts it, is nothing more than a view taken by the court of the individual liberty of the subject.

Nevertheless, picketing on the highway of private premises, despite causing a prima facie obstruction, is lawful if it is reasonable in all the circumstances (*Hirst and Another* v *Chief Constable of West Yorkshire, The Times,* 19 November 1986). Otton J said that the courts had long recognised the right of free speech and the right to peaceful protest on matters of public concern, subject to the need for peace and good order. And the control of open-air assemblies imposed for the first time by statute (Public Order Act 1986, s. 14) suggests that their legality is now not in doubt, subject to the fulfilment of the specified conditions. It should also be noted that the United Kingdom is a party to the European Convention on Human Rights 1950 (Cmd 8969) which provides in art. 11:

(1)   Everyone has the right to freedom of peaceful assembly and to freedom of association with others, including the right to form and to join trade unions for the protection of his interests.

(2)   No restrictions shall be placed on the exercise of these rights other than such as are prescribed by law and are necessary in a democratic society in the interests of national security or public safety, for the prevention of disorder or crime, for the protection of health or morals or for the protection of the rights and freedoms of others. This Article shall not prevent the imposition of lawful restrictions on the exercise of these rights by members of the armed forces, of the police or the administration of the State.

The Convention also provides (in art. 1) that: 'The High Contracting Parties shall secure to everyone within their jurisdiction the rights and freedoms defined in Section I of this Convention' (which includes art. 11). But the Convention, in the absence of implementing legislation, has no direct internal effect. Its only value is for the purpose of challenging decisions of the domestic courts at the European Commission of Human Rights, once domestic remedies have been exhausted. In *Christians against Racism & Fascism* v *United Kingdom* (1980) 21 DR 138 the Commission held that the right to freedom of peaceful assembly under art. 11(1) of the Convention is secured to everyone who has the intention of organising a peaceful demonstration. The possibility of violent counter-demonstrations could not take away that right (see 8.6.1.2). Other precedents for the right of assembly can be found in the Universal Declaration of Human Rights 1948 (Cmd 7662), the American Declaration of the Rights and Duties of Man 1948, and the International Covenant on Civil and Political Rights 1966.

8.3   MEANING OF 'PROCESSION' AND 'PUBLIC PLACE'

The police can only impose controls on a march or demonstration etc. under Part II of the Public Order Act 1986 if it is a *public procession.*

8.3.1 Procession

In the Public Order Act 1986 'public procession' means a procession in a public place (s. 16). This definition follows a definition in part of the Public Order Act 1936, s. 9, that is now repealed. Although 'public place' is defined (see 8.3.2), 'procession' is given no further definition.

In *Kent* v *Metropolitan Police Commissioner, The Times*, 15 May 1981 (see 8.7) the definition in the Public Order Act 1936, s. 9, of 'a procession in a public place' was considered to be 'very wide' and since the dictionary definition included 'a proceeding of body of persons . . . in orderly succession' the ban in question covered all kinds of procession: weddings, ceremonial processions and marches to Parliament. Any procession was likely to be covered by the definition. In *Flockhart* v *Robinson* [1950] 2 KB 498 it was said that the essence of a procession was a body of persons moving along a route. The definition of 'public place' is therefore important in understanding this Part of the Public Order Act 1986.

8.3.2 Public place

8.3.2.1 Public Order Act 1986, s. 16   'Public place' means any highway and any place to which the public or any section of the public has access, on payment or otherwise, as of right or by virtue of express or implied permission (Public Order Act 1986, s. 16).

The new definition of public place is wider than earlier definitions in that it includes all places of common resort and also all private property to which the public has access otherwise than as a trespasser. This includes obviously public places like the highway (including private roads), public transport, public houses and restaurants, parks and gardens, public footpaths, shops and public offices. It also includes places which can be attended on payment, such as clubs, dance-halls, and places of entertainment open to the public (or any section of it, e.g., adults) on payment of a fee. It includes places which the public can go to 'by virtue of . . . implied permission', such as some private land, for example, unfenced farm land or unfenced areas adjacent to the highway, or private land which is commonly walked on or played on without objection, or any land on which the public would in law be a visitor or licensee (see the Occupiers' Liability Act 1957) as opposed to a trespasser. The new definition in s. 16 of the Public Order Act 1986 would seem to overrule the decision in *R* v *Edwards and Roberts* (1978) 67 Cr App R 228 that lawful access to a private house through a garden did not make the garden a public place.

8.3.2.2 Public Order Act 1936, s. 9   The definition of 'public place' in the Public Order Act 1936, s. 9, as originally enacted, was

> 'Public place' means any highway, public park or garden, any sea beach, and any public bridge, road, lane, footway, square, court, alley or passage, whether a thoroughfare or not; and includes any open space to which, for the time being, the public have or are permitted to have access, whether on payment or otherwise.

This definition was amended by the Criminal Justice Act 1972, s. 33, to:

'Public place' includes any highway and any other premises or place to which at the material time the public have or are permitted to have access, whether on payment or otherwise.

This definition is not repealed by the Public Order Act 1986 but is retained for the purposes of the Public Order Act 1936, s. 1, which prohibits the wearing of uniforms in a public place for political purposes (see 3.6).

The inclusion of the highway and the expression 'access, whether on payment or otherwise', is common to other definitions—as in the carrying of offensive weapons in a public place (Prevention of Crime Act 1953, s. 1(4)), carrying firearms (Firearms Act 1968, s. 19), drunkenness in a public place (Criminal Justice Act 1967, s. 91) and in the retained definition of 'public meeting' in the Public Order Act 1936, s. 9 (the Public Meeting Act 1908 contains no definition).

8.3.2.3 Other definitions There are many references to 'public place' in legislation, and in construing the expression each statute must be considered by itself in the context of the particular statute and the evil it is designed to check (*Woods* v *Lindsay* 1910 SC(J) 88). The Street Offences Act 1959, s. 1, (soliciting for prostitution, see 6.9, above) penalises conduct 'in a street or public place' but does not define 'public place'. The Metropolitan Police Act 1839, s. 54 (offences in thoroughfares or public places, see chapter 6) contains no definition, but the Town Police Clauses Act 1847, s. 28 (commission of multifarious offences, from suffering to be at large any unmuzzled ferocious dog to throwing ashes, carrion, fish, offal or rubbish on any street) adopts for certain offences the definition of public place and street in the Public Health Acts Amendment Act 1907, s. 81, whereby any place of public resort or recreation ground and any unfenced ground adjoining or abutting upon any street shall be deemed to be an open and public place and a street. See also the Indecent Displays (Control) Act 1981, s. 1.

8.3.2.4 Cases 'A public place is one where the public go, no matter whether they have a right to go or not' (Grove J in *R* v *Wellard* (1884) 14 QBD 63). Whether a place is a public place is largely a matter of degree and fact (*R* v *Waters* (1963) 47 Cr App R 149). A field to which the public were admitted for one day was a public place (*R* v *Collinson* (1931) 23 Cr App R 49), as was the platform of a railway station (*Re Davis* (1857) 2 H & N 149), a railway carriage on its journey (*Langrish* v *Archer* (1882) 10 QBD 44), an omnibus on its journey (*R* v *Holmes* (1853) 3 Car & Kir 360), and a private house in which an auction sale is in progress is a 'place of public resort' (*Sewell* v *Taylor* (1859) 7 CB (NS) 160). However, buildings did not come within the definition of 'public place' in the Public Order Act 1936, s. 9(1), as originally enacted. A station platform was not within that definition because, although some parts were open to the air, it was an integral part of a station building (*Cooper* v *Shield* [1971] 2 QB 334, a threatening behaviour case).

An enclosure at the rear of an inn, entered through an open gateway, and in which cars were parked, was a public place (*Elkins* v *Cartlidge* [1947] 1 All ER 829), but a public house car-park bearing a notice that it was for the patrons of the inn only was no longer a public place one hour after closing time (*Sandy* v

Martin [1974] Crim LR 258). A shop car-park was not a public place when the shop was closed (*Marsh* v *Arscott* (1982) 75 Cr App R 211). In *Knox* v *Anderton* (1983) 76 Cr App R 156 the upper landing of a block of flats on a housing estate was held to be a public place—there were no barriers or doors to the stairways or landings to stop members of the public from entering. Tattersall's enclosure at a racecourse was a 'place of public resort' notwithstanding a charge for admission and a right to refuse entry (*Glynn* v *Simmonds* [1952] 2 All ER 47).

Where the public has access to one part of premises but not the other, for example behind the counter in a shop, the right approach to deciding whether it is a public place is to consider whether the premises is an entire unit (*Anderson* v *Miller* (1977) 64 Cr App R 178: under the counter, where a loaded revolver was kept, was a public place; see also *Cawley* v *Frost* [1976] 3 All ER 743, a football ground was a public place despite the fact that the public had been denied access to certain parts).

8.4   ADVANCE NOTICE OF PROCESSIONS

The Public Order Act 1986, s. 11, provides for the first time a national requirement to give advance written notice of most public processions. The requirement extends to processions but not to assemblies.

8.4.1   Background

Before the Public Order Act 1986 some 100 local Acts of Parliament required advance notice of processions, usually at least 24 or 36 hours before the event. But the vast majority of local authorities had not seen the need for a legal requirement to give notice—it was estimated that the police were in fact notified in at least 80% of the cases where no requirement existed (Lord Scarman on the Red Lion Square disorders, Cmnd 5919, para. 129). The authorities which possessed it had not used the criminal sanctions to enforce the provision. There is no report of any prosecution for failing to comply.

Lord Scarman originally thought that there was no need for an advance notice requirement: 'It does present really insuperable difficulty for the urgently called demonstration' (Cmnd 5919, para. 128). But in his later Brixton report he felt that subsequent events had shown that the need did exist (Cmnd 8427, para. 7.45). The government in its White Paper (Cmnd 9510, para. 4.2) relied on the conclusions in favour of a requirement set out in the Report of the House of Commons Select Committee on Home Affairs in 1980, in particular that a notice requirement might 'serve as a formal trigger for discussion between police and organisers designed to agree the ground rules for a march . . . and would underline for organisers their responsibilities for the safety and good behaviour of their supporters' (HC (1979–80) 756, vol. 1, para. 35).

8.4.2   The advance notice provision (Public Order Act 1986, s. 11)

8.4.2.1   Most, but not all, processions   Notice is required to be given for most, but not all, processions (s. 11(1)). The three categories of public procession for which notice is required are:

(a)   processions intended to demonstrate support for or opposition to the
views or actions of any person or body of persons,
(b)   processions intended to publicise a cause or campaign, and
(c)   processions intended to mark or commemorate an event.

These categories will cover most types of procession. They clearly include all
forms of political protest, whether against national, international or local
governments, whether criticising action, inaction or the expression of a
viewpoint. They cover (moving) rallies in support of political organisations and
single issue groups (like CND) or in support of more obscure campaigns and
causes. They cover marches to commemorate D-Day, the death of a person (cf.
funeral processions, 8.4.2.2) and other events. It is difficult to see what type of
procession is not covered by the three categories, other than school
'crocodiles', possibly Salvation Army processions (which were often
specifically exempted in local Acts), although it could certainly be argued that
they are publicising 'a cause or campaign', and Boy Scouts, Sea Scouts, Girl
Guides and other similar groups.

8.4.2.2   Exceptions   The above three categories do not apply to funeral
processions and processions commonly or customarily held, such as those held
annually (or more frequently) by Scouts or Guides (s. 11(2)).

Processions commonly or customarily held includes a wide range of public
processions of a national or local nature. The judges process annually to
Westminster Abbey. CND organises an annual protest demonstration in
London. Carnival processions take place in Notting Hill and, to celebrate the
Chinese New Year, in Soho. The Lord Mayor of London's show processes
through the City of London. Many local groups, church groups, Scouts etc.,
have annual local parades. The police will of course know of or be informed of
the vast majority of these processions.

8.4.2.3   Further   exception: 'not   reasonably   practicable'   There is no
requirement to give notice if 'it is not reasonably practicable' to do so (s. 11(1)).
The details of giving notice (see 8.4.2.5) allow for the late delivery of notice in
cases of spontaneous demonstrations. This exception in s. 11(1), however,
exempts organisers from giving any notice at all in circumstances when it is not
reasonably practicable to do so. These circumstances will be few. The
spontaneous demonstration usually takes some time to organise, so that notice
will be possible. This exception therefore seems to apply only to the procession
which takes place almost instantly, for example where a crowd has collected
and somebody says, 'Let's march to the Town Hall'. See *Flockhart* v *Robinson*
[1950] 2 KB 498.

8.4.2.4   The notice must be in writing (s. 11(1))   The notice must include (s.
11(3)):

(a)   the fact that a procession is to be held, and presumably the nature of the
proposed procession (although this is not specified in the Act),
(b)   the date, and the starting time,
(c)   the proposed route, and

(d)   the name and address of one of the organisers.

8.4.2.5   Delivery of the notice (s. 11(4)(b))   Delivery of the notice must be made:

(a)   to any police station in the police area in which it is proposed the procession will start, or, where it is proposed the procession will start in Scotland and cross into England, in the first police area in England on the proposed route (s. 11(4)),

(b)   either by hand or by recorded delivery post *at least six clear days* before the date of the procession (if sent by recorded post it must arrive at least six clear days before) (s. 11(5)(b)), or

(c)   if it is not reasonably practicable to deliver the notice at least six days before the procession, by hand (and not by post) as soon as is reasonably practicable (s. 11(6)). This allows for the spontaneous demonstration, one called at short notice in response to some event, for example to protest at US jets from English bases bombing Libya, or where parents of local children call for a pedestrian crossing after a child has been killed on a road near a school. It should, however, be noted that the spontaneous procession is not automatically exonerated from the effect of the criminal law. It will be up to the police, or ultimately the magistrates' court, to decide whether the failure to give notice in the particular case was 'not reasonably practicable'.

The seven-day period has been incorporated from Scots law (Civic Government (Scotland) Act 1982), but a noticeable difference in Scotland is that notice is given to the local authority and then passed on to the police.

8.4.3   Failure to comply: prosecution

It is a criminal offence to fail to comply with the advance notice requirements of the Public Order Act 1986, s. 11. The Public Order Act 1986 provides no immunities as a quid pro quo for the giving of notice on time. Other jurisdictions, for example, New South Wales, Australia (Public Assemblies Act 1979), have protected those who give notice and process peacefully from prosecution for obstruction of the highway or other public nuisance. This means that the consent of the police to the route etc. of the procession would protect the organiser and marchers from being prosecuted for unexceptional behaviour, thereby overruling previous court decisions as in *Arrowsmith* v *Jenkins* [1963] 2 QB 561 where a conviction for obstructing the highway was upheld despite the fact that the police had notice of the meeting, that there was no intention to obstruct the highway and that meetings had been held there before without complaint (see 6.5).

8.4.3.1   The offence (s. 11(7))   The *organiser(s)* (but not the participants) of a procession may be prosecuted, and on summary conviction in the magistrates' court fined up to a fine not exceeding level 3 on the standard scale (s. 11(10), if:

(a)   any of the notice requirements has not been satisfied, or

(b)   the date, starting time, or route of the procession differs from the details in the written notice.

The word 'organiser' is not defined and must therefore be given its ordinary meaning. Clearly there can be more than one organiser. Responsibility does not rest solely with the organiser named in the written notice, and in *Flockhart* v *Robinson* [1950] 2 KB 498 the person who indicated the route to be followed when a procession had formed spontaneously was held to be an organiser, as well as the person who planned the route. This decision might be considered to be too wide in the context of the 1986 Act (see 8.5.3).

It is a defence for the accused to prove on a balance of probabilities that:

(a)   he did not know of, and neither suspected nor had reason to suspect, that the notice requirements had not been satisfied or that the date etc. differed from the notice (s. 11(8)), or

(b)   the difference of date etc. arose from circumstances either beyond his control or from something done with the agreement or by the direction of a police officer (s. 11(9)).

8.5   POLICE CONTROLS OVER PUBLIC PROCESSIONS

Apart from the requirement to give the police advance written notice of a procession (Public Order Act 1986, s. 11, see 8.4.2), the Public Order Act 1986, Part II, creates a scheme of controls over public processions, involving the imposition of conditions on public processions (s. 12) or, in limited circumstances, the prohibition of public processions (s. 13).

8.5.1   Background

8.5.1.1   Public Order Act 1936, s. 3   The Public Order Act 1936, s. 3, was passed in the wake of fascist marches in the 1930s. It provided the police with the power to control public processions where the police had reasonable grounds for apprehending that the procession might occasion *serious public disorder*. This was the sole test for the imposition of such conditions 'as appear necessary', usually rerouting. The decision had to be taken by the chief officer of police (the chief constable or, in London, the Metropolitan Police Commissioner or the City of London Commissioner).

If the chief officer of police was of the opinion that his powers to impose conditions were insufficient to prevent serious public disorder he could apply for an order banning all or a class of processions for a period up to three months.

On the whole the police used these formal powers sparingly. The excessive use of coercion in the management of demonstrations is known to be counter-productive. The White Paper (Cmnd 9510) admitted (para. 4.19) that:

The police prefer to discuss the plans for a march with the organisers and to negotiate an informal agreement about the route and other matters. In general these arrangements work well: the Metropolitan Police have given only two examples of cases where they have imposed formal conditions in order to prevent serious public disorder in the last five years. [Both were examples of straightforward rerouting.]

Elsewhere, for example, in Leicester in 1974 and 1979, rerouting has usually been used to divert racist groups from marching through Asian communities.

8.5.1.2   Local powers   Other powers exist at a local level. In London the Police Commissioner can make regulations and give directions to keep order and prevent obstruction of the streets (Metropolitan Police Act 1839, s. 52). Outside London similar powers are granted to all district councils (see Town Police Clauses Act 1847, s. 21, Public Health Act 1875, s. 171, Local Government Act 1972, s. 180 and sch. 14, paras. 23 and 26(a)), and many local authorities pass by-laws controlling public meetings held in their area. See 5.11 and 6.4.

8.5.2   Imposing conditions (Public Order Act 1986, s. 12)

8.5.2.1   The new tests   The new tests for imposing conditions on a public procession (s. 12(1)) are:

(a)   it may result in *serious public disorder* (this re-enacts the test in the Public Order Act 1936, s. 3), or
(b)   it may result in *serious damage to property*, or
(c)   it may result in *serious disruption to the life of the community*, or
(d)   the purpose of the organiser(s) is *the intimidation of others* with a view to compelling them 'not to do an act they have a right to do, or to do an act they have a right not to do'.

Tests (a) and (b) are relatively clear. Test (c), however, serious disruption to the life of the community, is widely drawn and not without controversy. It is aimed at preventing marches from causing unreasonable disruption to local residents, other users of the highway, and adjoining shops and premises; to limit traffic congestion, to prevent a bridge from being blocked, to reduce the severe disruption sometimes suffered by pedestrians, business and commerce, or to keep Oxford Street or shopping centres or city centres free from demonstrators during business hours (Cmnd 9510, para. 4.22). This test more than any other extends the basis for imposing conditions beyond the concept of public disorder. Serious disruption may well be interpreted by the police as serious inconvenience. The balance between the freedom of assembly and the rights of pedestrians and motorists to use the highway unhindered by protestors may tilt in favour of the latter.

Test (d), the intimidation of others, is directed at those who organise processions with more malicious intent, whose overt purpose is to persuade people but whose covert purpose is to intimidate or coerce (Cmnd 9510, para. 4.23). The example given in the White Paper to illustrate this test was of a National Front counter-demonstration to a march by the Troops Out Movement in Manchester in 1984 with literature describing their purpose as being to 'stop this vermin . . . don't let them march'. This would appear to fall within the test as being intimidation of the Troops Out March with a view to compelling them not to do an act they have a right to do, namely to march through the streets of Manchester.

On the other hand the use of the words 'compelling them not to do an act they have a right to do' etc. might not cover a march by a racist group through an Asian community. There would be no obvious compulsion in relation to rights, except perhaps their right to be on the highway at the time that the march passes by. Such a march would be more likely to fall foul of the serious disruption to the community test. The words 'compelling' etc. are derived from the offence of intimidation contrary to the Conspiracy and Protection of Property Act 1875, s. 7, see 3.5, and this suggests the provision is directed particularly at the control of picketing (see 9.1.3).

8.5.2.2 Application of the tests The tests only have effect when *the senior police officer*, having regard to the time or place at which, and the circumstances in which, any public procession is being, or is intended to be, held and to its route, *reasonably believes* that any one or more of the tests is applicable to a particular public procession (s. 12(1)).
   The senior police officer is either:

(a)   the chief officer of police (the Metropolitan or City of London Police Commissioners, or outside London the Chief Constable) (s. 12(2)(b))—he may delegate to an assistant commissioner of police in London or a deputy or assistant chief constable outside London (s. 15)—or
(b)   the most senior in rank of the police officers at the scene (s. 12(2)(a)). The most senior ranking officer present might only be a police constable.

8.5.2.3 Conditions Once the senior police officer reasonably believes that one or more of the tests is applicable *he may give directions* imposing on the organisers or participants *such conditions as appear to him necessary* to prevent disorder, damage, disruption or intimidation (s. 12(1)).
   This section specifically provides for conditions controlling the route of the procession or prohibiting the procession from entering any particular public place (for the definition of 'public place', see 8.3.2). But it clearly also includes greater powers than simple rerouting. It is possible that conditions could be imposed restricting the number of people on the procession and its duration, as well as its route.
   But s. 12 does not permit the police to ban a procession (for bans, see 8.6) nor to disband a procession under way, although the police have other common law powers to prevent or curb a breach of the peace which would allow them to break up a procession in circumstances of violence or threatened violence (see chapter 5).
   The power to impose conditions can be exercised in advance or on the spot. If exercised in advance by the chief officer, the directions imposing the conditions must be given in writing (s. 12(3)), presumably to the organiser(s), although the Act is silent on this point despite the fact that the directions impose liabilities on participants as well as organisers (see 8.5.3). The condition need not be given in writing when it is imposed by the senior police officer on the spot.

8.5.3   Failure to comply with conditions: prosecution

The Public Order Act 1986 creates three summary offences of failing to comply with police conditions imposed on a public procession:

(a)   It is an offence if an *organiser* organises a procession and knowingly
fails to comply with a condition (s. 12(4)). The maximum penalty on summary
conviction is three months' imprisonment and/or a fine not exceeding level 4 (s.
12(8)).

In *Flockhart* v *Robinson* [1950] 2 KB 498 it was held that a person who
directed a spontaneous procession along its route or planned the route was the
person who organised it. This decision may be limited to its particular
facts—see the dissenting judgment of Finnemore J who found that the fact that
the organiser was the leader of the procession was not enough to constitute him
its organiser.

(b)   It is an offence if a *participant* takes part in a procession and knowingly
fails to comply with a condition (s. 12(5)). The maximum penalty on summary
conviction is a fine not exceeding level 3 (s. 12(9)).

It is a defence to charges (a) and (b) to prove that the failure to comply with
the condition arose from circumstances beyond the defendant's control (s.
12(4) and (5)).

(c)   It is an offence to *incite* somebody else knowingly to participate in a
procession in breach of a condition (s. 12(6)). The maximum penalty on
summary conviction is three months' imprisonment and/or a fine not exceeding
level 4 (s. 12(10)).

Power of arrest.   A constable in uniform may arrest without warrant anyone
he reasonably suspects is committing any of these three offences (s. 12(7)). For
general powers of arrest, see chapter 5.

8.6   PROHIBITING PUBLIC PROCESSIONS: BANS

The Public Order Act 1986, s. 13, makes limited provision for the banning of all
public processions or a class of public procession for a period not exceeding
three months.

8.6.1   Background

8.6.1.1   Public Order Act 1936, s. 3   The Public Order Act 1936 empowered
the chief officer of police to apply to the local authority for an order, to which
the Home Secretary had to consent, prohibiting the holding of public
processions for up to three months. Before requesting an order the chief officer
of police had to be satisfied that his power to impose conditions under the
Public Order Act 1936, s. 3(1), was not sufficient to enable him to prevent
serious public disorder. The banning order could not apply to a single
procession. It applied to all processions or any class of procession in the
relevant police area. In London the Metropolitan Police Commissioner or the
City of London Police Commissioner could apply directly to the Home
Secretary for a banning order. Non-compliance with an order was a criminal
offence.

8.6.1.2   Increasing use of banning orders   The government Green Paper
(Cmnd 7891) saw the order to prohibit processions as the ultimate preventive
measure, and expressed no desire to see bans being imposed more frequently
(para. 5.9). But despite injunctions by Home Secretaries to chief constables to

keep bans to the minimum because they were 'a serious curtailment of liberties' (Home Office Circular No. 55/1981), the power to ban processions has been used with increasing frequency in recent years. There were 11 banning orders in the period 1970 to 1980 and 75 in the period 1981 to 1984 (White Paper, Cmnd 9510, para. 4.7).

Blanket bans.   The effect of blanket bans has often been to prohibit public processions which would have been perfectly peaceful and orderly. In practice the Home Secretary has approved blanket bans which were sometimes designed to cover only one march. For example a 17-day ban in July 1981 of all public processions in Grimsby, Hull, Cleethorpes and Scunthorpe was imposed in order to stop a proposed National Front march in Grimsby. The standard formula is to ban 'all public processions other than those of a traditional or ceremonial character.' A May Day march organised by the Trades Council in Leeds was not considered to be of a ceremonial nature (*Daily Telegraph*, 22 September 1978: the secretary was fined £40 for organising an illegal march).

Class bans.   Class bans (they can be defined by exclusion of a generality of classes: per Sir Denys Buckley in *Kent* v *Metropolitan Police Commissioner, The Times*, 15 May 1981) are rarer. One example was the one-month ban in Birmingham, Coventry and Solihull in 1974 of any procession in connection with the death of James McDade, a member of the IRA.

Single processions.   The government, recognising that 'the innocent suffer with the guilty', did propose that the law should be amended to allow a single march to be banned (Cmnd 9510, para. 4.14), but this proposal did not appear in the Public Order Bill and does not appear in the Public Order Act 1986. In *Christians against Racism & Fascism* v *United Kingdom* (1980) 21 DR 138 the European Commission of Human Rights declared inadmissible an organisation's claim that a two-month ban on all public processions other than those of a religious, educational, festive or ceremonial character customarily held within the metropolitan police district was in breach of art. 11(1) of the Convention (see 8.2). The Commission held that, although the ban was designed to prevent one National Front march in the London Borough of Ilford, on the facts it was not unreasonable to prohibit all public processions other than customary ones.

8.6.2   Power to ban processions (Public Order Act 1986, s. 13)

8.6.2.1   The test   Where the chief officer of police reasonably believes that his powers to impose conditions under the Public Order Act 1986, s. 12, are insufficient to prevent the holding of public processions from resulting in *serious public disorder*, he is required (there is no discretion) to put into motion the procedure for applying for a banning order (s. 13(1) and (4)). The test for prohibiting public processions therefore remains the same as under the Public Order Act 1936, namely, the reasonable apprehension of serious public disorder (s. 13(1)). The Public Order Act 1986 has not added to this sole test (cf. conditions on processions and assemblies).

The chief officer is the chief constable outside London and the Metropolitan Police Commissioner and the City of London Police Commissioner in London.

The chief officer may delegate this function to a deputy or assistant chief constable outside London, or to an assistant commissioner of police in London (s. 15).

8.6.2.2   *Procedure outside London*

(a)   The chief constable applies to the council of the district in which the procession is to be held, specifying in the application the district (or part) concerned, the length of the ban required (up to three months), and whether the ban should extend to all processions or a class of procession (there is no power to request or make a ban of one particular procession) (s. 13(1)).

(b)   The council may (it does have a discretion), after obtaining the Home Secretary's consent, make an order. The order may be made in the terms of the application or it can be modified with the Home Secretary's consent (s. 13(2)).

Local authorities have no power of their own to seek a ban with or without the consent of the Home Secretary. The initiative must come from the police. Local authorities have, however, been known to refuse police requests, although the Home Secretary has not been known to refuse his consent once the local authority has agreed to an order.

8.6.2.3   *Procedure in London*   The Metropolitan Police Commissioner or, where applicable, the City of London Police Commissioner makes the order himself after obtaining the consent of the Home Secretary (s. 13(4)) and in the same terms as orders made prohibiting processions outside London (see 8.6.2.2). In London the Home Secretary is the local police authority. There is no separate body with responsibility for policing in London (nor did the GLC have such responsibility before it was abolished). Therefore local authorities in London have no part in the formal process of making banning orders, although they may seek to persuade the Commissioner in a particular case.

8.6.2.4   *Variation or revocation of an order*   An existing order may be varied or revoked during its currency by using the same procedure as for making the order (s. 13(5)). It is unclear whether the order can be relaxed for one particular procession if the full procedure is complied with (see *Kent* v *Metropolitan Police Commissioner, The Times*, 15 May 1981). The Act makes no reference to the renewal of orders, but there is nothing to prevent the making of a fresh order in the same or modified terms on the expiry of the existing order.

8.6.3   Challenge to an order

There is no procedure laid down in the Public Order Act 1986 (nor was there a procedure in the Public Order Act 1936) for appealing against the merits of a decision to make an order banning processions. The only form of challenge is by way of judicial review (see 8.7).

8.6.4   Failure to comply with a ban: prosecution

The 1986 Act creates *three summary offences* of failing to comply with an order prohibiting public processions:

(a) It is an offence knowingly *to organise* a banned procession (s. 13(7)). The maximum penalty on summary conviction is three months' imprisonment and/or a fine not exceeding level 4 (s. 13(11)).

(b) It is an offence *to take part* in a banned procession knowing that it is banned (s. 13(8)). The maximum penalty on summary conviction is a fine not exceeding level 3 (s. 13(12)).

(c) It is an offence *to incite* somebody else knowingly to take part in a banned procession (s. 13(9)). The maximum penalty on summary conviction is three months' imprisonment and/or a fine not exceeding level 4 (s. 13(13)).

Power of arrest. A constable in uniform may arrest without warrant anyone he reasonably suspects is committing any of these three offences (s. 13(10)). For general powers of arrest, see chapter 5.

8.6.5 The order

Orders made under the Public Order Act 1936 were made in the following form, and will presumably be made under the Public Order Act 1986 in a similar form (s. 13(6) provides that the order, if not made in writing, shall be recorded in writing as soon as practicable after being made):

WHEREAS I,——, Commissioner of Police of the Metropolis, am of the opinion that, by reason of particular circumstances existing in my police area, the powers conferred on me by subsection (1) of section 3 of the Public Order Act 1936, will not be sufficient to enable me to prevent serious public disorder being occasioned by the holding of public processions in the Metropolitan Police District,

Now I,——, Commissioner of Police of the Metropolis, with the consent of the Secretary of State, in pursuance of the powers conferred on me by subsection (3) of the said Act hereby by this order prohibit for the period of two months from 6 a.m. on Friday, 23 February 198–, the holding of the following class of public processions, that is to say, all public processions other than those of a religious, educational, festive or ceremonial character customarily held within the Metropolitan District.

signed
Commissioner of Police of the Metropolis

dated
New Scotland Yard, London SW1H 0BG

I hereby certify that the above order has been made by the Commissioner of Police with my consent.

signed
Secretary of State for the Home Department

8.7   JUDICIAL REVIEW

There is no statutory or other right of appeal against the imposition of conditions or a ban made under the Public Order Act 1986 (although the right of appeal has often been proposed, see, e.g., *Brownlie's Law of Public Order and National Security*, 2nd ed., p. 58, and Thornton, *We Protest*, p. 52).

In limited circumstances, however, judicial review will lie to quash the order of the chief officer of police. Judicial review is available because of the use of the words 'reasonably believes' as a prerequisite to the operation of the procedure to impose conditions or a ban. The chief officer, or a deputy or assistant chief constable to whom the chief officer has delegated his powers under ss. 12 to 14 (s. 15), or a senior officer (s. 12, see 8.5.2.2), must act *reasonably* in exercising his powers under Part II of the Act. The test of reasonableness of his decision, although a question of fact, is always treated as a question of law and therefore may be challenged by way of judicial review (*G v Chief Superintendent of Police, Stroud, The Times*, 29 November 1986). This also applies to the controls over assemblies (see chapter 9).

8.7.1   Limited scope of judicial review

Judicial review does not provide a right of appeal in the sense that a judge considers afresh the merits of the original decision (for a discussion of this topic, see Green Paper, Cmnd 7891, para. 55 et seq.). Judicial review is a challenge to the decision on the basis that it is unlawful either:

(a)   because the decision was improperly reached, for example, the procedure was not complied with or improper considerations were taken into account, or

(b)   because the decision was so unreasonable or capricious or arbitrary that no reasonable chief officer could have come to that conclusion (see *Associated Provincial Picture Houses Ltd* v *Wednesbury Corporation* [1948] 1 KB 223).

This means that if the correct procedure is complied with the courts will show extreme reluctance to interfere with decisions.

8.7.2   Operation of judicial review in public order cases

In *Kent* v *Metropolitan Police Commissioner, The Times*, 15 May 1981, the Campaign for Nuclear Disarmament tried unsuccessfully to challenge a 28-day ban on all public processions within the Metropolitan Police District (from Radlett to Croydon and from Kenley to Heathrow). Despite accepting that CND marches were commonly and peacefully held and that the court was dealing with one of the fundamental freedoms—the right to demonstrate and to protest on matters of public concern—the Court of Appeal declined to hold that the ban was wrong or unlawful in any way. Sir Denys Buckley said that the Commissioner's reasons for his order seemed meagre, but nevertheless the court could not say that the Commissioner was at fault in making the order, especially when the Home Secretary had agreed with it.

A similar reluctance was shown when the London Borough of Lewisham tried to obtain an order of mandamus against the Commissioner to ban a National Front march (*The Times*, 12 August 1977). Slynn J said:

> No doubt I have power to grant mandamus. Circumstances could arise in which I could make an order. For example if the Commissioner failed to take into account all relevant matters or if the Commissioner was of the opinion that his powers to prevent serious public disorder under subsection (1) [of the Public Order Act 1936, s. 3, imposition of conditions], . . . and other powers, were not sufficient to prevent public disorder, but nevertheless failed to take action. Or if the Commissioner took a view of the circumstances which was wholly untenable, I consider that the court could intervene. (Quoted in *Brownlie's Law of Public Order and National Security*, 2nd ed., p. 52.)

Nevertheless the court did not intervene.

Despite the injunction in the Green Paper (Cmnd 7891, para. 57) that the courts should not be involved in the examination of the merits of decisions because they are not best placed to take decisions about major public order matters in such a potentially controversial area, it is to be hoped that the courts will take a more active role in the control of banning orders in particular and in restricting them from being too widely drawn and, to use the wording of the White Paper (Cmnd 9510, para. 4.25), 'to ensure that demonstrators have an effective means of challenging any decision by the police to impose conditions which is not justified by a real risk of serious disorder, disruption or coercion'.

8.7.3 Applying for judicial review

The judicial review procedure is governed by Ord. 53 of the Rules of the Supreme Court under the statutory backing of the Supreme Court Act 1981, s. 31. Application for leave to apply for judicial review must be made to the Divisional Court of the High Court on Form 86A and supported by an affidavit. The application must be made promptly and in any event within three months from the date when the grounds for the application first arose.

The application may be for an order of mandamus, prohibition or certiorari, and for an injunction, a declaration or damages. Leave may be granted by a single judge on consideration of the papers alone. If he refuses leave a further application may be made to a judge in open court. If leave is granted the case goes forward to a full hearing. For further details see *The Supreme Court Practice* and *De Smith's Judicial Review of Administrative Action*, 4th ed.

9

New Controls over Public Assemblies

This chapter explains the new police powers to control public assemblies. The Public Order Act 1986, s. 14, provides for the first time a statutory control over public assemblies, that is, assemblies of 20 or more persons in the open air. The controls include the imposition of conditions on assemblies but not the power to ban them.

9.1 INTRODUCTION

9.1.1 Summary of new controls

Part II of the Public Order Act 1986 creates new police controls over public processions and assemblies (the controls over processions and marches are considered separately in chapter 8). In relation to assemblies the Public Order Act 1986 provides the police with a brand-new power to impose conditions on those organising or taking part in an assembly (s. 14). The conditions may prescribe the place and the duration of the assembly and the maximum numbers who may take part. There is no advance notice requirement (cf. processions, chapter 8) nor is there a power to prohibit a public assembly (cf. processions, chapter 8).

9.1.2 No previous statutory restrictions

There were no previous statutory restrictions on the holding of assemblies in public. The Public Order Act 1936 only imposed restrictions on processions. The static demonstration or open-air assembly or meeting fell outside the Act. It has been estimated that three quarters of the demonstrations held in London fall into the category of static demonstrations: meetings, counter-demonstrations outside meetings, demonstrations outside embassies, lobbies of Parliament, pickets and demonstrations in support of pickets (White Paper, Cmnd 9510, para. 5.1).

9.1.3 Picketing—the target

The Home Affairs Committee (HC (1979–80) 756, vol. 1, para. 72) had earlier recommended that statutory controls should be extended to static demonstrations on the highway. This—and subsequent government proposals—was particularly directed at the control of pickets and demonstrations in support of pickets. The White Paper refers to picketing at Warrington and 'of course the mass pickets during the miners' dispute' (Cmnd 9510, para. 5.1). Picketing is already heavily controlled by the law (see 6.8) but the pre-1986 Act controls operate at the time of the picket, for example, to prevent a breach of the peace or to control numbers, whereas the 1986 Act controls can operate both before and during the picket.

The government has stated that the right of peaceful picketing will not in any way be infringed and that it is not intended that the power should be used to undermine the right of pickets in reasonable numbers to stand by the entrance to a workplace (Cmnd 9510, para. 5.14). Nevertheless the 1986 Act controls could have a radical effect on the nature and extent of picketing without actually banning it altogether. In particular the directions as to place, duration and numbers will extend existing police powers considerably and legitimise police practices over picketing which have enjoyed uncertain legality hitherto.

9.1.4 Embassies

The government also considered (Cmnd 9510, para. 5.12) whether, following the shooting of a woman police constable outside the Libyan People's Bureau in April 1984, demonstrations outside embassies, particularly by foreign nationals, should be subject to special controls. But it concluded that it would be neither practicable nor desirable to make any changes to public order law in this respect: the police's existing statutory and common law powers, coupled with the new 1986 Act powers, were quite adequate.

9.2 A RIGHT OF ASSEMBLY?

There is no statutory right of assembly either in the Public Order Act 1986 or elsewhere. Nor does the common law specifically recognise the right of assembly (or free speech). Nevertheless, the existence of the right of public assembly has been recognised by judicial decision, extra-judicial opinion, and art. 11 of the European Convention on Human Rights. Furthermore, the creation for the first time of statutory controls on public assemblies suggests that their legality is not in doubt, subject to the fulfilment of the specified consideration.

For a full discussion of these considerations, see 8.2.

9.3 MEANING OF 'PUBLIC ASSEMBLY'

The Public Order Act 1986, s. 16, defines 'public assembly' as meaning an assembly of 20 or more persons in a public place which is wholly or partly open to the air.

'Public place' means any highway and any place to which the public or any section of the public has access, on payment or otherwise, as of right or by virtue of express or implied permission (s. 16). For a full discussion of this definition of 'public place' see 8.3.

This Part of the Public Order Act 1986 only governs, therefore:

(a)   the assembly which is held in public—private assemblies held indoors or outdoors such as private meetings (see chapter 10) cannot be controlled by these provisions, and

(b)   the assembly which is held out of doors or which at least is partly open to the air. This presumably includes a marquee with its sides up but not down, but presumably does not include an indoor hall which has its doors left open on a warm summer's day.

'Assembly' is not further defined. Nor is there a common law definition of 'assembly' (see, however, unlawful assembly, 2.3). The government intended that an 'assembly' would cover the whole range of public gatherings, from political rallies to religious services and from pop festivals to football matches. In *DPP* v *Roffey* [1959] Crim LR 283, in the context of the criminal offence of flying too near an assembly, it was said that an assembly means no more than a gathering of persons, and one which could be stationary or in motion. *Brownlie's Law of Public Order and National Security*, 2nd ed., p. 31, suggests that it includes any coming together of persons, including processions, political vigils, prayer meetings, demonstrations, a group at a cenotaph ceremony, families watching the changing of the guard, flag sellers acting in concert, sandwich-men walking in a line, and a cycling club *en route*.

How close the 20 or more persons have to be in order to make an assembly will be a question of fact which will no doubt call for judicial interpretation. The 1986 Act does not use the word 'together' in this context. It is, however, unlikely that six pickets at each of four factory entrances, and therefore exceeding the statutory minimum, will be classified as an assembly. This would give an unnecessarily wide meaning to 'public assembly'.

9.4   NO ADVANCE NOTICE REQUIREMENT

Unlike the law relating to processions (Public Order Act 1986, s. 11, see 8.4), there is no legal requirement to give advance notice, either to the police or to the local authority, of the holding of a public assembly.

Although the Home Affairs Committee (HC (1979–80) 756, vol. 1, para. 72) recommended that organisers should be required to give 72 hours' advance notice, the government felt (Cmnd 9510, para. 5.4) that an advance notice requirement would produce much unnecessary work for the police to little purpose, in that it would inundate the police with notifications of perfectly peaceful meetings.

9.5   POLICE CONTROLS OVER PUBLIC ASSEMBLIES

The Public Order Act 1986, s. 14, creates a scheme of controls over public assemblies, whereby the police, either at the time or in advance, may impose limiting conditions on the assembly, provided that certain tests are satisfied.

9.5.1   Imposing conditions (Public Order Act 1986, s. 14)

9.5.1.1   The tests   The tests for imposing conditions on a public assembly (s. 14(1)) are:

   (a)   it may result in *serious public disorder*, or
   (b)   it may result in *serious damage to property*, or
   (c)   it may result in *serious disruption to the life of the community*, or

(d)   the purpose of the organiser(s) is *the intimidation of others* with a view to compelling them 'not to do an act they have a right to do, or to do an act they have a right not to do'.

These tests are the same as the tests for imposing conditions on processions (Public Order Act 1986, s. 12(1), and see the discussion of these tests at 8.5.2).

9.5.1.2   Picketing etc.   The use of language in test (d), the intimidation of others etc., suggests that this test is directed primarily at picketing and demonstrations in support of picketing. This is confirmed by the White Paper (Cmnd 9510, para. 5.10) which gives picketing as 'the obvious example' and suggests that this test should apply either to picketing which obstructs the free passage of the highway or to other forms of picketing which are not obstructive but can nevertheless be intimidatory especially outside someone's home.

The use of the words 'right to do' and 'right not to do' are adapted from the offence of intimidation contrary to s. 7 of the Conspiracy and Protection of Property Act 1875 (see 3.5). The 'rights' in question are intended to refer to the right to go to work and the right to refuse to come out on strike. Whether they are rights in the sense of statutory or common law rights or even fundamental freedoms is dubious. The so-called right to go to work is in effect only the right to pass and repass along the highway (see chapter 6) to a place of work and the so-called right not to strike often conflicts with the collective decision-making process at places of work and creates contractual difficulties.

Intimidation for the purposes of the Conspiracy and Protection of Property Act 1875, s. 7, includes putting a person in fear by the exhibition of force or violence, and there is no limitation restricting the meaning of 'intimidation' to cases of violence or threats of violence to the person (*R* v *Jones* (1974) 59 Cr App R 120). It also includes threats of breaches of contract (*Rookes* v *Barnard* [1964] AC 1129). Intimidate is not a term of art; it must be given 'a reasonable and sensible interpretation' (*Gibson* v *Lawson* [1891] 2 QB 545). In *News Group Newspapers Ltd* v *Society of Graphical & Allied Trades 1982, The Times,* 1 August 1986, it was held that 'abuse, swearing and shouting' did not amount to a threat of violence for the purposes of intimidation (p. 28 of the transcript). See also *Thomas* v *National Union of Mineworkers (South Wales Area)* [1985] 2 WLR 1081.

9.5.1.3   Application of the tests   The tests only have effect when *the senior police officer*, having regard to the time or place at which and the circumstances in which any public assembly is being held or is intended to be held, *reasonably believes* that any one or more of the tests is applicable to a particular public assembly (Public Order Act 1986, s. 14(1)).

The senior police officer is either:

(a)   the chief officer of police (the Metropolitan or City of London Police Commissioners, or outside London the chief constable) (s. 14(2)(b))—the chief officer of police may delegate any of his functions under s. 14 to a deputy or assistant chief constable (outside London) or to an assistant commissioner of police (in London) (s. 15)—or

(b)   the most senior in rank of the police officers at the scene of an assembly

(s. 14(2)(a)). The most senior ranking officer present might only be a police constable.

9.5.1.4   The conditions   Once the senior police officer reasonably believes that one or more of the tests is applicable *he may give directions* (s. 14(1)). The directions may impose on the organisers or participants such conditions as to the *place, maximum duration* or *maximum numbers* of the assembly as appear to the senior police officer necessary to prevent disorder, damage, disruption or intimidation (s. 14(1)).

This contrasts with the directions which may be given in relation to processions imposing *any conditions* (s. 12(1), and see 8.5.2).

Section 14 does not permit the police to ban an assembly, nor to control its starting time, and within the wide discretion granted to the police the senior police officer making the decision and imposing the conditions must act reasonably otherwise his decision will be open to challenge in the courts (see 9.7).

Conditions restricting the *place* of an assembly may mean that a picket of factory premises is restricted to one particular entrance or that a protest against inadequate child-care facilities intended to be held outside the town hall could be rescheduled by the police on the grounds of serious disruption to the life of the community (traffic and shoppers) to a quieter spot or 'a less sensitive area' (Cmnd 9510, para. 5.7), perhaps a side entrance or even a local park. Restrictions on *duration* and *numbers* might mean that the town hall protest could go ahead but in a limited form, say with only 20 people for half an hour, giving time for the protest to be made and a petition to be handed in.

Restrictions on *numbers* could have a substantial impact upon mass picketing or mass demonstrations in support of picketing, as seen in recent years in the Warrington print dispute, in the miners' strike and outside the News International plant at Wapping. What will happen in practice remains to be seen. Presumably the imposition of conditions by way of numbers cannot reduce an assembly to under 20 because the group is thereafter no longer an assembly. Whether the police will in fact impose widespread conditions on assemblies and, if they do, whether they will make widespread arrests of those who breach the conditions (see 9.5.2) is at present speculation. Certainly the police have on the whole called for wider powers to control processions and assemblies and have welcomed the implementation of the Public Order Act 1986 powers. But the decision in *News Group Newspapers Ltd* v *Society of Graphical & Allied Trades 1982, The Times*, 1 August 1986, which suggests that mass demonstrations in support of pickets are not in themselves unlawful, may restrain the police from imposing conditions too readily upon this form of public assembly.

9.5.2   Failure to comply with conditions: prosecution

The Public Order Act 1986 creates three summary offences of failing to comply with police conditions on assemblies:

(a)   It is an offence if an organiser organises an assembly and knowingly fails to comply with a condition (s. 14(4)). The maximum penalty on summary conviction is three months' imprisonment and/or a fine not exceeding level 4 (s. 14(8)).

(b) It is an offence if a participant takes part in an assembly and knowingly fails to comply with a condition (s. 14(5)). The maximum penalty on summary conviction is a fine not exceeding level 3 (s. 14(9)).

It is a defence to charges (a) and (b) to prove that the failure to comply with the condition arose from circumstances beyond the defendant's control (s. 14(4) and (5)).

(c) It is an offence to incite somebody else knowingly to participate in an assembly in breach of a condition (s. 14(6)). The maximum penalty on summary conviction is three months' imprisonment and/or a fine not exceeding level 4 (s. 14(10)).

Power of arrest.   A constable in uniform may arrest without warrant anyone he reasonably suspects is committing any one of these three offences (s. 14(7)). For general powers of arrest, see chapter 5.

9.6 NO POWER TO PROHIBIT ASSEMBLIES

In contrast to the provisions relating to public processions which permit the prohibition of all processions or a class of procession in a police area (Public Order Act 1986, s. 13, and see 8.6), there is no power to prohibit an assembly or all assemblies or a class of assembly.

9.7 JUDICIAL REVIEW

There is no statutory or other right of appeal against the imposition of conditions on a public assembly under the Public Order Act 1986, s. 14. As with processions the only legal method of challenge to the imposition of conditions on an assembly is by way of judicial review. The scope of judicial review is limited. The remedy is concerned with reviewing, not the merits of the decision in respect of which the application is made, but the decision-making process itself. For a full discussion of judicial review, see 8.7.

In the case of assemblies, applications for leave to apply for judicial review could be mounted where the senior police officer has applied the tests unreasonably or conditions have been unreasonably imposed. It is unlikely that judicial review will become a fruitful avenue for frustrated protestors, although the imposition of conditions which so emaciate an assembly that it is tantamount to a prohibition on the holding of the assembly, for example, by moving to Hyde Park a protest against the use of American bombers intended to be held outside the American embassy in Grosvenor Square, might give rise to a successful action.

10

Public Meetings

This chapter deals with the three types of public meetings: outdoor meetings which are treated as public assemblies when at least 20 persons are present, indoor meetings and election meetings. Only outdoor meetings which are treated as assemblies are governed by the provisions of the Public Order Act 1986.

10.1 INTRODUCTION

The law has long recognised the right of public meeting, 'a right which has long passed out of the region of discussion or doubt' (*Ex parte Lewis* (1888) 21 QBD 191, 196).

10.1.1 Public Order Act 1986

The Public Order Act 1986 provides controls over *open-air meetings* at which at least 20 persons are present. For the purposes of the Public Order Act 1986 these meetings are called 'assemblies' (see chapter 9) and are subject to controls in Part II of the Act. But the Act provides no controls over public meetings held indoors or in closed premises, such as council meetings which are open to the public (except where it is likely that confidential information would be disclosed in breach of the obligation of confidence: Local Government Act 1972, s. 100A). The controls over open-air meetings (assemblies) have not been extended to indoor public meetings except those which are partly open to the air (Public Order Act 1986, s. 16)—presumably this means more than having the doors open in summer. It was felt that it was neither necessary nor desirable, because serious public disorder was less frequently associated with indoor meetings and because the existing law provided adequate coverage (White Paper, Cmnd 9510, para. 5.17).

Indoor public meetings are subject, however, to the following controls: police common law powers, the criminal offence of disorderly conduct at a public meeting (Public Meeting Act 1908, s. 1) and the new criminal offences contrary to ss. 4 and 5 of the Public Order Act 1986. There are also special provisions for election meetings in the Representation of the People Act 1983.

10.1.2 Private meetings

Private meetings are governed by the law of contract and the terms of the letting and hiring of halls. The public have no right to attend private meetings unless specifically invited, whether on payment or otherwise. Those who attend without permission or who breach the conditions of their attendance are trespassers and can be ejected from the meeting, if necessary by force (*Marshall* v *Tinnelly* (1937) 81 SJ 902). The organisers have the right to refuse anyone admission. Otherwise the attendance of persons at a meeting is governed by the terms of the contract. In clear cases an interlocutory injunction will be granted to prevent the wrongful exclusion of members from meetings of an association (*Woodford* v *Smith* [1970] 1 All ER 1091, a local ratepayers' and residents' association; and see 7.2.2.3).

The police have no right to attend private meetings unless they are invited by the organisers (see *Davis* v *Lisle* [1936] 2 KB 434, following *Great Central Railway Co.* v *Bates* [1921] 3 KB 578; *R* v *Prebble* (1858) 1 F & F 325). They do, however, have the right to enter to prevent crime or to deal with a breach of the peace or to pursue a criminal, and the new offences under the Public Order Act 1986 (see chapter 2) can be committed in private as well as in public so that the police will be entitled to enter private premises for the purposes of arrest. If there is no legal justification for the police entering private premises they will not be in the execution of their duty for the purposes of the offences of assault and obstruction contrary to the Police Act 1964, s. 51 (*Davis* v *Lisle*; *R* v *Prebble*; and see *R* v *Richards and Leeming* (1985) 81 Cr App R 125, a case of forcible entry; see also 5.12). A police constable who has entered private premises without permission becomes a trespasser at the very latest on being told to leave and refusing to do so (*Davis* v *Lisle*). The police were not entitled to remove drinkers at a late hour from a barn attached to a public house where there was no nuisance, no breach of the peace and no danger of one (*R* v *Prebble*).

10.2   DEFINITION OF 'PUBLIC MEETING'

There is no definition of 'public meeting' in the Public Order Act 1986. In an early draft of the Public Order Bill a definition was required for the offence of racial hatred by words or gestures. 'Public meeting' would have been defined for the purposes of this racial hatred offence as including any meeting in a public place and any meeting which the public or a section of it are permitted to attend, whether on payment or otherwise. But the definition was no longer required when the offence was amended so that it could also be committed in a private place (see chapter 4).

This leaves the similarly worded definition of a public meeting in the Public Order Act 1936, s. 9, namely, 'any meeting in a public place and any meeting which the public or any section thereof are permitted to attend, whether on payment or otherwise'. This definition was required in the 1936 Act for the offence under s. 5 of theatening behaviour etc., which could only be committed in a public place or at a public meeting. But s. 5 is now repealed and its replacements—the offences contrary to ss. 4 and 5 of the Public Order Act 1986—do not contain s. 5's wording of 'in any public place or at any public meeting'. The new offences can be committed in a public or a private place (with exceptions—see 2.5 and 2.6). Hence there is no definition in Part I (new offences) of the Public Order Act 1986. But the definition is retained in the 1936 Act for the offence prohibiting the wearing of uniforms 'in any public place or at any public meeting' (Public Order Act 1936, s. 1(1), and see 3.6).

There is no definition of 'public meeting' in either the Public Meeting Act 1908 or the Representation of the People Act 1983.

The existing definition of 'public meeting' (Public Order Act 1936, s. 9) is therefore likely to be applied to any public meeting covered in this chapter. First, it must be *a meeting*. This must apply to any small or larger group of persons meeting for a particular purpose. There is no reason why two persons could not constitute a meeting. Under the Public Order Act 1936 the purpose of the meeting is limited in the definition of 'meeting' to 'a meeting held for the purpose of the discussion of matters of public interest or for the purpose of the expression of views on such matters' (Public Order Act 1936, s. 9). This definition must now be restricted to the remaining purposes of the 1936 Act, namely the s. 1 offence of wearing uniforms. In any other context the meeting could be for a private or a public purpose. A meeting on the highway, for example, could be private in nature but held in public. It would also be an assembly, because held out of doors.

Secondly, the meeting must be held *in a public place*. For a full discussion of the meaning of 'public place' see 8.3. The essence of the definition is that the meeting must be held either on the highway (this would be unusual, but not necessarily unlawful: see *Burden* v *Rigler* [1911] 1 KB 337, and in any event if the numbers were more than 20 the meeting would become an assembly) or in any other premises or place to which the public have access, whether on payment or otherwise. This excludes private meetings held on private premises, such as private members' clubs, and meetings by invitation or limited ticket sale. A public meeting should be one which is genuinely open to the public, and usually on a first-come, first-served basis, although many public meetings keep sections of the meeting place reserved for interested parties, such as the organisers of the meeting or the officers of the club holding the meeting. It is irrelevant whether payment is required before entry or not. If the meeting is a ticket-holders-only meeting, the sale or provision of tickets must be made to the public or a section of it, although there is no need for extensive publicity, before a meeting becomes public.

Public access to the meetings, committees and subcommittees of local authorities and other bodies is provided for, except where publicity would be prejudicial to the public interest by reason of the confidential nature of the business to be transacted (Public Bodies (Admission to Meetings) Act 1960; Local Government (Access to Information) Act 1985).

10.3   CONTROL OF PUBLIC MEETINGS

10.3.1   General management

It is the responsibility of those holding public meetings to see that the premises are fit for the purpose of the meeting and the intended size of the meeting, to comply with the contractual conditions imposed by the lettors or hirers of the hall or meeting-place, including fire and safety arrangements, and to ensure that the meeting is conducted in an orderly manner.

10.3.2 Stewards

A reasonable number of clearly identifiable stewards (see Public Order Act 1936, s. 2(6)) or managers should be appointed where necessary to assist in the admittance and seating of members of the public and to ensure that disorder, beyond the bounds of reasonable heckling and participation from the floor, is properly controlled. This control may extend to the use of reasonable force where necessary in order to control disorder, to prevent crime such as stealing (Criminal Law Act 1967, s. 3) and to eject members of the public who have strayed beyond the bounds of reasonable participation.

Stewards must also be restrained from the unreasonable or excessive use of force, and should not (a) wear a uniform to promote a political object or signify association with a political organisation (Public Order Act 1936, s. 1), or (b) usurp the functions of the police or the armed forces (Public Order Act 1936, s. 2) or (c) use or display force to promote a political object (Public Order Act 1936, s. 2).

The chairman of a meeting convened by members of an association was held not to be liable for the acts of stewards who assaulted a member of the gallery, because there is no relationship of master and servant between chairman and stewards (*Lucas* v *Mason* (1875) LR 10 Ex 251). If a person is wrongly ejected or refused permission to attend a public meeting he may be able to challenge the decision by way of judicial review. A judge granted a Cumbrian district councillor leave to apply for judicial review under the Local Government (Access to Information) Act 1985 after he had been arrested for attending as an observer a working party meeting convened to discuss the efficiency of the council's operations (*The Guardian*, 14 June 1986). For further discussion of judicial review see 8.7.

10.3.3 Public Meeting Act 1908

The limited provisions of the Public Meeting Act 1908 s. 1, create three criminal offences summarised by the marginal note 'penalty on endeavour to break up a public meeting'. These offences do not apply to election meetings (Representation of the People Act 1983, sch. 8, and see 10.4.4):

(a)   It is an offence to act in a disorderly manner at a lawful public meeting for the purpose of preventing the transaction of the business for which the meeting was called (s. 1(1)). The words 'in a disorderly manner' are not defined (see 2.6). The offence is triable summarily only, with a maximum penalty of six months' imprisonment and/or a fine not exceeding level 5.

(b)   It is an offence to incite a person so to act (s. 1(2)). This offence is also triable summarily with the same maximum penalty.

(c)   It is an offence to refuse or fail to give your name and address to a constable who has, on the request of the chairman of the meeting, required you to give it, having reasonably suspected you of committing one of the above offences (i.e., acting or inciting somebody to act in a disorderly manner etc.). It is also an offence in these circumstances to give a false name and address (s. 1(3)). These offences contrary to s. 1(3) of the Public Meeting Act 1908 are punishable on summary conviction with a fine not exceeding level 1.

Power of arrest.   Before the Police and Criminal Evidence Act 1984 came into force in January 1986, the Public Meeting Act 1908, s. 1, contained a very limited power of arrest without warrant. It could only be exercised where a person had refused or failed to give his name and address or where the constable reasonably suspected him of giving a false name and address (s. 1(3)). The power was therefore rarely used.

But the power of arrest under the 1908 Act has not been retained in the arrest powers of Part III of the Police and Criminal Evidence Act 1984. The Public Meeting Act 1908, s. 1, is therefore governed by the Police and Criminal Evidence Act 1984, s. 25, which permits arrest without warrant where a constable has reasonable grounds for suspecting that an offence has been committed or attempted or is being committed or attempted and it appears to him that a summons is impracticable or inappropriate because any of the general arrest conditions is satisfied, namely that the name of the person cannot be readily ascertained by him or he has reasonable grounds for doubting its correctness, or the person has failed to furnish a satisfactory address or it may be false, or that the constable has reasonable grounds for believing that arrest is necessary to prevent the person causing or suffering physical injury or causing loss of or damage to property (Police and Criminal Evidence Act 1984, s. 25(3), see 5.2).

10.3.4   Police powers at common law

Where a public meeting is held in an obviously *public place*, like Trafalgar Square, the police will be present and entitled to deal with breaches of the peace and criminal offences, such as obstruction of the highway or obstruction of a police officer in the execution of his duty, when and if they occur (see generally chapter 5).

Where, however, a public meeting is held in *private premises*, such as a room in a town hall (which is private despite being owned by a public body) or the South Place Ethical Society halls in Red Lion Square in London, the right of the police to be present is less certain, particularly when those present or those holding the meeting have decided that police officers should be excluded. Generally, the police will not attend such meetings unless invited to do so. But in *Thomas* v *Sawkins* [1935] 2 KB 249 the Divisional Court seems to have decided that the police have the right, although uninvited, to attend public meetings held on private premises if they reasonably apprehend a breach of the peace. This decision has been much criticised and the extent of the court's ruling is uncertain. The meeting which was open to the public without payment was convened in order to protest against the Incitement to Disaffection Bill and to demand the dismissal of the Chief Constable of Glamorgan. The case was unusual in that Sawkins, a police sergeant, was ejected from the meeting by Thomas who subsequently brought a private prosecution against Sawkins for resisting his ejectment. In fact no breach of the peace took place. The magistrates found that the police were entitled to enter and remain during the meeting because they had reasonable grounds to believe that if they were not present there would be seditious speeches and other incitements to violence and a breach of the peace. They therefore concluded that there had been no assault. These findings were upheld on appeal when much emphasis was laid upon the fact that the meeting was in public.

The application of this case is not easy, and each case will depend on its own facts. The police might argue, for example, that a meeting convened to protest against the passage of a Public Order Bill might permit their attendance if held on the Broadwater Farm Estate but not if held in Hereford. But, it is submitted, the police will not be entitled to attend public meetings on private premises (except in a private capacity) unless there are clear grounds for believing that a breach of the peace will take place.

Annoyance and disturbance at a meeting by cries of 'Hear, hear!', putting questions to the speaker and making observations on his statements would not be a breach of the peace (*Wooding* v *Oxley* (1839) 9 C & P 1).

Once the police are lawfully present at a public meeting they can arrest and remove a person for a breach or threat of a breach of the peace (see 5.1).

10.3.5   Police powers under statute

In addition to the police powers at common law to prevent a breach of the peace, police officers, once lawfully in attendance at a public meeting (see 10.3.4), can:

(a)   make an arrest if the general arrest conditions of the Police and Criminal Evidence Act 1984, s. 25, apply (see 5.2), or

(b)   arrest anyone reasonably suspected of committing an offence of threatening behaviour etc. contrary to s. 4 of the Public Order Act 1986 (threatening behaviour etc., see 2.5), or

(c)   arrest a person under s. 5 of the Public Order Act 1986 (disorderly conduct) if he engages in further offensive conduct after being warned to stop (see 2.6.6).

If the conduct is more serious the police can arrest for affray, violent disorder or riot (see chapter 2). The s. 4 offence of threatening behaviour etc. is likely to be used in this context more frequently than the other offences.

10.4   ELECTION MEETINGS

The Public Order Act 1986 makes no changes to the law on the holding of public meetings at the time of national and local elections. Election meetings are governed by the provisions of the Representation of the People Act 1983 which permits a candidate in an election to use certain schools and halls for public election meetings free of charge, provided that he shall bear the expense of any damage caused (Representation of the People Act 1983, ss. 95 and 96).

The aim is to ensure that candidates of all parties, however impecunious, have a public platform for their views. Two conditions must be complied with: the purpose of the meeting must be to further the candidature of the person holding the meeting, and the meeting must be public.

10.4.1   Background

It was an election meeting which led to the violent events in Southall in April

1979 which in turn led to the government's review of public order law (May 1985, Cmnd 9510) and ultimately to the Public Order Act 1986. There were also serious disturbances in Leicester, West Bromwich and Bradford at other election meetings held by the National Front during the general election campaign in 1979. But the government decided to make no changes to the law or to its practical application despite widespread concern over abuses of the right to hold election meetings.

10.4.2   Refusal to allow meetings

Local authorities are under no general duty to make facilities available for ordinary public meetings. But they have no discretion to refuse election meetings unless the meeting will not further the candidature or it will not be a public meeting (see 10.4.3). All candidates in a local or general election are entitled to inspect the list of meeting halls and school premises available for meetings in the constituency and neighbouring constituencies. The candidate can be refused a particular hall if it is already booked.

In May 1986 the Court of Appeal upheld the right of a candidate of the British National Party to have a suitable school room made available for a public meeting in a local government election. The Inner London Education Authority had refused permission to the candidate on the grounds that violence would inevitably ensue and damage would be caused to the school in Bethnal Green. The reported decision in the case relates only to the procedural issue. The court held that the right which arose under the Representation of the People Act 1983, s. 96(1), was a private law right enforceable by an action in the Queen's Bench Division and not a public law right subject to judicial review under RSC, Ord. 53 (*Ettridge* v *Morrell, The Times*, 5 May 1986). In fact the court permitted the meeting to take place.

10.4.3   Public election meetings

One of the complaints about the use of public buildings free of charge for election meetings is that the meetings are often not truly public meetings. Sections 95 and 96 of the Representation of the People Act 1983 create special privileges for all parties fielding candidates, to permit debate on electoral issues in meetings which are genuinely open to the public. In practice public debate has sometimes been replaced by private meetings at public expense, with only a handful of sympathisers present. On occasions stewards have wrongly excluded from these meetings persons to whom they object.

Local councils have from time to time refused applications by National Front candidates to hold election meetings, in the belief that the meetings would not be genuinely open to the public. For example, in 1978 the Greater Manchester Council refused a series of applications made by the National Front in the Moss Side parliamentary by-election. The Divisional Court granted the aggrieved party leave to challenge the council's decision but refused to hear the case before the date of the election. The case was not pursued. In 1979 a similar refusal by Brent London Borough Council was challenged in the courts but rejected on technical grounds. Another challenge by the National Front to an Inner London Education Authority decision refusing permission was left too late and not pursued.

One of the problems hinges on the definition of 'public meeting'. Neither the Representation of the People Act 1983 nor the Public Meeting Act 1908 contains a definition and the definition in the Public Order Act 1936 (see 10.2) is inappropriate to the context. One remedy would be to provide a definition of 'public meeting' for election purposes as 'a meeting which any person may attend without restriction on entrance by ticket, invitation or otherwise, provided that a candidate or his agent may retain for the candidate's own purposes not more than one quarter of the seats available in the meeting room'. (See also White Paper, Cmnd 9510, para. 5.19.)

For further discussion, see *Southall 23 April 1979: The Report of the Unofficial Committee of Inquiry* (NCCL, 1980).

10.4.4 Criminal offences

Under the Representation of the People Act 1983, s. 97 (disturbances at election meetings), it is an 'illegal practice' to act, or incite others to act, in a disorderly manner for the purpose of preventing the transaction of the business for which the meeting was called together. The penalty on summary conviction is a fine not exceeding level 3 (Representation of the People Act 1983, s. 169). It is an offence punishable on summary conviction with a maximum penalty of a fine not exceeding level 1 to refuse or fail to give the correct name and address after the chairman has requested a constable to require that person to give it, the constable having reasonably suspected the person of causing a disturbance. The power of arrest for this offence has been repealed and replaced by the general arrest provisions of the Police and Criminal Evidence Act 1984, s. 25 (see 5.2).

10.5 TRAFALGAR SQUARE AND HYDE PARK

10.5.1 Trafalgar Square

There is no right of public meeting in Trafalgar Square (*Ex parte Lewis* (1888) 21 QBD 191). Trafalgar Square was a private possession of the Crown, but by Act of Parliament in 1844 was constituted as part of the metropolis under the control and supervision of the police, with the management and regulation of the square originally vested in the Commissioner of Woods and Forests. The management of the square is now conducted by the Department of the Environment.

Application to hold a public meeting in Trafalgar Square must be made to the Department of the Environment, 2 Marsham Street, London, SW1 (Trafalgar Square Regulation (SI 1952 No. 776), reg. 3). By convention (and not regulation) the application must be made within three months of the date for the meeting. Meetings can only be held on Saturdays (2 p.m. to sunset), Sundays (sunrise to sunset) and public holidays (sunrise to sunset). The maximum permitted sound amplification is 50 watts and the sound must not reach beyond the square. Applications are considered on their merits, and relevant bodies, such as the Metropolitan Police are consulted. An application must also be made to sell or distribute anything, or to carry on a trade or business, or to organise or conduct an assembly, parade or procession (reg. 3).

10.5.2 Hyde Park

There is no right in the public to hold meetings in the royal parks (*Bailey* v
Williamson (1873) LR 8 QB 118). The position is the same with most local
parks which are governed by by-laws (see 6.4), although some by-laws permit
public meetings in some specified public parks. Permission must be obtained
from the Royal Parks Division of the Department of the Environment to hold
assemblies and events in Hyde Park (see *Policy and Procedure for the Use of
Hyde Park for Special Events*, July 1969). Contact the Bailiff of the Royal Parks
Office, Department of the Environment, 2 Marsham Street, London, SW1.

11

Football Matches:
Exclusion Orders and Alcohol-related Offences

This chapter explains the new scheme of excluding offenders from association football matches which is introduced by Part IV of the Public Order Act 1986. It also deals with a number of alcohol-related offences at or on journeys to football matches under the provisions of the Sporting Events (Control of Alcohol etc.) Act 1985 and with limited additions to those provisions made by the Public Order Act 1986.

11.1   INTRODUCTION

The Public Order Act 1986 makes two changes to public order law relating to football matches. It introduces a new scheme of exclusion orders designed to tackle some of the problems of soccer hooliganism by excluding trouble-makers from football matches. A court will be able to impose on anyone found guilty of a football-related offence an order prohibiting him from attending prescribed football matches where the court believes that it will help to prevent violence or disorder. In addition the Public Order Act 1986, sch. 1, amends the Sporting Events (Control of Alcohol etc.) Act 1985 and Part V of the Criminal Justice (Scotland) Act 1980 by introducing new controls on alcohol in relation to sporting events as well as imposing restrictions on articles such as smoke-bombs. The Public Order Act 1986 makes no other specific provisions for dealing with football hooliganism.

   The violence at the Heysel stadium in Brussels and at English football grounds, particularly at Birmingham and Luton, in the 1984/85 season, together with the tragic fire at Bradford in which 56 people died, shocked football supporters across the world. Proposals for changes in the law came from two sources, the White Paper, *Review of Public Order Law* (May 1985, Cmnd 9510) and the Popplewell Inquiry Report (Committee of Inquiry into Crowd Safety and Control at Sports Grounds, January 1986, Cmnd 9710).

   The White Paper did not give undue prominence to football hooliganism, but proposed (para. 6.20) to restrict the availability of alcohol at or on the way to football matches along the lines of Scots law (Criminal Justice (Scotland) Act 1980, Part V). This proposal was enacted in England and Wales in the Sporting Events (Control of Alcohol etc.) Act 1985 which passed through the House of Commons in four working days. A similar private member's Bill (Football Grounds (Control) Bill) had fallen for lack of support in 1981.

   The second source of proposed change came from the Popplewell Report on safety in sport. Many of the Popplewell recommendations on safety and ground management are likely to be implemented despite the cost factor. For example, the recommendation that all grounds and stadiums with crowd capacities of more than 10,000 should require safety certificates from the local authority if they wished to continue to admit spectators has been implemented and came into force on 23 August 1986. The Home Secretary made an order under the Safety of Sports Grounds Act 1975 designating a further 26 football, 16 rugby union, three rugby league and seven cricket grounds for these purposes.

But other proposals made in the Popplewell Report are unlikely to be implemented nationally because of their impact upon civil liberties: a criminal offence of disorderly conduct at sports grounds, unfettered police powers of search at football grounds (although it should be noted that most clubs make it a condition of entry that spectators must submit to a police search if requested to do so), membership card schemes for supporters, offences of chanting obscene or racialist slogans and of running on to pitches. It should be noted that even without the implementation of these proposals official figures for the 1985/86 football season show a decrease in trouble at matches. Arrests at first-division matches fell by 51%, at second-division matches by 41%. Ejections from first-division matches fell by 33%, and at second-division matches by 30% (*The Times*, 26 July 1986).

In practice improvements at football grounds are more likely to come from the good management of clubs and the general goodwill of spectators than from sweeping changes in the law. Banning alcohol inside grounds does not prevent fans from getting drunk before the match. Much of the trouble at Birmingham was caused by those who had been drinking outside the ground and who had difficulty getting in when they arrived late. Moderate drinking inside grounds will always be preferable to 'stoking up' at great speed beforehand.

In fact the Sporting Events (Control of Alcohol etc.) Act 1985 has created more confusion than clarity. Football clubs up and down the country, apparently to the surprise of the legislators, have been granted exemptions by magistrates' courts for opening bars while executive boxes have been deprived of alcohol because they are premises from which the match may be 'directly viewed' (Sporting Events (Control of Alcohol etc.) Act 1985, s. 3(3)).

11.2   EXCLUSION ORDERS

Part IV of the Public Order Act 1986 gives the courts in England and Wales the power to make orders excluding offenders from football grounds on their conviction for an offence connected with football.

11.2.1   Prescribed football matches

The court's power to make an exclusion order does not apply to all football matches. It is limited to prescribed football matches (s. 30(1)). A prescribed football match is an association football match of any description which is prescribed by the Home Secretary by statutory instrument (Public Order Act 1986, s. 36). It is envisaged that the Home Secretary will prescribe the same sort of matches as those which are designated for the purposes of alcohol-related offences and licensing under the Sporting Events (Control of Alcohol etc.) Act 1985 (see 11.3.1). These include association football matches played by members of the Football League, international football matches, and matches in the competition for the European Cup, the Cup Winners' Cup or the UEFA Cup. The exclusion order scheme could also be extended by the Home Secretary to other sporting events (Public Order Act 1986, s. 37).

11.2.2 Offences connected with football

Exclusion orders can only be made when a person is convicted of an offence connected with football (Public Order Act 1986, s. 31). An offence connected with football is an offence which fulfils any one or more of three conditions:

(a) it is an offence committed at a football ground, or on entering or leaving or trying to enter or leave a football ground, within two hours before the start of the match or its advertised time (if earlier), even if the match is postponed, or within one hour after the end of the match or one hour after the advertised start if the match is postponed; or

(b) it is an offence committed while the defendant (or, in case (i) below, the victim) was on a journey, including breaks, even overnight breaks, to or from a match, *and* the offence

(i) involved the use or threat of violence (defined in the Public Order Act 1986, s. 8, see 2.2.4.4) to the person, or

(ii) involved the use or threat of violence towards property, or

(iii) was an offence under the Public Order Act 1986, s. 5 (disorderly conduct) or under Part III of the Public Order Act 1986 (racial hatred); or

(c) it is an offence committed on a journey to or from a football match in contravention of the offences banning alcohol under the Sporting Events (Control of Alcohol etc.) Act 1985 (as amended by the Public Order Act 1986, sch. 1), see 11.3.

11.2.3 Making an exclusion order

A court can only make an exclusion order if:

(a) the defendant is convicted of an offence connected with football (see 11.2.2), and

(b) the court is satisfied that making an order against the particular defendant will help to prevent violence or disorder at or in connection with prescribed football matches (Public Order Act 1986, s. 30(2)), and

(c) some other penalty (or a probation order or a conditional or absolute discharge) is imposed (s. 30(3)).

An exclusion order cannot therefore be made if the only sanction available to the court (either under the common law breach of the peace powers or by complaint under the Magistrates' Courts Act 1980, s. 115, see 5.1) is a binding-over order. Nor should a court make an order under (b) above if there is no likelihood of the offender going to another football match or if the circumstances suggest that the offence was out of character and unlikely to be repeated.

11.2.4 A copy of the order

Once made, a copy of the order must be given to the defendant, sent to the chief constable of the area where the offence was committed, and sent to anyone prescribed by order of the Home Secretary (Public Order Act 1986, s. 34). It is envisaged that the prescribed person referred to in the Public Order Act 1986, s. 34, will be someone nominated by the football authorities to act as a liaison officer with the clubs.

11.2.5 Effect of an exclusion order

11.2.5.1 Duration of the order   An exclusion order prohibiting a person from entering any premises for the purpose of attending a prescribed football match shall specify the period of the order which shall be for at least three months (Public Order Act 1986, s. 32).

There is no maximum limit, therefore a ban for life would be lawful if reasonable in all the circumstances of the case, for example, in the case of a defendant who had repeatedly committed crimes of violence at football matches. Clearly lengthy periods are contemplated (see 11.2.8). If the defendant is already subject to an exclusion order the minimum three-month period shall run consecutively to the existing period (s. 32(2)).

11.2.5.2 Photographing offender   If, and only if, the prosecution applies, the court making an exclusion order can also make an order that the defendant should be photographed (Public Order Act 1986, s. 35). A police officer may arrest without warrant a person who fails to comply with an order for the taking of photographs (s. 35(4)). For the taking of photographs, see also the Code of Practice for the Identification of Persons by Police Officers made under the Police and Criminal Evidence Act 1984.

11.2.6 Breach of an exclusion order

11.2.6.1 The breach   A person subject to an exclusion order is in breach of the exclusion order if he enters premises for the purpose of attending any prescribed football match (Public Order Act 1986, s. 32(3)). He is not in breach of the order if he enters a football ground for any other purpose, for example, to buy tickets for friends, nor if he is convicted of a subsequent offence connected with football unless it involved his entering the ground to attend a match.

The real difficulty with exclusion orders will be their enforcement, particularly at away matches. This is a weakness in the scheme which will not easily be overcome. If exclusion orders are persistently flouted with immunity their value will be token.

11.2.6.2 An offence   A breach of an exclusion order is a criminal offence punishable on summary conviction with a maximum penalty of one month's imprisonment and/or a fine not exceeding level 3 (Public Order Act 1986, s. 32(3)). This offence only becomes an offence connected with football, so that a further exclusion order can be imposed, if one of the three conditions (see 11.2.2) applies. Most defendants who breach an exclusion order will be subject to the first condition (unless they were caught more than two hours before the match), and therefore the court before which they are convicted will be able to impose a fresh exclusion order.

Arrest. A police constable may arrest any person whom he reasonably suspects to have entered premises in breach of an exclusion order (Public Order Act 1986, s. 32(4)). The constable does not have to be in uniform.

11.2.7 Appeals

If a *magistrates' court* has imposed the exclusion order the defendant can appeal against the imposition of the order or its length (in addition to any appeal against any other sentence or other order imposed at the same time) to the Crown Court (Magistrates' Courts Act 1980, s. 108). The appeal is by way of rehearing (Supreme Court Act 1981, s. 79) and the Crown Court can revoke the order, reduce the length of the period imposed *or* increase the length of the order (Supreme Court Act 1981, s. 48).

If a *Crown Court* has imposed the exclusion order the defendant can appeal to the Court of Appeal against the imposition of the order or its length, but the Court of Appeal has no power to increase the length of the period of the order (Criminal Appeal Act 1968, ss. 9 and 50).

11.2.8 Application to terminate an exclusion order

In addition to the appeal procedure, a defendant who has been subject to an exclusion order for at least one year may apply to the court which made the order to terminate the order (Public Order Act 1986, s. 33). The court can terminate the order forthwith or from a date specified in the order or refuse the application (Public Order Act 1986, s. 33(2)). No further application can be made within six months after an application has been refused (s. 33(3)).

This provision is analogous to the procedure for applying for removal of disqualification from driving (Road Traffic Act 1972, s. 95). In particular in both cases the court must have regard to the applicant's character, his conduct since the order was made, the nature of the offence, and any other circumstances of the case (Public Order Act 1986, s. 33(2)).

The power to rescind or suspend orders under the Magistrates' Courts Act 1980, s. 63(2), does not apply to exclusion orders (Public Order Act 1986, s. 33(6)).

11.3 SPORTING EVENTS (CONTROL OF ALCOHOL ETC.) ACT 1985: ALCOHOL-RELATED OFFENCES AND LICENSING

The Sporting Events (Control of Alcohol etc.) Act 1985 penalises the carrying of alcoholic drinks to or from designated sporting events, possessing alcohol or articles capable of causing injury at designated sports grounds, drunkenness at or on journeys to or from sporting events, and makes provision for control of the sale or supply of alcohol at sports grounds.

Section 40(1) of and sch. 1 to the Public Order Act 1986 provide amendments to the Sporting Events (Control of Alcohol etc.) Act 1985 (and similar amendments to the Criminal Justice (Scotland) Act 1980 on which the 1985 Act is based). In particular the Public Order Act 1986, sch. 1, extends alcohol offences on journeys to football matches to minibuses and penalises possession of smoke-bombs and fireworks.

11.3.1   Sports grounds and sporting events

The Sporting Events (Control of Alcohol etc.) Act 1985 applies to sports grounds and sporting events designated under the Act by the Home Secretary, and to journeys to and from such events. The Home Secretary has designated the following grounds and events for the purposes of this Act as from 9 August 1985 (Sports Grounds and Sporting Events (Designation) Order 1985, SI No. 1151):

(a)   *Sports grounds.* The home grounds of all association football clubs which are members of the Football Association Ltd or the Football Association of Wales Ltd, any other ground in England and Wales used occasionally or temporarily by such a club, Wembley Stadium, any other ground in England and Wales used for an international association football match, and Shielfield Park, Berwick-upon-Tweed.

(b)   *Sporting events.* Association football matches played by members of the Football League, international association football matches, association football matches (whether at home or abroad) in the competition for the European Cup, the Cup Winners' Cup, or the UEFA Cup, association football matches within the jurisdiction of the Scottish Football Association Ltd and association football matches at a sports ground outside Great Britain in which one of the participating teams represents the Football Association Ltd, the Football Association of Wales Ltd or a club which is a member of the Football League.

The 1985 Act does not, however, apply to such events where they are free for the spectators and at which all the competitors take part without reward (s. 9(6)).

11.3.2   Alcohol-related offences

The Sporting Events (Control of Alcohol etc.) Act 1985 creates:

(a)   an offence of being drunk on a public service vehicle (a bus or coach) or a train on a journey to or from any sporting events designated by the Home Secretary (s. 1(4)), punishable with a maximum penalty on summary conviction of a fine not exceeding level 2 (s. 8);

(b)   an offence of being drunk in or while entering or trying to enter a designated sports ground during the period of a designated sporting event (s. 2(2)), punishable with a maximum penalty on summary conviction of a fine not exceeding level 2 (s. 8);

(c)   an offence of being in possession of:

(i)   intoxicating liquor, or

(ii)   any drink container (whether empty or full, whole, crushed or broken) (presumably this includes soft drink containers and Thermos flasks), except medicine containers, capable of causing injury to a person, at a sporting event designated by the Home Secretary or while entering or trying to enter a designated sports ground during the period of a designated sports event (s. 2(1) and (3)), punishable with a maximum penalty on summary conviction of three months' imprisonment and/or a fine not exceeding level 3 (s. 8);

(d)   an offence of knowingly causing or permitting intoxicating liquor to be carried on such vehicles as referred to in (a) above (s. 1(2)), punishable with a maximum penalty on summary conviction of a fine not exceeding level 4 (s. 8);

(e)   an offence of selling or supplying or authorising the sale or supply of intoxicating liquor in breach of licensing conditions imposed or outside the permitted hours (s. 3(10)), punishable with a maximum penalty on summary conviction of three months' imprisonment and/or a fine not exceeding level 3 (s. 8);

(f)   an offence of failing to comply with a requirement by a constable to close a bar and keep it closed where it appears to a constable in uniform that the sale or supply of intoxicating liquor at the bar is detrimental to the orderly conduct or safety of spectators (s. 6), punishable with a maximum penalty on summary conviction of three months' imprisonment and/or a fine not exceeding level 3 (s. 8).

11.3.3   Powers of enforcement

A constable may enter a designated sports ground to enforce the provisions of the Sporting Events (Control of Alcohol etc.) Act 1985 (s. 7(1)). He may search a person he has reasonable grounds to suspect is committing or has committed an offence under the Act (s. 7(2)), he may arrest such a person (s. 7(2)), and he may stop and search a train or public service vehicle if he has reasonable grounds to suspect that a vehicle offence (s. 1) is being or has been committed (s. 7(3)). He may also close a bar where it appears to him that the sale or supply of intoxicating liquor is detrimental to the orderly conduct or safety of spectators (s. 6(1)).

11.3.4   Restrictions on licensing

The Sporting Events (Control of Alcohol etc.) Act 1985, s. 3, prohibits the sale or supply of intoxicating liquor from licensed premises or registered club premises situated within the area of a designated sports ground during the period of a designated sporting event. The period is two hours before the start of the event, during the event and one hour after the event (s. 9(4)).

These restrictions may be eased by application to the magistrate's court (s. 3(2)) which may permit the sale or supply of intoxicating liquour or modify the period or impose such conditions as it thinks fit. The court may not ease the restrictions in relation to any part of the ground from which the designated sports event may be directly viewed (s. 3(3)). This means that there can be no drinking on the terraces. It has also meant that executive boxes overlooking the field of play have not been allowed to supply alcohol to the customers.

Many clubs up and down the country have applied successfully for the restrictions to be removed or eased. In London, for example, by the end of 1985 exemption orders were in force at 15 different clubs. At Arsenal all private and public bars in the east and west stands were exempted. At

Tottenham Hotspur, West Ham and Orient all private bars were exempted. At Chelsea all private bars plus a pre-lunch bar in the executive suite were exempted. At Queens Park Rangers all private bars were exempted as well as executive boxes, provided curtains were installed in the boxes to prevent a view of the match. At Wembley all bars were exempted with a restriction of two pints per person.

For the procedure for applying for exemption orders see the schedule to the Act.

11.3.5   Changes made by the Public Order Act 1986

The Public Order Act 1986, sch. 1, amends the Sporting Events (Control of Alcohol etc.) Act 1985 in the following respects:

(a)   *Minibuses.* It adds s. 1A to the 1985 Act and thereby extends s. 1 (offences in connection with alcohol on coaches and trains) to include vehicles which are not public service vehicles but are adapted to carry more than eight passengers (mostly minibuses).

(b)   *Fireworks, smoke-bombs etc.* It adds s. 2A to the 1985 Act and thereby creates the offence of possessing at a designated sporting event, without lawful authority, any article or substance whose main purpose is the emission of a flare or of smoke or a visible gas (particularly distress flares, fog signals, and pellets and capsules intended to be used as fumigators or for testing pipes, but not matches, cigarette lighters or heaters), punishable on summary conviction with a maximum penalty of three months' imprisonment and/or a fine not exceeding level 3.

(c)   *Licensing.* It adds ss. 5A, 5B and 5C to the 1985 Act and thereby extends the licensing restrictions on the sale or supply of alcohol under occasional licences in force (s. 5A) or at registered clubs (s. 5B) or at non-retail outlets (s. 5C) in the area (whose geographical limits are not defined) of a designated sports ground.

(d)   *Scotland.* Similar amendments in relation to minibuses and fireworks, smoke-bombs etc. are made to the Criminal Justice (Scotland) Act 1980.

Appendix 1   Public Order Act 1986

1986, c. 64. An Act to abolish the common law offences of riot, rout, unlawful assembly and affray and certain statutory offences relating to public order; to create new offences relating to public order; to control public processions and assemblies; to control the stirring up of racial hatred; to provide for the exclusion of certain offenders from sporting events; to create a new offence relating to the contamination of or interference with goods; to confer power to direct certain trespassers to leave land; to amend section 7 of the Conspiracy and Protection of Property Act 1875, section 1 of the Prevention of Crime Act 1953, Part V of the Criminal Justice (Scotland) Act 1980 and the Sporting Events (Control of Alcohol etc.) Act 1985; to repeal certain obsolete or unnecessary enactments; and for connected purposes. [Royal assent 7 November 1986.]

Be it enacted by the Queen's most Excellent Majesty, by and with the advice and consent of the Lords Spiritual and Temporal, and Commons, in this present Parliament assembled, and by the authority of the same, as follows:—

Part I   New offences

Riot
1.—(1)   Where 12 or more persons who are present together use or threaten unlawful violence for a common purpose and the conduct of them (taken together) is such as would cause a person of reasonable firmness present at the scene to fear for his personal safety, each of the persons using unlawful violence for the common purpose is guilty of riot.
(2)   It is immaterial whether or not the 12 or more use or threaten unlawful violence simultaneously.
(3)   The common purpose may be inferred from conduct.
(4)   No person of reasonable firmness need actually be, or be likely to be, present at the scene.
(5)   Riot may be committed in private as well as in public places.
(6)   A person guilty of riot is liable on conviction on indictment to imprisonment for a term not exceeding 10 years or a fine or both.

Violent disorder
2.—(1)   Where three or more persons who are present together use or threaten unlawful violence and the conduct of them (taken together) is such as would cause a person of reasonable firmness present at the scene to fear for his personal safety, each of the persons using or threatening unlawful violence is guilty of violent disorder.

(2)   It is immaterial whether or not the three or more use or threaten unlawful violence simultaneously.

(3)   No person of reasonable firmness need actually be, or be likely to be, present at the scene.

(4)   Violent disorder may be committed in private as well as in public places.

(5)   A person guilty of violent disorder is liable on conviction on indictment to imprisonment for a term not exceeding five years or a fine or both, or on summary conviction to imprisonment for a term not exceeding six months or a fine not exceeding the statutory maximum or both.

Affray

3.—(1)   A person is guilty of affray if he uses or threatens unlawful violence towards another and his conduct is such as would cause a person of reasonable firmness present at the scene to fear for his personal safety.

(2)   Where two or more persons use or threaten the unlawful violence, it is the conduct of them taken together that must be considered for the purposes of subsection (1).

(3)   For the purposes of this section a threat cannot be made by the use of words alone.

(4)   No person of reasonable firmness need actually be, or be likely to be, present at the scene.

(5)   Affray may be committed in private as well as in public places.

(6)   A constable may arrest without warrant anyone he reasonably suspects is committing affray.

(7)   A person guilty of affray is liable on conviction on indictment to imprisonment for a term not exceeding three years or a fine or both, or on summary conviction to imprisonment for a term not exceeding six months or a fine not exceeding the statutory maximum or both.

Fear or provocation of violence

4.—(1)   A person is guilty of an offence if he—

(a)   uses towards another person threatening, abusive or insulting words or behaviour, or

(b)   distributes or displays to another person any writing, sign or other visible representation which is threatening, abusive or insulting,

with intent to cause that person to believe that immediate unlawful violence will be used against him or another by any person, or to provoke the immediate use of unlawful violence by that person or another, or whereby that person is likely to believe that such violence will be used or it is likely that such violence will be provoked.

(2)   An offence under this section may be committed in a public or a private place, except that no offence is committed where the words or behaviour are used, or the writing, sign or other visible representation is distributed or displayed, by a person inside a dwelling and the other person is also inside that or another dwelling.

(3)   A constable may arrest without warrant anyone he reasonably suspects is committing an offence under this section.

(4)   A person guilty of an offence under this section is liable on summary conviction to imprisonment for a term not exceeding six months or a fine not exceeding level 5 on the standard scale or both.

Harassment, alarm or distress
5.—(1)   A person is guilty of an offence if he—

(a)   uses threatening, abusive or insulting words or behaviour, or disorderly behaviour, or
(b)   displays any writing, sign or other visible representation which is threatening, abusive or insulting,

within the hearing or sight of a person likely to be caused harassment, alarm or distress thereby.

(2)   An offence under this section may be committed in a public or a private place, except that no offence is committed where the words or behaviour are used, or the writing, sign or other visible representation is displayed, by a person inside a dwelling and the other person is also inside that or another dwelling.

(3)   It is a defence for the accused to prove—

(a)   that he had no reason to believe that there was any person within hearing or sight who was likely to be caused harassment, alarm or distress, or
(b)   that he was inside a dwelling and had no reason to believe that the words or behaviour used, or the writing, sign or other visible representation displayed, would be heard or seen by a person outside that or any other dwelling, or
(c)   that his conduct was reasonable.

(4)   A constable may arrest a person without warrant if—

(a)   he engages in offensive conduct which the constable warns him to stop, and
(b)   he engages in further offensive conduct immediately or shortly after the warning.

(5)   In subsection (4) 'offensive conduct' means conduct the constable reasonably suspects to constitute an offence under this section, and the conduct mentioned in paragraph (a) and the further conduct need not be of the same nature.

(6)   A person guilty of an offence under this section is liable on summary conviction to a fine not exceeding level 3 on the standard scale.

Mental element: miscellaneous
6.—(1)   A person is guilty of riot only if he intends to use violence or is aware that his conduct may be violent.

(2)   A person is guilty of violent disorder or affray only if he intends to use or threaten violence or is aware that his conduct may be violent or threaten violence.

(3)   A person is guilty of an offence under section 4 only if he intends his words or behaviour, or the writing, sign or other visible representation, to be

threatening, abusive or insulting, or is aware that it may be threatening, abusive or insulting.

(4)   A person is guilty of an offence under section 5 only if he intends his words or behaviour, or the writing, sign or other visible representation, to be threatening, abusive or insulting, or is aware that it may be threatening, abusive or insulting or (as the case may be) he intends his behaviour to be or is aware that it may be disorderly.

(5)   For the purposes of this section a person whose awareness is impaired by intoxication shall be taken to be aware of that of which he would be aware if not intoxicated, unless he shows either that his intoxication was not self-induced or that it was caused solely by the taking or administration of a substance in the course of medical treatment.

(6)   In subsection (5) 'intoxication' means any intoxication, whether caused by drink, drugs or other means, or by a combination of means.

(7)   Subsections (1) and (2) do not affect the determination for the purposes of riot or violent disorder of the number of persons who use or threaten violence.

Procedure: miscellaneous
7.—(1)   No prosecution for an offence of riot or incitement to riot may be instituted except by or with the consent of the Director of Public Prosecutions.

(2)   For the purposes of the rules against charging more than one offence in the same count or information, each of sections 1 to 5 creates one offence.

(3)   If on the trial on indictment of a person charged with violent disorder or affray the jury find him not guilty of the offence charged, they may (without prejudice to section 6(3) of the Criminal Law Act 1967) find him guilty of an offence under section 4.

(4)   The Crown Court has the same powers and duties in relation to a person who is by virtue of subsection (3) convicted before it of an offence under section 4 as a magistrates' court would have on convicting him of the offence.

Interpretation
8.   In this Part—

'dwelling' means any structure or part of a structure occupied as a person's home or as other living accommodation (whether the occupation is separate or shared with others) but does not include any part not so occupied, and for this purpose 'structure' includes a tent, caravan, vehicle, vessel or other temporary or movable structure;
    'violence' means any violent conduct, so that—

(a)   except in the context of affray, it includes violent conduct towards property as well as violent conduct towards persons, and

(b)   it is not restricted to conduct causing or intended to cause injury or damage but includes any other violent conduct (for example, throwing at or towards a person a missile of a kind capable of causing injury which does not hit or falls short).

Offences abolished
9.—(1)   The common law offences of riot, rout, unlawful assembly and affray are abolished.

(2)   The offences under the following enactments are abolished—

(a)   section 1 of the Tumultuous Petitioning Act 1661 (presentation of petition to monarch or Parliament accompanied by excessive number of persons),

(b)   section 1 of the Shipping Offences Act 1793 (interference with operation of vessel by persons riotously assembled),

(c)   section 23 of the Seditious Meetings Act 1817 (prohibition of certain meetings within one mile of Westminster Hall when Parliament sitting), and

(d)   section 5 of the Public Order Act 1936 (conduct conducive to breach of the peace).

Construction of other instruments
10.—(1)   In the Riot (Damages) Act 1886 and in section 515 of the Merchant Shipping Act 1894 (compensation for riot damage) 'riotous' and 'riotously' shall be construed in accordance with section 1 above.

(2)   In Schedule 1 to the Marine Insurance Act 1906 (form and rules for the construction of certain insurance policies) 'rioters' in rule 8 and 'riot' in rule 10 shall, in the application of the rules to any policy taking effect on or after the coming into force of this section, be construed in accordance with section 1 above unless a different intention appears.

(3)   'Riot' and cognate expressions in any enactment in force before the coming into force of this section (other than the enactments mentioned in subsections (1) and (2) above) shall be construed in accordance with section 1 above if they would have been construed in accordance with the common law offence of riot apart from this Part.

(4)   Subject to subsections (1) to (3) above and unless a different intention appears, nothing in this Part affects the meaning of 'riot' or any cognate expression in any enactment in force, or other instrument taking effect, before the coming into force of this section.

Part II   Processions and assemblies

Advance notice of public processions
11.—(1)   Written notice shall be given in accordance with this section of any proposal to hold a public procession intended—

(a)   to demonstrate support for or opposition to the views or actions of any person or body of persons,

(b)   to publicise a cause or campaign, or

(c)   to mark or commemorate an event,

unless it is not reasonably practicable to give any advance notice of the procession.

(2)   Subsection (1) does not apply where the procession is one commonly or customarily held in the police area (or areas) in which it is proposed to be held or is a funeral procession organised by a funeral director acting in the normal course of his business.

(3)   The notice must specify the date when it is intended to hold the procession, the time when it is intended to start it, its proposed route, and the

name and address of the person (or of one of the persons) proposing to organise it.

(4)   Notice must be delivered to a police station—

(a)   in the police area in which it is proposed the procession will start, or

(b)   where it is proposed the procession will start in Scotland and cross into England, in the first police area in England on the proposed route.

(5)   If delivered not less than six clear days before the date when the procession is intended to be held, the notice may be delivered by post by the recorded delivery service; but section 7 of the Interpretation Act 1978 (under which a document sent by post is deemed to have been served when posted and to have been delivered in the ordinary course of post) does not apply.

(6)   If not delivered in accordance with subsection (5), the notice must be delivered by hand not less than six clear days before the date when the procession is intended to be held or, if that is not reasonably practicable, as soon as delivery is reasonably practicable.

(7)   Where a public procession is held, each of the persons organising it is guilty of an offence if—

(a)   the requirements of this section as to notice have not been satisfied, or

(b)   the date when it is held, the time when it starts, or its route, differs from the date, time or route specified in the notice.

(8)   It is a defence for the accused to prove that he did not know of, and neither suspected nor had reason to suspect, the failure to satisfy the requirements or (as the case may be) the difference of date, time or route.

(9)   To the extent that an alleged offence turns on a difference of date, time or route, it is a defence for the accused to prove that the difference arose from circumstances beyond his control or from something done with the agreement of a police officer or by his direction.

(10)   A person guilty of an offence under subsection (7) is liable on summary conviction to a fine not exceeding level 3 on the standard scale.

Imposing conditions on public processions
12.—(1)   If the senior police officer, having regard to the time or place at which and the circumstances in which any public procession is being held or is intended to be held and to its route or proposed route, reasonably believes that—

(a)   it may result in serious public disorder, serious damage to property or serious disruption to the life of the community, or

(b)   the purpose of the persons organising it is the intimidation of others with a view to compelling them not to do an act they have a right to do, or to do an act they have a right not to do,

he may give directions imposing on the persons organising or taking part in the procession such conditions as appear to him necessary to prevent such disorder, damage, disruption or intimidation, including conditions as to the route of the procession or prohibiting it from entering any public place specified in the directions.

(2) In subsection (1) 'the senior police officer' means—

(a) in relation to a procession being held, or to a procession intended to be held in a case where persons are assembling with a view to taking part in it, the most senior in rank of the police officers present at the scene, and

(b) in relation to a procession intended to be held in a case where paragraph (a) does not apply, the chief officer of police.

(3) A direction given by a chief officer of police by virtue of subsection (2)(b) shall be given in writing.

(4) A person who organises a public procession and knowingly fails to comply with a condition imposed under this section is guilty of an offence, but it is a defence for him to prove that the failure arose from circumstances beyond his control.

(5) A person who takes part in a public procession and knowingly fails to comply with a condition imposed under this section is guilty of an offence, but it is a defence for him to prove that the failure arose from circumstances beyond his control.

(6) A person who incites another to commit an offence under subsection (5) is guilty of an offence.

(7) A constable in uniform may arrest without warrant anyone he reasonably suspects is committing an offence under subsection (4), (5) or (6).

(8) A person guilty of an offence under subsection (4) is liable on summary conviction to imprisonment for a term not exceeding three months or a fine not exceeding level 4 on the standard scale or both.

(9) A person guilty of an offence under subsection (5) is liable on summary conviction to a fine not exceeding level 3 on the standard scale.

(10) A person guilty of an offence under subsection (6) is liable on summary conviction to imprisonment for a term not exceeding three months or a fine not exceeding level 4 on the standard scale or both, notwithstanding section 45(3) of the Magistrates' Courts Act 1980 (inciter liable to same penalty as incited).

(11) In Scotland this section applies only in relation to a procession being held, and to a procession intended to be held in a case where persons are assembling with a view to taking part in it.

Prohibiting public processions

13.—(1) If at any time the chief officer of police reasonably believes that, because of particular circumstances existing in any district or part of a district, the powers under section 12 will not be sufficient to prevent the holding of public processions in that district or part from resulting in serious public disorder, he shall apply to the council of the district for an order prohibiting for such period not exceeding three months as may be specified in the application the holding of all public processions (or of any class of public procession so specified) in the district or part concerned.

(2) On receiving such an application, a council may with the consent of the Secretary of State make an order either in the terms of the application or with

such modifications as may be approved by the Secretary of State.

(3)   Subsection (1) does not apply in the City of London or the metropolitan police district.

(4)   If at any time the Commissioner of Police for the City of London or the Commissioner of Police of the Metropolis reasonably believes that, because of particular circumstances existing in his police area or part of it, the powers under section 12 will not be sufficient to prevent the holding of public processions in that area or part from resulting in serious public disorder, he may with the consent of the Secretary of State make an order prohibiting for such period not exceeding three months as may be specified in the order the holding of all public processions (or of any class of public procession so specified) in the area or part concerned.

(5)   An order made under this section may be revoked or varied by a subsequent order made in the same way, that is, in accordance with subsections (1) and (2) or subsection (4), as the case may be.

(6)   Any order under this section shall, if not made in writing, be recorded in writing as soon as practicable after being made.

(7)   A person who organises a public procession the holding of which he knows is prohibited by virtue of an order under this section is guilty of an offence.

(8)   A person who takes part in a public procession the holding of which he knows is prohibited by virtue of an order under this section is guilty of an offence.

(9)   A person who incites another to commit an offence under subsection (8) is guilty of an offence.

(10)   A constable in uniform may arrest without warrant anyone he reasonably suspects is committing an offence under subsection (7), (8) or (9).

(11)   A person guilty of an offence under subsection (7) is liable on summary conviction to imprisonment for a term not exceeding three months or a fine not exceeding level 4 on the standard scale or both.

(12)   A person guilty of an offence under subsection (8) is liable on summary conviction to a fine not exceeding level 3 on the standard scale.

(13)   A person guilty of an offence under subsection (9) is liable on summary conviction to imprisonment for a term not exceeding three months or a fine not exceeding level 4 on the standard scale or both, notwithstanding section 45(3) of the Magistrates' Courts Act 1980.

Imposing conditions on public assemblies

14.—(1)   If the senior police officer, having regard to the time or place at which and the circumstances in which any public assembly is being held or is intended to be held, reasonably believes that—

    (a)   it may result in serious public disorder, serious damage to property or serious disruption to the life of the community, or

    (b)   the purpose of the persons organising it is the intimidation of others with a view to compelling them not to do an act they have a right to do, or to do an act they have a right not to do,

he may give directions imposing on the persons organising or taking part in the assembly such conditions as to the place at which the assembly may be (or continue to be) held, its maximum duration, or the maximum number of persons who may constitute it, as appear to him necessary to prevent such disorder, damage, disruption or intimidation.

(2) In subsection (1) 'the senior police officer' means—

(a) in relation to an assembly being held, the most senior in rank of the police officers present at the scene, and

(b) in relation to an assembly intended to be held, the chief officer of police.

(3) A direction given by a chief officer of police by virtue of subsection (2)(b) shall be given in writing.

(4) A person who organises a public assembly and knowingly fails to comply with a condition imposed under this section is guilty of an offence, but it is a defence for him to prove that the failure arose from circumstances beyond his control.

(5) A person who takes part in a public assembly and knowingly fails to comply with a condition imposed under this section is guilty of an offence, but it is a defence for him to prove that the failure arose from circumstances beyond his control.

(6) A person who incites another to commit an offence under subsection (5) is guilty of an offence.

(7) A constable in uniform may arrest without warrant anyone he reasonably suspects is committing an offence under subsection (4), (5) or (6).

(8) A person guilty of an offence under subsection (4) is liable on summary conviction to imprisonment for a term not exceeding three months or a fine not exceeding level 4 on the standard scale or both.

(9) A person guilty of an offence under subsection (5) is liable on summary conviction to a fine not exceeding level 3 on the standard scale.

(10) A person guilty of an offence under subsection (6) is liable on summary conviction to imprisonment for a term not exceeding three months or a fine not exceeding level 4 on the standard scale or both, notwithstanding section 45(3) of the Magistrates' Courts Act 1980.

Delegation
15.—(1) The chief officer of police may delegate, to such extent and subject to such conditions as he may specify, any of his functions under sections 12 to 14 to a deputy or assistant chief constable; and references in those sections to the person delegating shall be construed accordingly.

(2) Subsection (1) shall have effect in the City of London and the metropolitan police district as if 'a deputy or assistant chief constable' read 'an assistant commissioner of police'.

Interpretation
16. In this Part—

'the City of London' means the City as defined for the purposes of the Acts relating to the City of London police;

'the metropolitan police district' means that district as defined in section 76 of the London Government Act 1963;

'public assembly' means an assembly of 20 or more persons in a public place which is wholly or partly open to the air;

'public place' means—

    (a)   any highway, or in Scotland any road within the meaning of the Roads (Scotland) Act 1984, and

    (b)   any place to which at the material time the public or any section of the public has access, on payment or otherwise, as of right or by virtue of express or implied permission;

'public procession' means a procession in a public place.

Part III   Racial hatred

Meaning of 'racial hatred'

17.   In this Part 'racial hatred' means hatred against a group of persons in Great Britain defined by reference to colour, race, nationality (including citizenship) or ethnic or national origins.

Acts intended or likely to stir up racial hatred

Use of words or behaviour or display of written material

18.—(1)   A person who uses threatening, abusive or insulting words or behaviour, or displays any written material which is threatening, abusive or insulting, is guilty of an offence if—

    (a)   he intends thereby to stir up racial hatred, or

    (b)   having regard to all the circumstances racial hatred is likely to be stirred up thereby.

(2)   An offence under this section may be committed in a public or a private place, except that no offence is committed where the words or behaviour are used, or the written material is displayed, by a person inside a dwelling and are not heard or seen except by other persons in that or another dwelling.

(3)   A constable may arrest without warrant anyone he reasonably suspects is committing an offence under this section.

(4)   In proceedings for an offence under this section it is a defence for the accused to prove that he was inside a dwelling and had no reason to believe that the words or behaviour used, or the written material displayed, would be heard or seen by a person outside that or any other dwelling.

(5)   A person who is not shown to have intended to stir up racial hatred is not guilty of an offence under this section if he did not intend his words or behaviour, or the written material, to be, and was not aware that it might be, threatening, abusive or insulting.

(6)   This section does not apply to words or behaviour used, or written material displayed, solely for the purpose of being included in a programme broadcast or included in a cable programme service.

Publishing or distributing written material
19.—(1)   A person who publishes or distributes written material which is threatening, abusive or insulting is guilty of an offence if—

(a)   he intends thereby to stir up racial hatred, or
(b)   having regard to all the circumstances racial hatred is likely to be stirred up thereby.

(2)   In proceedings for an offence under this section it is a defence for an accused who is not shown to have intended to stir up racial hatred to prove that he was not aware of the content of the material and did not suspect, and had no reason to suspect, that it was threatening, abusive or insulting.

(3)   References in this Part to the publication or distribution of written material are to its publication or distribution to the public or a section of the public.

Public performance of play
20.—(1)   If a public performance of a play is given which involves the use of threatening, abusive or insulting words or behaviour, any person who presents or directs the performance is guilty of an offence if—

(a)   he intends thereby to stir up racial hatred, or
(b)   having regard to all the circumstances (and, in particular, taking the performance as a whole) racial hatred is likely to be stirred up thereby.

(2)   If a person presenting or directing the performance is not shown to have intended to stir up racial hatred, it is a defence for him to prove—

(a)   that he did not know and had no reason to suspect that the performance would involve the use of the offending words or behaviour, or
(b)   that he did not know and had no reason to suspect that the offending words or behaviour were threatening, abusive or insulting, or
(c)   that he did not know and had no reason to suspect that the circumstances in which the performance would be given would be such that racial hatred would be likely to be stirred up.

(3)   This section does not apply to a performance given solely or primarily for one or more of the following purposes—

(a)   rehearsal,
(b)   making a recording of the performance, or
(c)   enabling the performance to be broadcast or included in a cable programme service;

but if it is proved that the performance was attended by persons other than those directly connected with the giving of the performance or the doing in relation to it of the things mentioned in paragraph (b) or (c), the performance shall, unless the contrary is shown, be taken not to have been given solely or primarily for the purposes mentioned above.

(4)   For the purposes of this section—

(a)   a person shall not be treated as presenting a performance of a play by reason only of his taking part in it as a performer,

(b)   a person taking part as a performer in a performance directed by another shall be treated as a person who directed the performance if without reasonable excuse he performs otherwise than in accordance with that person's direction, and

(c)   a person shall be taken to have directed a performance of a play given under his direction notwithstanding that he was not present during the performance;

and a person shall not be treated as aiding or abetting the commission of an offence under this section by reason only of his taking part in a performance as a performer.

(5)   In this section 'play' and 'public performance' have the same meaning as in the Theatres Act 1968.

(6)   The following provisions of the Theatres Act 1968 apply in relation to an offence under this section as they apply to an offence under section 2 of that Act—

> section 9 (script as evidence of what was performed),
> section 10 (power to make copies of script),
> section 15 (powers of entry and inspection).

Distributing, showing or playing a recording
21.—(1)   A person who distributes, or shows or plays, a recording of visual images or sounds which are threatening, abusive or insulting is guilty of an offence if—

(a)   he intends thereby to stir up racial hatred, or
(b)   having regard to all the circumstances racial hatred is likely to be stirred up thereby.

(2)   In this Part 'recording' means any record from which visual images or sounds may, by any means, be reproduced; and references to the distribution, showing or playing of a recording are to its distribution, showing or playing to the public or a section of the public.

(3)   In proceedings for an offence under this section it is a defence for an accused who is not shown to have intended to stir up racial hatred to prove that he was not aware of the content of the recording and did not suspect, and had no reason to suspect, that it was threatening, abusive or insulting.

(4)   This section does not apply to the showing or playing of a recording solely for the purpose of enabling the recording to be broadcast or included in a cable programme service.

Broadcasting or including programme in cable programme service
22.—(1)   If a programme involving threatening, abusive or insulting visual images or sounds is broadcast, or included in a cable programme service, each of the persons mentioned in subsection (2) is guilty of an offence if—

(a)   he intends thereby to stir up racial hatred, or
(b)   having regard to all the circumstances racial hatred is likely to be stirred up thereby.

(2)   The persons are—

    (a)   the person providing the broadcasting or cable programme service,

    (b)   any person by whom the programme is produced or directed, and

    (c)   any person by whom offending words or behaviour are used.

(3)   If the person providing the service, or a person by whom the programme was produced or directed, is not shown to have intended to stir up racial hatred, it is a defence for him to prove that—

    (a)   he did not know and had no reason to suspect that the programme would involve the offending material, and

    (b)   having regard to the circumstances in which the programme was broadcast, or included in a cable programme service, it was not reasonably practicable for him to secure the removal of the material.

(4)   It is a defence for a person by whom the programme was produced or directed who is not shown to have intended to stir up racial hatred to prove that he did not know and had no reason to suspect—

    (a)   that the programme would be broadcast or included in a cable programme service, or

    (b)   that the circumstances in which the programme would be broadcast or so included would be such that racial hatred would be likely to be stirred up.

(5)   It is a defence for a person by whom offending words or behaviour were used and who is not shown to have intended to stir up racial hatred to prove that he did not know and had no reason to suspect—

    (a)   that a programme involving the use of the offending material would be broadcast or included in a cable programme service, or

    (b)   that the circumstances in which a programme involving the use of the offending material would be broadcast or so included, or in which a programme broadcast or so included would involve the use of the offending material, would be such that racial hatred would be likely to be stirred up.

(6)   A person who is not shown to have intended to stir up racial hatred is not guilty of an offence under this section if he did not know, and had no reason to suspect, that the offending material was threatening, abusive or insulting.

(7)   This section does not apply—

    (a)   to the broadcasting of a programme by the British Broadcasting Corporation or the Independent Broadcasting Authority, or

    (b)   to the inclusion of a programme in a cable programme service by the reception and immediate retransmission of a broadcast by either of those authorities.

(8)   The following provisions of the Cable and Broadcasting Act 1984 apply to an offence under this section as they apply to a 'relevant offence' as defined in section 33(2) of that Act—

    section 33 (scripts as evidence),
    section 34 (power to make copies of scripts and records),
    section 35 (availability of visual and sound records);

and sections 33 and 34 of that Act apply to an offence under this section in connection with the broadcasting of a programme as they apply to an offence in connection with the inclusion of a programme in a cable programme service.

Racially inflammatory material

Possession of racially inflammatory material
23.—(1) A person who has in his possession written material which is threatening, abusive or insulting, or a recording of visual images or sounds which are threatening, abusive or insulting, with a view to—

(a) in the case of written material, its being displayed, published, distributed, broadcast or included in a cable programme service, whether by himself or another, or
(b) in the case of a recording, its being distributed, shown, played, broadcast or included in a cable programme service, whether by himself or another,

is guilty of an offence if he intends racial hatred to be stirred up thereby or, having regard to all the circumstances, racial hatred is likely to be stirred up thereby.

(2) For this purpose regard shall be had to such display, publication, distribution, showing, playing, broadcasting or inclusion in a cable programme service as he has, or it may reasonably be inferred that he has, in view.

(3) In proceedings for an offence under this section it is a defence for an accused who is not shown to have intended to stir up racial hatred to prove that he was not aware of the content of the written material or recording and did not suspect, and had no reason to suspect, that it was threatening, abusive or insulting.

(4) This section does not apply to the possession of written material or a recording by or on behalf of the British Broadcasting Corporation or the Independent Broadcasting Authority or with a view to its being broadcast by either of those authorities.

Powers of entry and search
24.—(1) If in England and Wales a justice of the peace is satisfied by information on oath laid by a constable that there are reasonable grounds for suspecting that a person has possession of written material or a recording in contravention of section 23, the justice may issue a warrant under his hand authorising any constable to enter and search the premises where it is suspected the material or recording is situated.

(2) If in Scotland a sheriff or justice of the peace is satisfied by evidence on oath that there are reasonable grounds for suspecting that a person has possession of written material or a recording in contravention of section 23, the sheriff or justice may issue a warrant authorising any constable to enter and search the premises where it is suspected the material or recording is situated.

(3) A constable entering or searching premises in pursuance of a warrant issued under this section may use reasonable force if necessary.

(4) In this section 'premises' means any place and, in particular, includes—

(a) any vehicle, vessel, aircraft or hovercraft,

(b)   any offshore installation as defined in section 1(3)(b) of the Mineral Workings (Offshore Installations) Act 1971, and

(c)   any tent or movable structure.

Power to order forfeiture

25.—(1)   A court by or before which a person is convicted of—

(a)   an offence under section 18 relating to the display of written material, or

(b)   an offence under section 19, 21 or 23,

shall order to be forfeited any written material or recording produced to the court and shown to its satisfaction to be written material or a recording to which the offence relates.

(2)   An order made under this section shall not take effect—

(a)   in the case of an order made in proceedings in England and Wales, until the expiry of the ordinary time within which an appeal may be instituted or, where an appeal is duly instituted, until it is finally decided or abandoned;

(b)   in the case of an order made in proceedings in Scotland, until the expiration of the time within which, by virtue of any statute, an appeal may be instituted or, where such an appeal is duly instituted, until the appeal is finally decided or abandoned.

(3)   For the purposes of subsection (2)(a)—

(a)   an application for a case stated or for leave to appeal shall be treated as the institution of an appeal, and

(b)   where a decision on appeal is subject to a further appeal, the appeal is not finally determined until the expiry of the ordinary time within which a further appeal may be instituted or, where a further appeal is duly instituted, until the further appeal is finally decided or abandoned.

(4)   For the purposes of subsection (2)(b) the lodging of an application for a stated case or note of appeal against sentence shall be treated as the institution of an appeal.

Supplementary provisions

Savings for reports of parliamentary or judicial proceedings

26.—(1)   Nothing in this Part applies to a fair and accurate report of proceedings in Parliament.

(2)   Nothing in this Part applies to a fair and accurate report of proceedings publicly heard before a court or tribunal exercising judicial authority where the report is published contemporaneously with the proceedings or, if it is not reasonably practicable or would be unlawful to publish a report of them contemporaneously, as soon as publication is reasonably practicable and lawful.

Procedure and punishment

27.—(1)   No proceedings for an offence under this Part may be instituted in England and Wales except by or with the consent of the Attorney General.

(2)   For the purposes of the rules in England and Wales against charging

more than one offence in the same count or information, each of sections 18 to 23 creates one offence.

(3)   A person guilty of an offence under this Part is liable—

(a)   on conviction on indictment to imprisonment for a term not exceeding two years or a fine or both;

(b)   on summary conviction to imprisonment for a term not exceeding six months or a fine not exceeding the statutory maximum or both.

Offences by corporations

28.—(1)   Where a body corporate is guilty of an offence under this Part and it is shown that the offence was committed with the consent or connivance of a director, manager, secretary or other similar officer of the body, or a person purporting to act in any such capacity, he as well as the body corporate is guilty of the offence and liable to be proceeded against and punished accordingly.

(2)   Where the affairs of a body corporate are managed by its members, subsection (1) applies in relation to the acts and defaults of a member in connection with his functions of management as it applies to a director.

Interpretation

29.   In this Part—

'broadcast' means broadcast by wireless telegraphy (within the meaning of the Wireless Telegraphy Act 1949) for general reception, whether by way of sound broadcasting or television;

'cable programme service' has the same meaning as in the Cable and Broadcasting Act 1984;

'distribute', and related expressions, shall be construed in accordance with section 19(3) (written material) and section 21(2) (recordings);

'dwelling' means any structure or part of a structure occupied as a person's home or other living accommodation (whether the occupation is separate or shared with others) but does not include any part not so occupied; and for this purpose 'structure' includes a tent, caravan, vehicle, vessel or other temporary or movable structure;

'programme' means any item which is broadcast or included in a cable programme service;

'publish', and related expressions, in relation to written material, shall be construed in accordance with section 19(3);

'racial hatred' has the meaning given by section 17;

'recording' has the meaning given by section 21(2), and 'play' and 'show', and related expressions, in relation to a recording, shall be construed in accordance with that provision;

'written material' includes any sign or other visible representation.

Part IV   Exclusion orders

Exclusion orders

30.—(1)   A court by or before which a person is convicted of an offence to which section 31 applies may make an order (an exclusion order) prohibiting him from entering any premises for the purpose of attending any prescribed football match there.

(2)   No exclusion order may be made unless the court is satisfied that making such an order in relation to the accused would help to prevent violence or disorder at or in connection with prescribed football matches.

(3)   An exclusion order may only be made—

(a)   in addition to a sentence imposed in respect of the offence of which the accused is convicted, or

(b)   in addition to a probation order or an order discharging him absolutely or conditionally.

(4)   An exclusion order may be made as mentioned in subsection (3)(b) notwithstanding anything in sections 2, 7 and 13 of the Powers of Criminal Courts Act 1973 (which relate to orders there mentioned and their effect).

Offences connected with football
31.—(1)   This section applies to any offence which fulfils one or more of the following three conditions.

(2)   The first condition is that the offence was committed during any period relevant to a prescribed football match (as determined under subsections (6) to (8)), while the accused was at, or was entering or leaving or trying to enter or leave, the football ground concerned.

(3)   The second condition is that the offence—

(a)   involved the use or threat of violence by the accused towards another person and was committed while one or each of them was on a journey to or from an association football match,

(b)   involved the use or threat of violence towards property and was committed while the accused was on such a journey, or

(c)   was committed under section 5 or Part III while the accused was on such a journey.

(4)   The third condition is that the offence was committed under section 1(3) or (4) or 1A(3) or (4) of the Sporting Events (Control of Alcohol etc.) Act 1985 (alcohol on journeys to or from certain sporting events) and the designated sporting event concerned was an association football match.

(5)   For the purposes of subsection (3) a person's journey includes breaks (including overnight breaks).

(6)   The period beginning two hours before the start of the match or (if earlier) two hours before the time at which it is advertised to start, and ending one hour after the end of it, is a period relevant to it.

(7)   Where the match is advertised to start at a particular time on a particular day and is postponed to a later day, the period in the advertised day beginning two hours before and ending one hour after that time is also a period relevant to it.

(8)   Where the match is advertised to start at a particular time on a particular day and does not take place, the period in that day beginning two hours before and ending one hour after that time is a period relevant to it.

Effect of order

32.—(1)   An exclusion order shall have effect for such period as is specified in the order.

(2)   The period shall be not less than three months or, in the case of a person already subject to an exclusion order, not less than three months plus the unexpired period of the earlier order or, if there is more than one earlier order, of the most recent order.

(3)   A person who enters premises in breach of an exclusion order is guilty of an offence and liable on summary conviction to imprisonment for a term not exceeding 1 month or a fine not exceeding level 3 on the standard scale or both.

(4)   A constable who reasonably suspects that a person has entered premises in breach of an exclusion order may arrest him without warrant.

Application to terminate order

33.—(1)   A person in relation to whom an exclusion order has had effect for at least one year may apply to the court by which it was made to terminate it.

(2)   On such an application the court may, having regard to the person's character, his conduct since the order was made, the nature of the offence which led to it and any other circumstances of the case, either by order terminate the order (as from a date specified in the terminating order) or refuse the application.

(3)   Where an application under this section is refused, a further application in respect of the exclusion order shall not be entertained if made within the period of six months beginning with the day of the refusal.

(4)   The court may order the applicant to pay all or any part of the costs of an application under this section.

(5)   In the case of an exclusion order made by a magistrates' court, the reference in subsection (1) to the court by which it was made includes a reference to any magistrates' court acting for the same petty sessions area as that court.

(6)   Section 63(2) of the Magistrates' Courts Act 1980 (power to suspend or rescind orders) does not apply to an exclusion order.

Information

34.—(1)   Where a court makes an exclusion order, the clerk of the court (in the case of a magistrates' court) or the appropriate officer (in the case of the Crown Court)—

(a)   shall give a copy of it to the person to whom it relates,

(b)   shall (as soon as reasonably practicable) send a copy of it to the chief officer of police for the police area in which the offence leading to the order was committed, and

(c)   shall (as soon as reasonably practicable) send a copy of it to any prescribed person.

(2)   Where a court terminates an exclusion order under section 28, the clerk of the court (in the case of a magistrates' court) or the appropriate officer (in the case of the Crown Court)—

(a)   shall give a copy of the terminating order to the person to whom the exclusion order relates,

(b)   shall (as soon as reasonably practicable) send a copy of the terminating order to the chief officer of police for the police area in which the offence leading to the exclusion order was committed, and

(c)   shall (as soon as reasonably practicable) send a copy of the terminating order to any prescribed person.

(3)   References in this section to the clerk of a magistrates' court shall be construed in accordance with section 141 of the Magistrates' Courts Act 1980, reading references to that Act as references to this section.

(4)   In this section 'prescribed' means prescribed by order made by the Secretary of State.

(5)   The power to make an order under this section shall be exercisable by statutory instrument subject to annulment in pursuance of a resolution of either House of Parliament.

Photographs
35.—(1)   The court by which an exclusion order is made may make an order which—

(a)   requires a constable to take a photograph of the person to whom the exclusion order relates or to cause such a photograph to be taken, and

(b)   requires that person to go to a specified police station not later than seven clear days after the day on which the order under this section is made, and at a specified time of day or between specified times of day, in order to have his photograph taken.

(2)   In subsection (1) 'specified' means specified in the order made under this section.

(3)   No order may be made under this section unless an application to make it is made to the court by or on behalf of the person who is the prosecutor in respect of the offence leading to the exclusion order.

(4)   If the person to whom the exclusion order relates fails to comply with an order under this section a constable may arrest him without warrant in order that his photograph may be taken.

Prescribed football matches
36.—(1)   In this Part 'prescribed football match' means an association football match of any description prescribed by order made by the Secretary of State.

(2)   The power to make an order under this section shall be exercisable by statutory instrument subject to annulment in pursuance of a resolution of either House of Parliament.

Extension to other sporting events
37.—(1)   The Secretary of State may by order provide for sections 30 to 35 to apply as if—

(a)   any reference to an association football match included a reference to a sporting event of a kind specified in the order, and

(b)   any reference to a prescribed football match included a reference to such a sporting event of a description specified in the order.

(2)   An order under subsection (1) may make such modifications of those sections, as they apply by virtue of the order, as the Secretary of State thinks fit.

(3)   The power to make an order under this section shall be exercisable by statutory instrument, and no such order shall be made unless a draft of the order has been laid before and approved by resolution of each House of Parliament.

Part V   Miscellaneous and general

Contamination of or interference with goods with intention of causing public alarm or anxiety, etc.

38.—(1)   It is an offence for a person, with the intention—

(a)   of causing public alarm or anxiety, or
(b)   of causing injury to members of the public consuming or using the goods, or
(c)   of causing economic loss to any person by reason of the goods being shunned by members of the public, or
(d)   of causing economic loss to any person by reason of steps taken to avoid any such alarm or anxiety, injury or loss,

to contaminate or interfere with goods, or make it appear that goods have been contaminated or interfered with, or to place goods which have been contaminated or interfered with, or which appear to have been contaminated or interfered with, in a place where goods of that description are consumed, used, sold or otherwise supplied.

(2)   It is also an offence for a person, with any such intention as is mentioned in paragraph (a), (c) or (d) of subsection (1), to threaten that he or another will do, or to claim that he or another has done, any of the acts mentioned in that subsection.

(3)   It is an offence for a person to be in possession of any of the following articles with a view to the commission of an offence under subsection (1)—

(a)   materials to be used for contaminating or interfering with goods or making it appear that goods have been contaminated or interfered with, or
(b)   goods which have been contaminated or interfered with, or which appear to have been contaminated or interfered with.

(4)   A person guilty of an offence under this section is liable—

(a)   on conviction on indictment to imprisonment for a term not exceeding 10 years or a fine or both, or
(b)   on summary conviction to imprisonment for a term not exceeding six months or a fine not exceeding the statutory maximum or both.

(5)   In this section 'goods' includes substances whether natural or manufactured and whether or not incorporated in or mixed with other goods.

(6)   The reference in subsection (2) to a person claiming that certain acts have been committed does not include a person who in good faith reports or warns that such acts have been, or appear to have been, committed.

Power to direct trespassers to leave land
39.—(1)   If the senior police officer reasonably believes that two or more persons have entered land as trespassers and are present there with the common purpose of residing there for any period, that reasonable steps have been taken by or on behalf of the occupier to ask them to leave and—

(a)   that any of those persons has caused damage to property on the land or used threatening, abusive or insulting words or behaviour towards the occupier, a member of his family or an employee or agent of his, or
(b)   that those persons have between them brought 12 or more vehicles on to the land,

he may direct those persons, or any of them, to leave the land.
(2)   If a person knowing that such a direction has been given which applies to him—

(a)   fails to leave the land as soon as reasonably practicable, or
(b)   having left again enters the land as a trespasser within the period of three months beginning with the day on which the direction was given,

he commits an offence and is liable on summary conviction to imprisonment for a term not exceeding three months or a fine not exceeding level 4 on the standard scale, or both.
(3)   A constable in uniform who reasonably suspects that a person is committing an offence under this section may arrest him without warrant.
(4)   In proceedings for an offence under this section it is a defence for the accused to show—

(a)   that his original entry on the land was not as a trespasser, or
(b)   that he had a reasonable excuse for failing to leave the land as soon as reasonably practicable or, as the case may be, for again entering the land as a trespasser.

(5)   In this section—

'land' does not include—

(a)   buildings other than—

(i)   agricultural buildings within the meaning of section 26(4) of the General Rate Act 1967, or
(ii)   scheduled monuments within the meaning of the Ancient Monuments and Archaeological Areas Act 1979;

(b)   land forming part of a highway;

'occupier' means the person entitled to possession of the land by virtue of an estate or interest held by him;
'property' means property within the meaning of section 10(1) of the Criminal Damage Act 1971;

'senior police officer' means the most senior in rank of the police officers present at the scene;

'trespasser', in relation to land, means a person who is a trespasser as against the occupier of the land;

'vehicle' includes a caravan as defined in section 29(1) of the Caravan Sites and Control of Development Act 1960;

and a person may be regarded for the purposes of this section as having the purpose of residing in a place notwithstanding that he has a home elsewhere.

Amendments, repeals and savings

40.—(1)   Schedule 1, which amends the Sporting Events (Control of Alcohol etc.) Act 1985 and Part V of the Criminal Justice (Scotland) Act 1980, shall have effect.

(2)   Schedule 2, which contains miscellaneous and consequential amendments, shall have effect.

(3)   The enactments mentioned in Schedule 3 (which include enactments related to the subject matter of this Act but already obsolete or unnecessary) are repealed to the extent specified in column 3.

(4)   Nothing in this Act affects the common law powers in England and Wales to deal with or prevent a breach of the peace.

(5)   As respects Scotland, nothing in this Act affects any power of a constable under any rule of law.

Commencement

41.—(1)   This Act shall come into force on such day as the Secretary of State may appoint by order made by statutory instrument, and different days may be appointed for different provisions or different purposes.

(2)   Nothing in a provision of this Act applies in relation to an offence committed or act done before the provision comes into force.

(3)   Where a provision of this Act comes into force for certain purposes only, the references in subsection (2) to the provision are references to it so far as it relates to those purposes.

Extent

42.—(1)   The provisions of this Act extend to England and Wales except so far as they—

(a)   amend or repeal an enactment which does not so extend, or

(b)   relate to the extent of provisions to Scotland or Northern Ireland.

(2)   The following provisions of this Act extend to Scotland—

in Part I, section 9(2) except paragraph (a);

in Part II, sections 12 and 14 to 16;

Part III;

Part V, except sections 38, 39, 40(4), subsections (1) and (3) of this section and any provision amending or repealing an enactment which does not extend to Scotland.

(3)   The following provisions of this Act extend to Northern Ireland—

sections 38, 41, this subsection, section 43 and paragraph 6 of Schedule 2.

Short title
43.   This Act may be cited as the Public Order Act 1986.

Schedule 1   Sporting events

Part I   England and Wales

Introduction

1.   The Sporting Events (Control of Alcohol etc.) Act 1985 shall be amended as mentioned in this Part.

Vehicles

2.   The following shall be inserted after section 1 (offences in connection with alcohol on coaches and trains)—

'*Alcohol on certain other vehicles*
1A.—(1)   This section applies to a motor vehicle which—

(a)   is not a public service vehicle but is adapted to carry more than eight passengers, and
(b)   is being used for the principal purpose of carrying two or more passengers for the whole or part of a journey to or from a designated sporting event.

(2)   A person who knowingly causes or permits intoxicating liquor to be carried on a motor vehicle to which this section applies is guilty of an offence—

(a)   if he is its driver, or
(b)   if he is not its driver but is its keeper, the servant or agent of its keeper, a person to whom it is made available (by hire, loan or otherwise) by its keeper or the keeper's servant or agent, or the servant or agent of a person to whom it is so made available.

(3)   A person who has intoxicating liquor in his possession while on a motor vehicle to which this section applies is guilty of an offence.
(4)   A person who is drunk on a motor vehicle to which this section applies is guilty of an offence.
(5)   In this section—

"keeper", in relation to a vehicle, means the person having the duty to take out a licence for it under section 1(1) of the Vehicles (Excise) Act 1971,
"motor vehicle" means a mechanically propelled vehicle intended or adapted for use on roads, and
"public service vehicle" has the same meaning as in the Public Passenger Vehicles Act 1981.'

Fireworks etc.

3.   The following shall be inserted after section 2 (offences in connection with alcohol, containers etc. at sports grounds)—

'*Fireworks etc.*

2A.—(1)   A person is guilty of an offence if he has an article or substance to which this section applies in his possession—

(a)   at any time during the period of a designated sporting event when he is in any area of a designated sports ground from which the event may be directly viewed, or

(b)   while entering or trying to enter a designated sports ground at any time during the period of a designated sporting event at the ground.

(2)   It is a defence for the accused to prove that he had possession with lawful authority.

(3)   This section applies to any article or substance whose main purpose is the emission of a flare for purposes of illuminating or signalling (as opposed to igniting or heating) or the emission of smoke or a visible gas; and in particular it applies to distress flares, fog signals, and pellets and capsules intended to be used as fumigators or for testing pipes, but not to matches, cigarette lighters or heaters.

(4)   This section also applies to any article which is a firework.'

Licensing etc.

4.   The following shall be inserted after section 5—

'*Private facilities for viewing events*

5A.—(1)   In relation to a room in a designated sports ground—

(a)   from which designated sporting events may be directly viewed, and

(b)   to which the general public are not admitted,

sections 2(1)(a) and 3(1)(a) of this Act have effect with the substitution for the reference to the period of a designated sporting event of a reference to the restricted period defined below.

(2)   Subject to any order under subsection (3) below, the restricted period of a designated sporting event for the purposes of this section is the period beginning 15 minutes before the start of the event or (if earlier) 15 minutes before the time at which it is advertised to start and ending 15 minutes after the end of the event, but—

(a)   where an event advertised to start at a particular time on a particular day is postponed to a later day, the restricted period includes the period in the day on which it is advertised to take place beginning 15 minutes before and ending 15 minutes after that time, and

(b)   where an event advertised to start at a particular time on a particular day does not take place, the period is the period referred to in paragraph (a) above.

(3)   The Secretary of State may by order provide, in relation to all designated sporting events or in relation to such descriptions of event as are specified in the order—

(a)   that the restricted period shall be such period, shorter than that mentioned in subsection (2) above, as may be specified in the order, or

(b)   that there shall be no restricted period.

(4)   An order under this section shall be made by statutory instrument which shall be subject to annulment in pursuance of a resolution of either House of Parliament.

Occasional licences

5B.—(1)   An occasional licence which is in force for any place situated in the area of a designated sports ground, and which would (apart from this section) authorise the sale of intoxicating liquor at the place during the whole or part of the period of a designated sporting event at the ground, shall not authorise such sale.

(2)   Where the sale of intoxicating liquor would (apart from this section) be authorised by an occasional licence, its holder is guilty of an offence if he sells or authorises the sale of such liquor and by virtue of this section the licence does not authorise the sale.

(3)   A person is guilty of an offence if he consumes intoxicating liquor at a place, or takes such liquor from a place, at a time when an occasional licence which would (apart from this section) authorise the sale of the liquor at the place does not do so by virtue of this section.

Clubs

5C.—(1)   Subsections (3) and (5) of section 39 of the Licensing Act 1964 (clubs), and subsection (4) of that section as it applies to subsection (3), shall not apply as regards the supply of intoxicating liquor in the area of a designated sports ground during the period of a designated sporting event at the ground or as regards the keeping of intoxicating liquor for such supply; but subsections (2) to (5) below shall apply.

(2)   During the period of such an event at the ground, intoxicating liquor shall not be supplied by or on behalf of a registered club to a member or guest in the area of the ground except at premises in respect of which the club is registered.

(3)   A person supplying or authorising the supply of intoxicating liquor in contravention of subsection (2) above is guilty of an offence.

(4)   A person who, during the period of such an event, obtains or consumes intoxicating liquor supplied in contravention of subsection (2) above is guilty of an offence.

(5)   If intoxicating liquor is kept in any premises or place by or on behalf of a club for supply to members or their guests in contravention of subsection (2) above, every officer of the club is guilty of an offence unless he shows that it was so kept without his knowledge or consent.

Non-retail sales

5D.—(1)   During the period of a designated sporting event at a designated sports ground, intoxicating liquor shall not be sold in the area of the ground except by sale by retail.

(2)   A person selling or authorising the sale of intoxicating liquor in contravention of subsection (1) above is guilty of an offence.

(3)   A person who, during the period of such an event, obtains or consumes intoxicating liquor sold in contravention of subsection (1) above is guilty of an offence.'

Supplementary

5.   In sections 2 and 3, after subsection (1) insert—

'(1A)   Subsection (1)(a) above has effect subject to section 5A(1) of this Act.'

6.   In section 7(3) (power to stop and search vehicles), after 'public service vehicle (within the meaning of section 1 of this Act)' insert 'or a motor vehicle to which section 1A of this Act applies'.

7.—(1)   Section 8 (penalties) shall be amended as follows.

(2)   In paragraph (a) after '1(2)' there shall be inserted 'or 1A(2)'.

(3)   In paragraph (b) after '1(3)' there shall be inserted ', 1A(3)', after '2(1)' there shall be inserted ', 2A(1)' and after '3(10)' there shall be inserted ', 5B(2), 5C(3), 5D(2)'.

(4)   In paragraph (c) after '1(4)' there shall be inserted ', 1A(4)'.

(5)   At the end there shall be inserted—

'(d)   in the case of an offence under section 5B(3), 5C(4) or 5D(3), to a fine not exceeding level 3 on the standard scale, and

(e)   in the case of an offence under section 5C(5), to a fine not exceeding level 1 on the standard scale.'.

Minor amendment

8.   Section 3(9) (notice varying order about sale or supply of intoxicating liquor) shall have effect, and be taken always to have had effect, as if in paragraph (b) 'order' read 'notice'.

Part II   Scotland

Introduction

9.   Part V of the Criminal Justice (Scotland) Act 1980 (sporting events: control of alcohol etc.) shall be amended as mentioned in this Part.

Vehicles

10.   After section 70 there shall be inserted the following—

'Alcohol on certain other vehicles

70A.—(1)   This section applies to a motor vehicle which is not a public service vehicle but is adapted to carry more than eight passengers and is being operated for the principal purpose of conveying two or more passengers for the whole or part of a journey to or from a designated sporting event.

(2)   Any person in possession of alcohol on a vehicle to which this section applies shall be guilty of an offence and liable on summary conviction to imprisonment for a period not exceeding 60 days or a fine not exceeding level 3 on the standard scale or both.

(3)   Any person who is drunk on a vehicle to which this section applies shall be guilty of an offence and liable on summary conviction to a fine not exceeding level 2 on the standard scale.

(4)   Any person who permits alcohol to be carried on a vehicle to which this section applies and—

(a)   is the driver of the vehicle, or

(b)   where he is not its driver, is the keeper of the vehicle, the employee or agent of the keeper, a person to whom it is made available (by hire, loan or otherwise) by the keeper or the keeper's employee or agent, or the employee or agent of a person to whom it is so made available,

shall, subject to section 71 of this Act, be guilty of an offence and liable on summary conviction to a fine not exceeding level 3 on the standard scale.'.

11.   In section 71 (defences in connection with carriage of alcohol) for 'or 70' there shall be substituted ', 70 or 70A(4)'.

12.   In section 75 (police powers of enforcement) for 'or 70' there shall be substituted ', 70 or 70A'.

13.   In section 77 (interpretation of Part V)—

(a)   the following definitions shall be inserted in the appropriate places alphabetically—

' "keeper", in relation to a vehicle, means the person having the duty to take out a licence for it under section 1(1) of the Vehicles (Excise) Act 1971;

"motor vehicle" means a mechanically propelled vehicle intended or adapted for use on roads;'; and

(b)   in the definition of 'public service vehicle' for the words 'Part I of the Transport Act 1980' there shall be substituted the words 'the Public Passenger Vehicles Act 1981';'.

Fireworks etc.

14.—(1)   After section 72 there shall be inserted the following—

'Possession of fireworks etc. at sporting events

72A.—(1)   Any person who has entered the relevant area of a designated sports ground and is in possession of a controlled article or substance at any time during the period of a designated sporting event shall be guilty of an offence.

(2)   Any person who, while in possession of a controlled article or substance, attempts to enter the relevant area of a designated sports ground at any time during the period of a designated sporting event at the ground shall be guilty of an offence.

(3)   A person guilty of an offence under subsection (1) or (2) above shall be liable on summary conviction to imprisonment for a period not exceeding 60 days or to a fine not exceeding level 3 on the standard scale or both.

(4)   It shall be a defence for a person charged with an offence under subsection (1) or (2) above to show that he had lawful authority to be in possession of the controlled article or substance.

(5)   In subsections (1) and (2) above "controlled article or substance" means—

(a)   any article or substance whose main purpose is the emission of a flare for purposes of illuminating or signalling (as opposed to igniting or heating) or the emission of smoke or a visible gas; and in particular it includes distress flares, fog signals, and pellets and capsules intended to be used as fumigators or for testing pipes, but not matches, cigarette lighters or heaters; and

(b)   any article which is a firework.'.

(2)   In section 75 (police powers of enforcement) at the end of subparagraph (ii) of paragraph (e) there shall be inserted—

'; or

(iii)   a controlled article or substance as defined in section 72A(5) of this Act.'.

Schedule 2   Other amendments

Conspiracy and Protection of Property Act 1875 (c. 86)

1.—(1)   In section 7 of the Conspiracy and Protection of Property Act 1875 (offence to intimidate etc. with a view to compelling another to abstain from doing or to do an act) for the words from 'shall' to the end there shall be substituted 'shall be liable on summary conviction to imprisonment for a term not exceeding six months or a fine not exceeding level 5 on the standard scale or both.'.

(2)   And the following shall be added at the end of that section—

'A constable may arrest without warrant anyone he reasonably suspects is committing an offence under this section.'.

Prevention of Crime Act 1953 (c. 14)

2.   In section 1 of the Prevention of Crime Act 1953 (offence to have offensive weapon) at the end of subsection (4) (offensive weapon includes article

intended by person having it for use by him) there shall be added 'or by some other person'.

Civic Government (Scotland) Act 1982 (c. 45)

3.—(1)   Part V of the Civic Government (Scotland) Act 1982 (public processions) shall be amended in accordance with this paragraph.
   (2)   In section 62 (notification of processions)—

      (a)   in subsection (1)—

         (i)   after 'below' there shall be inserted '(a)'; and
         (ii)   at the end there shall be inserted—

'; and
         (b)   to the chief constable.';

      (b)   in subsection (2)—

         (i)   in paragraph (a), after 'council' there shall be inserted 'and to the office of the chief constable';
         (ii)   in paragraph (b), for 'that office' there shall be substituted 'those offices';

      (c)   in subsection (4)—

         (i)   after 'area' there shall be inserted '(a)'; and
         (ii)   after 'them' there shall be inserted—

'; and
         (b)   intimated to the chief constable,'; and

      (d)   in subsection (12), in the definition of 'public place', for 'the Public Order Act 1936' there shall be substituted 'Part II of the Public Order Act 1986'.

   (3)   In section 63 (functions of regional and islands councils in relation to processions)—

      (a)   after subsection (1) there shall be inserted—

'(1A)   Where notice of a proposal to hold a procession has been given or falls to be treated as having been given in accordance with section 62(1) of this Act—

      (a)   if a regional or islands council have made an order under subsection (1) above they may at any time thereafter, after consulting the chief constable, vary or revoke the order and, where they revoke it, make any order which they were empowered to make under that subsection;
      (b)   if they have decided not to make an order they may at any time thereafter, after consulting the chief constable, make any order which they were empowered to make under that subsection.';

      (b)   in subsection (2) after '(1)' there shall be inserted 'or (1A)';
      (c)   in subsection (3)—

(i)   in paragraph (a)(i), after '(1)' there shall be inserted 'or (1A) above';

(ii)   in paragraph (a)(ii), for 'such an order' there shall be substituted 'an order under subsection (1) above or to revoke an order already made under subsection (1) or (1A) above';

(iii)   at the end of paragraph (a)(ii), for 'and' there shall be substituted—

'(iii)   where they have, under subsection (1A) above, varied such an order, a copy of the order as varied and a written statement of the reasons for the variation; and';

(iv)   in paragraph (b), after '(1)' there shall be inserted 'or (1A)', and after 'made' where third occurring there shall be inserted 'and, if the order has been varied under subsection (1A) above, that it has been so varied'; and

(v)   at the end of paragraph (b) there shall be inserted—

'; and

(c)   where they have revoked an order made under subsection (1) or (1A) above in relation to a proposal to hold a procession, make such arrangements as will ensure that persons who might take or are taking part in that procession are made aware of the fact that the order has been revoked.'.

(4)   In section 64 (appeals against orders under section 63)—

(a)   in subsection (1) for the words from 'against' to the end there shall be substituted—

'against—

(a)   an order made under section 63(1) or (1A) of this Act; or
(b)   a variation under section 63(1A) of this Act of an order made under section 63(1) or (1A),

in relation to the procession.';

(b)   in subsection (4) after 'make' there shall be inserted 'or, as the case may be, to vary'; and

(c)   in subsection (7) after 'order' there shall be inserted 'or, as the case may be, the variation of whose order'.

(5)   In section 65 (offences and enforcement)—

(a)   in paragraphs (b) and (c) of subsection (1), after '(1)' there shall be inserted 'or (1A)'; and

(b)   in paragraphs (b) and (c) of subsection (2), after '(1)' there shall be inserted 'or (1A)'.

(6)   In section 66 (relationship with Public Order Act 1936)—

(a)   for 'the Public Order Act 1936' there shall be substituted 'Part II of the Public Order Act 1986';

(b)   in paragraph (a), for 'or order made under section 3' there shall be substituted 'under section 12', and 'or that order' shall be omitted; and

(c)   in paragraph (b), 'or order under the said section 3' shall be omitted.

Criminal Justice Act 1982 (c. 48)

4.   The following shall be inserted at the end of Part II of Schedule 1 to the Criminal Justice Act 1982 (statutory offences excluded from provisions for early release of prisoners)—

PUBLIC ORDER ACT 1986
27.   Section 1 (riot).
28.   Section 2 (violent disorder).
29.   Section 3 (affray).'.

Cable and Broadcasting Act 1984 (c. 46)

5.—(1)   The Cable and Broadcasting Act 1984 as it extends to England and Wales and Scotland is amended as follows.

(2)   Omit section 27 (inclusion of programme in cable programme service likely to stir up racial hatred).

(3)   In section 28 (amendment of the law of defamation), at the end add—

'(6)   In this section "words" includes pictures, visual images, gestures and other methods of signifying meaning.'.

(4)   In section 33(2), in the definition of 'relevant offence' omit 'an offence under section 27 above or'.

6.—(1)   Section 27 of the Cable and Broadcasting Act 1984 as it extends to Northern Ireland is amended as follows.

(2)   For subsections (1) to (5) substitute—

'(1)   If a programme involving threatening, abusive or insulting visual images or sounds is included in a cable programme service, each of the persons mentioned in subsection (2) below is guilty of an offence if—

(a)   he intends thereby to stir up racial hatred, or
(b)   having regard to all the circumstances racial hatred is likely to be stirred up thereby.

(2)   The persons are—

(a)   the person providing the cable programme service,
(b)   any person by whom the programme is produced or directed, and
(c)   any person by whom offending words or behaviour are used.

(3)   If the person providing the service, or a person by whom the programme was produced or directed, is not shown to have intended to stir up racial hatred, it is a defence for him to prove that—

(a)   he did not know and had no reason to suspect that the programme would involve the offending material, and
(b)   having regard to the circumstances in which the programme was included in a cable programme service, it was not reasonably practicable for him to secure the removal of the material.

(4)   It is a defence for a person by whom the programme was produced or directed who is not shown to have intended to stir up racial hatred to prove that he did not know and had no reason to suspect—

(a)   that the programme would be included in a cable programme service, or

(b)   that the circumstances in which the programme would be so included would be such that racial hatred would be likely to be stirred up.

(5)   It is a defence for a person by whom offending words or behaviour were used and who is not shown to have intended to stir up racial hatred to prove that he did not know and had no reason to suspect—

(a)   that a programme involving the use of the offending material would be included in a cable programme service, or

(b)   that the circumstances in which a programme involving the use of the offending material would be so included, or in which a programme so included would involve the use of the offending material, would be such that racial hatred would be likely to be stirred up.

(5A)   A person who is not shown to have intended to stir up racial hatred is not guilty of an offence under this section if he did not know, and had no reason to suspect, that the offending material was threatening, abusive or insulting.

(5B)   A person guilty of an offence under this section is liable—

(a)   on conviction on indictment to imprisonment for a term not exceeding two years or a fine or both;

(b)   on summary conviction to imprisonment for a term not exceeding six months or a fine not exceeding the statutory maximum or both.'.

(3)   In subsection (8) (consents to prosecutions), for the words from 'shall not be instituted' to the end substitute 'shall not be instituted except by or with the consent of the Attorney-General for Northern Ireland.'.

(4)   In subsection (9) (interpretation) for ' "racial group" means a group of persons' substitute ' "racial hatred" means hatred against a group of persons in Northern Ireland'.

(5)   After subsection (10) insert—

'(11)   This section extends to Northern Ireland only.'.

Police and Criminal Evidence Act 1984 (c. 60)

7.   In section 17(1)(c) of the Police and Criminal Evidence Act 1984 (entry for purpose of arrest for certain offences) in subparagraph (i) the words from '4' to 'peace)' shall be omitted and after subparagraph (ii) there shall be inserted—

'(iii)   section 4 of the Public Order Act 1986 (fear or provocation of violence);'.

Schedule 3   Repeals

Chapter	Short title	Extent of repeal
13 Chas. 2 Stat. 1. c. 5.	Tumultuous Petitioning Act 1661.	The whole Act.
33 Geo. 3. c. 67.	Shipping Offences Act 1793.	The whole Act.
57 Geo. 3. c. 19.	Seditious Meetings Act 1817.	The whole Act.
5 Geo. 4. c. 83.	Vagrancy Act 1824.	In section 4, the words from 'every person being armed' to 'arrestable offence' and from 'and every such gun' to the end.
2 & 3 Vict. c. 47.	Metropolitan Police Act 1839.	In section 54, paragraph 13.
2 & 3 Vict. c. xciv.	City of London Police Act 1839.	In section 35, paragraph 13.
3 Edw. 7. c. ccl.	Erith Tramways and Improvement Act 1903.	Section 171.
1 Edw. 8 & 1 Geo. 6. c. 6.	Public Order Act 1936.	Section 3. Section 4. Section 5. Section 5A. In section 7, in subsection (2) the words 'or section 5 or 5A' and in subsection (3) the words ', four or five'. Section 8(6). In section 9, in subsection (1) the definition of 'public procession' and in subsection (3) the words 'by the council of any borough or district or'.
7 & 8 Geo. 6. c. xxi.	Middlesex County Council Act 1944.	Section 309.
1967 c. 58.	Criminal Law Act 1967.	Section 11(3). In Schedule 2, paragraph 2(1)(b).
1968 c. 54.	Theatres Act 1968.	Section 5. In sections 7(2), 8, 9(1), 10(1)(a) and (b), 15(1)(a) and 18(2), the references to section 5.
1976 c. 74.	Race Relations Act 1976.	Section 70. Section 79(6).
1976 c. xxxv.	County of South Glamorgan Act 1976.	Section 25. In Part I of Schedule 3, the entry relating to section 25.

1980 c. 62.	Criminal Justice (Scotland) Act 1980.	In section 75(e)(i), the word 'or' at the end.
1980 c. x.	County of Merseyside Act 1980.	In section 30(2), paragraph (b), the word 'and' preceding that paragraph and the words from 'and may make' to the end.
		In section 30(5), the words 'in the said section 31 or'.
		Section 31.
		In section 137(2), the reference to section 31.
1980 c. xi.	West Midlands County Council Act 1980.	Section 38, except subsection (4).
		In section 116(2), the reference to section 38.
1980 c. xiii.	Cheshire County Council Act 1980.	Section 28, except subsection (4).
		In section 108(2), the reference to section 28.
1980 c. xv.	Isle of Wight Act 1980.	Section 26, except subsection (4).
		In section 63(2), the reference to section 26.
1981 c. ix.	Greater Manchester Act 1981.	Section 56, except subsection (4).
		In section 179(2), the reference to section 56.
1981 c. xxv.	East Sussex Act 1981.	Section 29.
		In section 102(2), the reference to section 29.
1982 c. 45.	Civic Government (Scotland) Act 1982.	Section 62(10).
		In section 63(3)(a)(i), the word 'or' at the end.
		In section 66, in paragraph (a), the words 'or that order', and in paragraph (b) the words 'or order under the said section 3'.
1982 c. 48.	Criminal Justice Act 1982.	In Part I of Schedule 1, the entries relating to riot and affray.
1984 c. 46.	Cable and Broadcasting Act 1984.	Section 27.
		In section 33(2), the words 'an offence under section 27 above or'.
1984 c. 60.	Police and Criminal Evidence Act 1984.	In section 17(1)(c)(i) the words from '4' to 'peace)'.
1985 c. 57.	Sporting Events (Control of Alcohol etc.) Act 1985.	In section 8, the word 'and' at the end of paragraph (b).

Appendix 2   Public Order Act 1936

1 Edw. 8 & 1 Geo. 6, c. 6. An Act to prohibit the wearing of uniforms in connection with political objects and the maintenance by private persons of associations of military or similar character; and to make further provision for the preservation of public order on the occasion of public processions and meetings and in public places. [Royal assent 18 December 1936.]

Prohibition of uniforms in connection with political objects
1.—(1)   Subject as hereinafter provided, any person who in any public place or at any public meeting wears uniform signifying his association with any political organisation or with the promotion of any political object shall be guilty of an offence:

Provided that, if the chief officer of police is satisfied that the wearing of any such uniform as aforesaid on any ceremonial, anniversary, or other special occasion will not be likely to involve risk of public disorder, he may, with the consent of a Secretary of State, by order permit the wearing of such uniform on that occasion either absolutely or subject to such conditions as may be specified in the order.

(2)   Where any person is charged before any court with an offence under this section, no further proceedings in respect thereof shall be taken against him without the consent of the Attorney-General [except such as are authorised by [section 6 of the Prosecution of Offences Act 1979[1]][2]], so, however, that if that person is remanded in custody he shall, after the expiration of a period of eight days from the date on which he was so remanded, be entitled to be [released on bail[3]] without sureties unless within that period the Attorney-General has consented to such further proceedings as aforesaid.

Notes
1.   Words substituted by the Prosecution of Offences Act 1979, sch. 1.
2.   Words substituted by the Criminal Jurisdiction Act 1975, sch. 5, para. 1.
3.   Words substituted by the Bail Act 1976, sch. 2, para. 10.

Prohibition of quasi-military organisations
2.—(1)   If the members or adherents of any association of persons, whether incorporated or not, are—

(a)   organised or trained or equipped for the purpose of enabling them to be employed in usurping the functions of the police or of the armed forces of the Crown; or
(b)   organised and trained or organised and equipped either for the purpose of enabling them to be employed for the use or display of physical force in promoting any political object, or in such manner as to arouse

reasonable apprehension that they are organised and either trained or equipped for that purpose;

then any person who takes part in the control or management of the association, or in so organising or training as aforesaid any members or adherents thereof, shall be guilty of an offence under this section:

Provided that in any proceedings against a person charged with the offence of taking part in the control or management of such an association as aforesaid it shall be a defence to that charge to prove that he neither consented to nor connived at the organisation, training, or equipment of members or adherents of the association in contravention of the provisions of this section.

(2) No prosecution shall be instituted under this section without the consent of the Attorney-General.

(3) If upon application being made by the Attorney-General it appears to the High Court that any association is an association of which members or adherents are organised, trained, or equipped in contravention of the provisions of this section, the Court may make such order as appears necessary to prevent any disposition without the leave of the Court of property held by or for the association and in accordance with rules of court may direct an inquiry and report to be made as to any such property as aforesaid and as to the affairs of the association and make such further orders as appear to the Court to be just and equitable for the application of such property in or towards the discharge of the liabilities of the association lawfully incurred before the date of the application or since that date with the approval of the Court, in or towards the repayment of moneys to persons who became subscribers or contributors to the association in good faith and without knowledge of any such contravention as aforesaid, and in or towards any costs incurred in connection with any such inquiry and report as aforesaid or in winding up or dissolving the association, and may order that any property which is not directed by the Court to be so applied as aforesaid shall be forfeited to the Crown.

(4) In any criminal or civil proceedings under this section proof of things done or of words written, spoken or published (whether or not in the presence of any party to the proceedings) by any person taking part in the control or management of an association or in organising, training or equipping members or adherents of an association shall be admissible as evidence of the purposes for which, or the manner in which, members or adherents of the association (whether those persons or others) were organised, or trained, or equipped.

(5) If a judge of the High Court is satisfied by information on oath that there is reasonable ground for suspecting that an offence under this section has been committed, and that evidence of the commission thereof is to be found at any premises or place specified in the information, he may, on an application made by an officer of police of a rank not lower than that of inspector, grant a search warrant authorising any such officer as aforesaid named in the warrant together with any other persons named in the warrant and any other officers of police to enter the premises or place at any time within one month from the date of the warrant, if necessary by force, and to search the premises or place and every person found therein, and to seize anything found on the premises or place or on any such person which the officer has reasonable ground for

suspecting to be evidence of the commission of such an offence as aforesaid:

Provided that no woman shall, in pursuance of a warrant issued under this subsection, be searched except by a woman.

(6) Nothing in this section shall be construed as prohibiting the employment of a reasonable number of persons as stewards to assist in the preservation of order at any public meeting held upon private premises, or the making of arrangements for that purpose or the instruction of the persons to be so employed in their lawful duties as such stewards, or their being furnished with badges or other distinguishing signs.

Powers for the preservation of public order on the occasion of processions
3.—(1) If the chief officer of police, having regard to the time or place at which and the circumstances in which any public procession is taking place or is intended to take place and to the route taken or proposed to be taken by the procession, has reasonable ground for apprehending that the procession may occasion serious public disorder, he may give directions imposing upon the persons organising or taking part in the procession such conditions as appear to him necessary for the preservation of public order, including conditions prescribing the route to be taken by the procession and conditions prohibiting the procession from entering any public place specified in the directions:

Provided that no conditions restricting the display of flags, banners, or emblems shall be imposed under this subsection except such as are reasonably necessary to prevent risk of a breach of the peace.

(2)   If at any time the chief officer of police is of opinion that by reason of particular circumstances existing in any borough or . . .[1] district or in any part thereof the powers conferred on him by the last foregoing subsection will not be sufficient to enable him to prevent serious public disorder being occasioned by the holding of public processions in that borough, district or part, he shall apply to the council of the borough or district for an order prohibiting for such period not exceeding three months as may be specified in the application the holding of all public processions or of any class of public procession so specified either in the borough or . . .[1] district or in that part thereof, as the case may be, and upon receipt of the application the council may, with the consent of a Secretary of State, make an order either in terms of the application or with such modifications as may be approved by the Secretary of State.

This subsection shall not apply within the City of London as defined for the purposes of the Acts relating to the City police or within the Metropolitan police district.

(3) If at any time the Commissioner of the City of London police or the Commissioner of police of the Metropolis is of opinion that, by reason of particular circumstances existing in his police area or in any part thereof, the powers conferred on him by subsection (1) of this section will not be sufficient to enable him to prevent serious public disorder being occasioned by the holding of public processions in that area or part, he may, with the consent of the Secretary of State, make an order prohibiting for such period not exceeding three months as may be specified in the order the holding of all public processions or of any class of public procession so specified either in the police area or in that part thereof, as the case may be.

(4) Any person who knowingly fails to comply with any directions given or conditions imposed under this section, or organises or assists in organising any public procession held or intended to be held in contravention of an order made under this

section or incites any person to take part in such a procession, shall be guilty of an offence.[2]

Notes
1.   Words omitted by virtue of the Local Government Act 1972, s. 179(3).
2.   This section is repealed by the Public Order Act 1986, sch. 3.

Prohibition of offensive weapons at public meetings and processions
4.—(1)   Any person who, while present at any public meeting or on the occasion of any public procession, has with him any offensive weapon, otherwise than in pursuance of lawful authority, shall be guilty of an offence.

(2)   For the purposes of this section, a person shall not be deemed to be acting in pursuance of lawful authority unless he is acting in his capacity as a servant of the Crown or of either House of Parliament or of any local authority or as a constable or as a member of a recognised corps or as a member of a fire brigade [or as a member of a visiting force within the meaning of any of the provisions of Part I of the Visiting Forces Act 1952 or of a headquarters or organisation designated for the purposes of the International Headquarters and Defence Organisations Act 1964[1]].[2]

Notes
1.   Words added by the Visiting Forces and International Headquarters (Application of Law) Order 1965 (SI 1965 No. 1536), sch. 3.
2.   This section is repealed by the Public Order Act 1986, sch. 3.

Prohibition of offensive conduct conducive to breaches of the peace
5.   Any person who in any public place or at any public meeting—

(a)   uses threatening, abusive or insulting words or behaviour, or
(b)   distributes or displays any writing, sign or visible representation which is threatening, abusive or insulting,

with intent to provoke a breach of the peace or whereby a breach of the peace is likely to be occasioned, shall be guilty of an offence [and shall on summary conviction be liable to imprisonment for a term not exceeding six months or to a fine not exceeding [level 5 on the standard scale[1]] or to both[2]].[3]

Notes
1.   Words substituted by virtue of the Criminal Justice Act 1982, s. 46 (in the law of England and Wales) and the Criminal Procedure (Scotland) Act 1975, s. 289G (in the law of Scotland).
2.   Words added by the Criminal Law Act 1977, sch. 1 (in the law of England and Wales) and Criminal Procedure (Scotland) Act 1975, sch. 7A (in the law of Scotland).
3.   This section was substituted by the Race Relations Act 1965, s. 7, and is repealed by the Public Order Act 1986, sch. 3.

Incitement to racial hatred
5A.—(1)   A person commits an offence if—

(a)   he publishes or distributes written matter which is threatening, abusive or insulting; or
(b)   he uses in any public place or at any public meeting words which are threatening, abusive or insulting,

in a case where, having regard to all the circumstances, hatred is likely to be stirred up against any racial group in Great Britain by the matter or words in question.

(2)   Subsection (1) above does not apply to the publication or distribution of written matter consisting of or contained in—

(a)   a fair and accurate report of proceedings publicly heard before any court or tribunal exercising judicial authority, being a report which is published contemporaneously with those proceedings or, if it is not reasonably practicable or would be unlawful to publish a report of them contemporaneously, is published as soon as publication is reasonably practicable and (if previously unlawful) lawful; or

(b)   a fair and accurate report of proceedings in Parliament.

(3)   In any proceedings for an offence under this section alleged to have been committed by the publication or distribution of any written matter, it shall be a defence for the accused to prove that he was not aware of the content of the written matter in question and neither suspected nor had reason to suspect it of being threatening, abusive or insulting.

(4)   Subsection (3) above shall not prejudice any defence which it is open to a person charged with an offence under this section to raise apart from that subsection.

(5)   A person guilty of an offence under this section shall be liable—

(a)   on summary conviction, to imprisonment for a term not exceeding six months or to a fine not exceeding [the prescribed sum[1]], or both;

(b)   on conviction on indictment, to imprisonment for a term not exceeding two years or to a fine, or both;

but no prosecution for such an offence shall be instituted in England and Wales except by or with the consent of the Attorney-General.

(6)   In this section—

'publish' and 'distribute' mean publish or distribute to the public at large or to any section of the public not consisting exclusively of members of an association of which the person publishing or distributing is a member;

'racial group' means a group of persons defined by reference to colour, race, nationality or ethnic or national origins, and in this definition 'nationality' includes citizenship.

'written matter' includes any writing, sign or visible representation.[2]

Notes
1.   Words substituted by virtue of the Magistrates' Courts Act 1980, s. 32(2).
2.   This section was inserted by the Race Relations Act 1976, s. 70, and is repealed by the Public Order Act 1986, sch. 3.

Amendment of 8 Edw. 7. c. 66
6.   Section one of the Public Meeting Act 1908 (which provides that any person who at a lawful public meeting acts in a disorderly manner for the purpose of preventing the transaction of the business for which the meeting was called together, or incites others so to act, shall be guilty of an offence) shall have effect as if the following subsection were added thereto—

'(3)   If any constable reasonably suspects any person of committing an offence under the foregoing provisions of this section, he may if requested so to do by the chairman of the meeting require that person to declare to him immediately his name and address and, if that person refuses or fails so to declare his name and address or gives a false name and address he shall be guilty of an offence under this subsection and liable on summary conviction thereof to a fine not exceeding [level 1 on the standard scale[1]], and if he refuses or fails so to declare his name and address or if the constable reasonably suspects him of giving a false name and address, the constable may without warrant arrest him.'

Note
1.   Words substituted by virtue of the Criminal Justice Act 1982, s. 46 (in the law of England and Wales) and the Criminal Procedure (Scotland) Act 1975, s. 289G (in the law of Scotland).

Enforcement
7.—(1)   Any person who commits an offence under section 2 of this Act shall be liable on summary conviction to imprisonment for a term not exceeding six months or to a fine not exceeding the prescribed sum,[1] or to both such imprisonment and fine, or, on conviction on indictment, to imprisonment for a term not exceeding two years or to a fine[2], or to both such imprisonment and fine.

(2)   Any person guilty of [any offence under this Act other than an offence under section 2 or section 5 [or 5A[3]][4]] shall be liable on summary conviction to imprisonment for a term not exceeding three months or to a fine not exceeding [level 4 on the standard scale[5]], or to both such imprisonment and fine.

(3)   A constable may without warrant arrest any person reasonably suspected by him to be committing an offence under section 1, 4 or 5[6] of this Act.

Notes
1.   By virtue of the Magistrates' Courts Act 1980, s. 32(2) (in the law of England and Wales), and the Criminal Procedure (Scotland) Act 1975, s. 289B(1) (in the law of Scotland), the maximum fine is the prescribed sum.
2.   By virtue of the Criminal Law Act 1977, s. 32(1) (in the law of England and Wales), and the Criminal Procedure (Scotland) Act 1975, s. 193A (in the law of Scotland), the liability is to a fine of any amount.
3.   Words added by the Race Relations Act 1976, s. 70(3).
4.   Words substituted by the Public Order Act 1963, s. 1(2), and words in smaller type repealed by the Public Order Act 1986, sch. 3.
5.   Words substituted by virtue of the Criminal Law Act 1977, sch. 6, and the Criminal Justice Act 1982, s. 46 (in the law of England and Wales), and the Criminal Procedure (Scotland) Act 1975, sch. 7C and s. 289G (in the law of Scotland).
6.   Words in smaller type repealed by the Public Order Act 1986, sch. 3.

Application to Scotland
8.   This Act shall apply to Scotland subject to the following modifications:—

(1)   Subsection (2) of section 1 and subsection (2) of section 2 of this Act shall not apply.

(2)   In subsection (3) of section 2 the Lord Advocate shall be substituted for the Attorney-General and the Court of Session shall be substituted for the High Court.

(3)   Subsection (5) of section 2 shall have effect as if for any reference to a judge of the High Court there were substituted a reference to the sheriff and any application for a search warrant under the said subsection shall be made by the procurator fiscal instead of such officer as is therein mentioned.

(4)   The power conferred on the sheriff by subsection (5) of section 2, as modified by the last foregoing paragraph, shall not be exercisable by an [honorary sheriff[1]].

(5)   . . .[2].

(6)   In subsection (2) of section 3 and in subsection (3) of section 9 of this Act for references to a borough or . . .[3] district [there shall be substituted references to a region[4]].[5]

Notes

1.   Words substituted by virtue of the Sheriff Courts (Scotland) Act 1971, s. 4(2).

2.   Subsection (5) repealed by the District Courts (Scotland) Act 1975, sch. 2.

3.   Word omitted by virtue of the Local Government Act 1972, s. 179(3).

4.   Words substituted by the District Courts (Scotland) Act 1975, sch. 1, para. 25.

5.   Subsection (6) repealed by the Public Order Act 1986, sch. 3.

Interpretation etc.

9.—(1)   In this Act the following expressions have the meanings hereby respectively assigned to them, that is to say:—

. . .[1]

'Meeting' means a meeting held for the purpose of the discussion of matters of public interest or for the purpose of the expression of views on such matters;

'Private premises' means premises to which the public have access (whether on payment or otherwise) only by permission of the owner, occupier, or lessee of the premises;

'Public meeting' includes any meeting in a public place and any meeting which the public or any section thereof are permitted to attend, whether on payment or otherwise;

['Public place' includes any highway and any other premises or place to which at the material time the public have or are permitted to have access, whether on payment or otherwise[2]];

'Public procession' means a procession in a public place;[3]

'Recognised corps' means a rifle club, miniature rifle club or cadet corps approved by a Secretary of State under the Firearms Acts 1920 to 1936, for the purposes of those Acts.

(2)   The powers conferred by this Act on the Attorney-General may, in the event of a vacancy in the office or in the event of the Attorney-General being

unable to act owing to illness or absence, be exercised by the Solicitor-General.

(3)   Any order made under this Act by the council of any borough or . . .[4] district or[5] by a chief officer of police may be revoked or varied by a subsequent order made in like manner.

(4)   The powers conferred by this Act on any chief officer of police may, in the event of a vacancy in the office or in the event of the chief officer of police being unable to act owing to illness or absence, be exercised by the person duly authorised in accordance with directions given by a Secretary of State to exercise those powers on behalf of the chief officer of police.

Notes

1.   Words repealed by the Police Act 1964, sch. 10, pt 1 (in the law of England and Wales), and the Police (Scotland) Act 1967, sch. 5, pt 1 (in the law of Scotland).
2.   Words substituted by the Criminal Justice Act 1972, s. 33.
3.   Words in smaller type repealed by the Public Order 1986, sch. 3.
4.   Word omitted by virtue of the Local Government Act 1972, s. 179(3).
5.   Words in smaller type repealed by the Public Order Act 1986, sch. 3.

Short title and extent

10.—(1)   This Act may be cited as the Public Order Act 1936.

(2)   This Act shall not extend to Northern Ireland.

(3)   . . .[1].

Note

1.   Subsection (3) repealed by the Statute Law Revision Act 1950.

Appendix 3 Police and Criminal Evidence Act 1984, Sections 24 to 26 and Schedule 2

1984, c. 60. An Act to make further provision in relation to the powers and duties of the police, persons in police detention, criminal evidence, police discipline and complaints against the police; to provide for arrangements for obtaining the views of the community on policing and for a rank of deputy chief constable; to amend the law relating to the Police Federations and Police Forces and Police Cadets in Scotland; and for connected purposes. [Royal assent 31 October 1984.]

Be it enacted by the Queen's most Excellent Majesty, by and with the advice and consent of the Lords Spiritual and Temporal, and Commons, in this present Parliament assembled, and by the authority of the same, as follows:—

Part III Arrest

Arrest without warrant for arrestable offences
24.—(1) The powers of summary arrest conferred by the following subsections shall apply—

    (a) to offences for which the sentence is fixed by law;
    (b) to offences for which a person of 21 years of age or over (not previously convicted) may be sentenced to imprisonment for a term of five years (or might be so sentenced but for the restrictions imposed by section 33 of the Magistrates' Courts Act 1980); and
    (c) to the offences to which subsection (2) below applies,

and in this Act 'arrestable offence' means any such offence.
    (2) The offences to which this subsection applies are—

    (a) offences for which a person may be arrested under the customs and excise Acts, as defined in section 1(1) of the Customs and Excise Management Act 1979;
    (b) offences under the Official Secrets Acts 1911 and 1920 that are not arrestable offences by virtue of the term of imprisonment for which a person may be sentenced in respect of them;
    (c) offences under section [. . .[1]] 22 (causing prostitution of women) or 23 (procuration of girl under 21) of the Sexual Offences Act 1956;
    (d) offences under section 12(1) (taking motor vehicle or other conveyance without authority etc.) or 25(1) (going equipped for stealing, etc.) of the Theft Act 1968; and
    (e) offences under section 1 of the Public Bodies Corrupt Practices Act 1889 (corruption in office) or section 1 of the Prevention of Corruption Act

1906 (corrupt transactions with agents).

(3) Without prejudice to section 2 of the Criminal Attempts Act 1981, the powers of summary arrest conferred by the following subsections shall also apply to the offences of—

(a) conspiring to commit any of the offences mentioned in subsection (2) above;
(b) attempting to commit any such offence;
(c) inciting, aiding, abetting, counselling or procuring the commission of any such offence;

and such offences are also arrestable offences for the purposes of this Act.

(4) Any person may arrest without a warrant—

(a) anyone who is in the act of committing an arrestable offence;
(b) anyone whom he has reasonable grounds for suspecting to be committing such an offence.

(5) Where an arrestable offence has been committed, any person may arrest without a warrant—

(a) anyone who is guilty of the offence;
(b) anyone whom he has reasonable grounds for suspecting to be guilty of it.

(6) Where a constable has reasonable grounds for suspecting that an arrestable offence has been committed, he may arrest without a warrant anyone whom he has reasonable grounds for suspecting to be guilty of the offence.

(7) A constable may arrest without a warrant—

(a) anyone who is about to commit an arrestable offence;
(b) anyone whom he has reasonable grounds for suspecting to be about to commit an arrestable offence.

Note
1. Words repealed by the Sexual Offences Act 1985, sch.

General arrest conditions
25.—(1) Where a constable has reasonable grounds for suspecting that any offence which is not an arrestable offence has been committed or attempted, or is being committed or attempted, he may arrest the relevant person if it appears to him that service of a summons is impracticable or inappropriate because any of the general arrest conditions is satisfied.

(2) In this section 'the relevant person' means any person whom the constable has reasonable grounds to suspect of having committed or having attempted to commit the offence or of being in the course of committing or attempting to commit it.

(3) The general arrest conditions are—

(a) that the name of the relevant person is unknown to, and cannot be readily ascertained by, the constable;

(b)   that the constable has reasonable grounds for doubting whether a name furnished by the relevant person as his name is his real name;

(c)   that—

(i)   the relevant person has failed to furnish a satisfactory address for service; or

(ii) the constable has reasonable grounds for doubting whether an address furnished by the relevant person is a satisfactory address for service;

(d)   that the constable has reasonable grounds for believing that arrest is necessary to prevent the relevant person—

(i)   causing physical injury to himself or any other person;

(ii)   suffering physical injury;

(iii)   causing loss of or damage to property;

(iv)   committing an offence against public decency; or

(v)   causing an unlawful obstruction of the highway;

(e)   that the constable has reasonable grounds for believing that arrest is necessary to protect a child or other vulnerable person from the relevant person.

(4)   For the purposes of subsection (3) above an address is a satisfactory address for service if it appears to the constable—

(a)   that the relevant person will be at it for a sufficiently long period for it to be possible to serve him with a summons; or

(b)   that some other person specified by the relevant person will accept service of a summons for the relevant person at it.

(5)   Nothing in subsection (3)(d) above authorises the arrest of a person under subparagraph (iv) of that paragraph except where members of the public going about their normal business cannot reasonably be expected to avoid the person to be arrested.

(6)   This section shall not prejudice any power of arrest conferred apart from this section.

Repeal of statutory powers of arrest without warrant or order

26.—(1)   Subject to subsection (2) below, so much of any Act (including a local Act) passed before this Act as enables a constable—

(a)   to arrest a person for an offence without a warrant; or

(b)   to arrest a person otherwise than for an offence without a warrant or an order of a court,

shall cease to have effect.

(2)   Nothing in subsection (1) above affects the enactments specified in Schedule 2 to this Act.

Schedule 2   Preserved powers of arrest

1892 c. 43.   Section 17(2) of the Military Lands Act 1892.
1911 c. 27.   Section 12(1) of the Protection of Animals Act 1911.

1920 c. 55.	Section 2 of the Emergency Powers Act 1920.
1936 c. 6.	Section 7(3) of the Public Order Act 1936.
1952 c. 52.	Section 49 of the Prison Act 1952.
1952 c. 67.	Section 13 of the Visiting Forces Act 1952.
1955 c. 18.	Sections 186 and 190B of the Army Act 1955.
1955 c. 19.	Section 186 and 190B of the Air Force Act 1955.
1957 c. 53.	Sections 104 and 105 of the Naval Discipline Act 1957.
1959 c. 37.	Section 1(3) of the Street Offences Act 1959.
1969 c. 54.	Sections 28(2) and 32 of the Children and Young Persons Act 1969.
1971 c. 77.	Section 24(2) of the Immigration Act 1971 and paragraphs 17, 24 and 33 of Schedule 2 and paragraph 7 of Schedule 3 to that Act.
1972 c. 20.	Sections 5(5), 7 and 100 of the Road Traffic Act 1972.
1976 c. 63.	Section 7 of the Bail Act 1976.
1977 c. 45.	Sections 6(6), 7(11), 8(4), 9(7) and 10(5) of the Criminal Law Act 1977.
1980 c. 5.	Section 16 of the Child Care Act 1980.
1980 c. 9.	Schedule 5 to the Reserve Forces Act 1980.
1981 c. 22.	Sections 60(5) and 61(1) of the Animal Health Act 1981.
1983 c. 2.	Rule 36 in Schedule 1 to the Representation of the People Act 1983[1]
1983 c. 20.	Sections 18, 35(10), 36(8), 38(7), 136(1) and 138 of the Mental Health Act 1983.
1984 c. 8.	Sections 12 and 13 of the Prevention of Terrorism (Temporary Provisions) Act 1984.
1984 c. 47.	Section 5(5) of the Repatriation of Prisoners Act 1984.

Note
1.   Words added by the Representation of the People Act 1985, s. 25(1).

Bibliography

J.F. Archbold, *Pleading, Evidence and Practice in Criminal Cases*, 42nd ed. (London: Sweet & Maxwell, 1985)

I. Brownlie, *Brownlie's Law of Public Order and National Security*, 2nd ed. by M. Supperstone (London: Butterworths, 1981)

Command Papers:

Universal Declaration of Human Rights (Cmd 7662)

European Convention on Human Rights (Cmd 8969)

Royal Commission on Trade Unions and Employers' Associations: Report (Cmnd 3623)

The Red Lion Square Disorders of 15 June 1974 (Lord Scarman's report) (Cmnd 5919)

Review of the Operation of the Prevention of Terrorism (Temporary Provisions) Acts 1974 and 1976 (Shackleton report) (Cmnd 7324)

Review of the Public Order Act 1936 and Related Legislation (Green Paper) (Cmnd 7891)

The Brixton Disorders 10–12 April 1981 (Lord Scarman's report) (Cmnd 8427)

Review of the Operation of the Prevention of Terrorism (Temporary Provisions) Act 1976 (Jellicoe report) (Cmnd 8803)

Review of Public Order Law (White Paper) (Cmnd 9510)

Committee of Inquiry into Crowd Safety and Control at Sports Grounds: Final Report (Cmnd 9710)

S.A. De Smith, *Constitutional and Administrative Law*, 5th ed. by H. Street and R. Brazier (Harmondsworth: Penguin, 1985)

S.A. De Smith, *De Smith's Judicial Review of Administrative Action*, 4th ed. by J.M. Evans (London: Stevens, 1980)

Department of the Environment, *Consultation Paper on Squatting*

Encyclopedia of Local Government Law (London: Sweet & Maxwell, (1980–)

Bob Fine and R. Millar (eds), *Policing the Miners' Strike* (London: Lawrence & Wishart, 1985)

Halsbury's Laws of England, 4th ed. (London: Butterworths, 1973–)

Home Affairs Committee, *The Law Relating to Public Order* (HC (1979–80) 756 I and II)

Home Office Circular No. 109/1959

Home Office Circular No. 55/1981

M. Kettle and L. Hodges, *Uprising!* (London: Pan, 1982)

Law Commission, *Conspiracy and Criminal Law Reform* (Law Com. No. 76)

Law Commission, *Report on the Mental Element in Crime* (Law Com. No. 89)

Law Commission, *Criminal Law: Offences Relating to Public Order* (Law Com. No. 123)

Law Commission, *Report on the Codification of Criminal Law* (Law Com. No. 143)

Law Commission Working Paper No. 54

Law Commission Working Paper No. 82

A. Lester and G. Bindman, *Race and Law* (Harmondsworth: Penguin, 1972)

T. Erskine May, *Erskine May's Treatise on the Law, Privileges, Proceedings and Usage of Parliament*, 20th ed. by Sir Charles Gordon (London: Butterworths, 1983)

NCCL, *The New Prevention of Terrorism Act: The Case for Repeal* (London: NCCL, 1985)

NCCL, *No Way in Wapping* (London: NCCL, 1986)

NCCL, *Southall 23 April 1979: The Report of the Unofficial Committee of Inquiry* (London: NCCL, 1980)

NCCL, *Stonehenge* (London: NCCL, 1986)

Sir W.O. Russell, *Russell on Crime*, 12th ed. (London: Stevens, 1964)

P. Sieghart, *The International Law of Human Rights* (Oxford: Clarendon Press, 1982)

J.C. Smith and B. Hogan, *Criminal Law*, 5th ed. (London: Butterworths, 1983)

Stone's Justices' Manual 1986, edited by J. Richman and A.T. Draycott (London: Butterworths, 1986)

H. Street, *The Law of Torts*, 7th ed. (London: Butterworths, 1983)

P. Thornton, *We Protest* (London: NCCL, 1985)

D.G.T. Williams, *Keeping the Peace* (London: Hutchinson, 1967)

Sir P.H. Winfield, *Winfield and Jolowicz on Tort*, 12th ed. (London: Sweet & Maxwell, 1984)

Index

Abusive
  definition 35
Affray 25–32
  alternative verdicts 30–1
  background 25–6
  common law 26
  elements of new offence 27–9
  mental element 29–30
  mode of trial 30
  new offence 26–7
  numbers 27
  participation 27
  penalty 31–2
  persons of reasonable firmness present at
    scene 28–9
  power of arrest 30
  prosecution 30
  public or private place 27
  unlawful violence 28
  uses or threatens unlawful violence 27–8
Arrest 78–9
  arrestable offence, for 78–9, 80
  fingerprinting, for 79
  information to be given on 80
  non-arrestable offence, for 79–80
  powers under Police and Criminal
    Evidence Act 1984 78–9
  private person, by 81
  Public Order Act 1986, under 80
    arrestable offences 80
    non-arrestable offences 80
  statutory powers 79
  warrant, with 81
Arrest, power of
  affray, and 30
  contaminating or interfering with
    goods 54
  disorderly conduct, and 44
  incitement to racial hatred 70
  obstructing police in execution of
    duty 86
  offensive weapons, and 48
  riot, and 16
  threatening behaviour, and 38–9
  trespass, and 126
  violent disorder, and 24
Arson 51
Assembly, right of 133–5, 151

Assembly, right of—*continued*
  European Convention on Human Rights
    135
Assault 49–50
  sport, and 50
Attorney-General
  consent to prosecution for incitement to
    racial hatred 70–1
Awareness 14–15
  intoxication, and 15–16

Bail conditions 82
Banners 108
Battery 49–50
Begging 111
Binding over 76–8
  consent 77
  evidence 77
Bomb hoaxes 58
Breach of the peace 73–6
  criminal offence, not 75–6
  exercise of police preventive powers,
    and 74–5
  meaning of 73–4
Burglary 127–8
By-laws 91–3
  civil proceedings 92
  criminal proceedings 92
  criminal trespass, and 128
  licensing 92–3

Conspiracy
  trespass, to 121–2
Contaminating or interfering with goods
  53–5
  intention 54
  mode of trial 55
  new offences 53
  penalty 55
  possession of articles 54
  power of arrest 54
  threats 54
Corporations
  incitement to racial hatred, and 71
Criminal damage 50–3
  arson 51
  destroying or damaging property 51
  endangering life 51

Criminal damage—*continued*
    threats to destroy or damage property
        51–2
Criminal trespass 126–7
    adverse occupation of residential
        premises 127
    being found on enclosed premises 128
    by-laws 128
    offensive weapon, and 127
    premises of foreign missions 127
    violence for security entry 126

Damage
    definition 52
Definitions
    abusive 35
    affray 26–7
    assembly 152
    assault 49
    awareness 14–15
    battery 49–50
    breach of the peace 73–4
    broadcast 67
    common purpose 12
    constable 85
    contaminated or interfered with 53
    damage 52
    disorderly behaviour 41–2
    disorderly conduct 41
    display 69
    gestures 62
    goods 54
    harassment, alarm or distress 42–3
    highway 88
    in the execution of his duty 85–6
    insulting 35–6
    intimidation 56, 153
    intoxication 15
    land 123
    meeting 158
    obstruct 84–5
    obstructing the highway 94–6
    occupier 124
    offensive conduct 44
    offensive weapon 47
    person of reasonable firmness 13
    play 66
    possession 69
    premises 127
    procession 136
    property 52, 124
    public assembly 151–2, 157–8
    public meeting 157–8
    public nuisance 112
    public performance 66
    public place 10, 47, 136–8, 151–2
    publication or distribution 64–5
    racial hatred 63

Definitions—*continued*
    recklessness 15
    recording 67
    reside 123–4
    riot 8
    sporting events 170
    sports grounds 170
    terrorism 58
    threatening 35
    trespass 116–17
    unlawful violence 11, 22, 28
    use or threaten 11–12
    vehicle 124
    violence 10–11, 22–3, 27–8, 38
    violent disorder 20–1
    wilfully 84, 94
    words 11
    written material 63
Director of Public Prosecutions
    consent to riot prosecution 16–17
Disorderly conduct 39–45
    background 40
    charge: duplicity 44
    defences 43-4
    disorderly behaviour 41
    elements of new offence 41–3
    harassment, alarm or distress 39–45
    mental element 43
    mode of trial 45
    new offence 41
    offensive conduct 44
    penalty 45
    power of arrest 44
    prosecution 44
    public and private places 41
    threatening, abusive or sight of a person
        likely to be caused harassment, alarm
        or distress 42–3
Door-to-door collections 106
Door-to-door selling
    summary of law 110

Election meetings 161–3
    criminal offences 163
    public 162–3
    refusal to allow 162
Entry and search, powers of
    incitement to racial hatred, and 71–2

Fascists 57
Fines
    Public Order Act 1986, under 4–5
Fingerprinting
    arrest for 79
Football exclusion orders
    racial hatred 72
Football grounds
    violence at 50

Football matches 165–72
    exclusion orders 166–9
        appeals 169
        application to terminate 169
        breach 168–9
        copy of 168
        duration of 168
        effect of 168
        making 167
        offences, and 167
        photographing offender 168
        prescribed matches 166–7

Highway 88–114
    by-laws, see By-laws
    definition 88
    leafleting 105–12
    litter 104–5
    obstruction of 89, 93–6
        elements of offence 93–6
        'destructs' 94–6
        wilfully 94
        without lawful authority or excuse
            93–4
    picketing, see Picketing
    public nuisance, see Public nuisance
    removal of vehicles from 96
    restrictions on right to use 90–1
        criminal offences 90
        local Acts 90
        Parliament, access to 90
        Public Order Act 1986 90
        Road Traffic Act 1972 90
        Road Traffic Regulation Act 1984
            90
    right of passage 88–90
    right to pass and repass along 89
    road-blocks, see Road-blocks
    street collections 105–12
    street offences 101–4
House to house collections
    summary of law 108–9
Hyde Park 164

Indecency
    men, between 103
Incitement to racial hatred 60–72
    arrest 70
    Attorney-General's consent to
        prosecution 70–1
    broadcasting 67–8
    corporations, offences by 71
    distributing, showing or playing a
        recording 67
    entry and search 71–2
    fair and accurate reports of parliamentary
        or judicial proceedings 71
    forfeiture 72

Incitement to racial hatred—continued
    including programme in cable programme
        service 67–8
    new offences 62–70
    penalties 71
    play, public performance of 65–6
    possession of racially inflammatory
        material 68–70
        purpose of offence 69
        specific defence 69–70
    Public Order Act 1936, s. 5A 61
    Public Order Act 1986, Part III 61–2
    publishing or distributing written
        material 64–5
        meaning 64–5
    Race Relations Act 1965, s. 6 61
    summary of changes made by Act of 1986
        60
    words or gestures, use of 62–4
        'intends to stir up hatred' 64
        public or private place 62
        racial hatred 63
        'racial hatred is likely to be stirred up'
            64
        specific defence 64
        threatening, abusive or insulting words
            or behaviour 62–3
        written material 63
Insulting
    definition 35–6
Intimidation 55–6
    meaning of 56
    offence 55
        ingredients of 56
    watching and besetting, including 55–6
Intoxication
    awareness, and 15–16

Judicial review 148–9
    applying for 149
    limited scope 148
    operation in public order cases 148–9
    public assemblies, and 155

Kerb-crawling 103–4

Leaflets 106–7
Litter 104–5
Marches 132–49
    new controls over 132–49
Military organisations 57

New public order offences 6–45
Newspapers
    selling 107
Northern Ireland
    application of Public Order Act 1986 to
        3–4

Obstructing police in execution of duty   84–7
    constable   85
    'in the execution of his duty'   85–6
    ingredients of offence   84–6
    Misuse of Drugs Act 1971, under 86–7
    'obstruct'   84–5
    power of arrest   86
    'wilfully'   84
Offensive conduct
    meaning of   44
Offensive weapons   46–9
    'he has with him'   46–7
    meaning of   47
    offence   46–8
    penalty   48
    power of arrest   48
    provisions concerning   48–9
    public place, in   47
    without lawful authority or reasonable
        excuse   48

Peace Convoy   129–31
    confiscation of vehicles   131
    Farmer Attwell, case of   129–30
    freedom of movement   130–1
    sites for travellers   130
Petitions   106–7
Picketing   98–101
    consumer   100–1
    industrial   98–100
    legal restrictions on   99–100
Placards   108
Play, public performance of
    incitement to racial hatred, and   65–6
Police and Criminal Evidence Act 1984
    215–18
Police powers   73–87
    arrest, see Arrest
    bail conditions   82
    binding over, see Binding over
    breach of the peace, see Breach of the
        peace
    Metropolitan Police Act 1839   82–3
    obstruction, see Obstructing police in
        course of duty
    Police and Criminal Evidence Act 1984,
        under   78–9
    preventive powers   73–8
    Public Order Act 1986, under   80
    'reading the Riot Act'   81
    road blocks   81
    Town Police Clauses Act 1847   82–3
Private meetings   156–7
Property
    definition   52
Prosecution
    affray, and   30
    disorderly conduct   44

Prosecution—continued
    riot, for   16–17
    threatening behaviour, for   39
    violent disorder, for   24
Processions   132–49
    advance notice provision   138–41
        delivery of notice   140
        exceptions   139
        failure to comply   140–1
        writing, must be in   139–40
    meaning of   135–6
    new controls over   132–49
    police controls over   141–4
        conditions   143
        failure to comply with conditions
            143–4
        imposing conditions   142–3
        intimidation   142–3
        local powers   142
        Public Order Act 1936, s. 3   141–2
        Public Order Act 1986, s. 12   142–3
        'serious damage to property'   142
        'serious disruption to the life of the
            community'   142
        'serious public disorder'   142
    prohibiting   144–7
        background   144–5
        challenge to order   146
        failure to comply with order   146–7
        increasing use of banning orders
            144–5
        judicial review, see Judicial review
        London, outside   146
        order   147
        powers   145–6
        Public Order Act 1936, s. 3   144
Prostitution   101–2
Public assemblies   150–5
    assembly, right of   151
    embassies   151
    failure to comply with conditions   154–5
    imposing conditions   152–4
        application of tests   153–4
        conditions   154
        picketing, and   153
        tests   152–3
    judicial review   155
    meaning of   151–2
    new controls over   150–5
    no advance notice requirement   152
    no power to prohibit   155
    no previous statutory restrictions   150
    picketing, and   150–1
    police controls   152
Public meetings   156–64
    common law   160–1
    control of   158–61
    definition   157–8

Public meetings—*continued*
  general management   158
  Hyde Park   164
  indoor   156
  police powers under statute   161
  private premises, on   160–1
  Public Meeting Act 1908   159–60
  Public Order Act 1986   156
  Trafalgar Square   163
Public nuisance   112–14
  examples   112–14
  meaning of   112
Public Order Act 1936   1
  text   207–14
Public Order Act 1986
  amendments to Bill   2
  background to   1–2
  codification, not   3
  commencement   2
  fine scales   4–5
  new offences   6–45
  Northern Ireland, application to   3–4
  penalties   4–5
  Scotland, application to   3–4
  text   173–206
Public Order Bill   2
  amendments to   2
Public place
  definition   47, 136–8

Quasi-military organisations   57

Racial hatred
  definition   63
  incitement to, *see* Incitement to
    racial hatred
Riot   7–19
  background   7–8
  common law   8
  damage, compensation for   19
  new offence   8–9
    alternative verdicts   17–18
    awareness   14
    charge: duplicity   17
    elements of   9–14
    for a common purpose   12
    mental element   14–16
    mode of trial   17
    penalty   18
    person of reasonable firmness present
      at scene   12–13
    persons present together   9–10
    power of arrest   16
    prosecution   16–17
    public or private place   10
    'reading the Riot Act'   18–19
    twelve or more persons   9
    unlawful violence   11

Riot—*continued*
    use or threaten unlawful violence
      10–12
    uses violence for common purpose
      13–14
Road blocks   81, 96–8
  common law   97–8
  Metropolitan Police Act 1839, s. 52,
    under   98
  Police and Criminal Evidence Act 1984,
    under   96–7
  Road Traffic Act 1972, under   97

Scotland
  application of Public Order Act 1986 to
    3–4
Solicitation
  men, by   102–3
Sport
  assault, and   50
Sporting events
  alcohol-related offences   169–72
    changes made by Public Order Act 1986
      172
    powers of enforcement   171
    restrictions on licensing   171–2
  meaning of   170
Sports grounds
  meaning of   170
Street collections   106
  summary of law   108–9
Street Collections (Metropolitan Police
    District) Regulations 1979   111–12
  form of statement   113
Street offences   101–4
Street trading
  summary of law   110

Terrorist offences   57–8
Threatening
  definition   35
Threatening behaviour (fear or provocation
    of violence)   32–9
  alternative verdicts   39
  background   32–3
  charge: duplicity   39
  elements of new offence   34–8
  mental element   38
  mode of trial   39
  new offence   33–4
  penalty   39
  power of arrest   38–9
  prosecution   39
  public and private places   34
  repealed offence   33
  threatening, abusive or insulting   34–6
  unlawful violence   38
  'whereby' clauses   37–8

Threatening behaviour (fear or provocation
        of violence)—*continued*
    'with intent' clauses   36–7
Trafalgar Square   163
Trespass   115–31
    civil law   116–21
        owners' and occupiers' remedies
            117–21
    conspiracy to   121–2
    criminal, *see* Criminal trespass
    criminal law   121–9
    damages   118
    direction to leave   122–4
        direction   122
        four preconditions   123
        'reasonably believe'   123
        senior police officer   122
    injunction   118–21
    meaning of   116–17
    new criminal law   122–6
    new criminal offence   125
        specific defences   125–6
    police, action by   128–9
    possession order   117–21
        summary procedure   118
    power of arrest   126
    power to direct trespassers to leave land
        122

Trespass—*continued*
    re-entry, right of   121

Uniforms, prohibition of   57

Violence
    definition   10–11, 22–3
Violent disorder   19–25
    alternative verdicts   25
    background   19–20
    charge: duplicity   24
    elements of new offence   21–4
    mental element   24
    mode of trial   24–5
    new offence   20–1
    penalty   25
    person of reasonable firmness present at
        scene   23
    persons present together   21
    power of arrest   24
    prosecution   24
    public or private place   21–2
    three or more persons   21
    use or threaten unlawful violence   22–3,
        23–4

Warrant
    arrest with   81